Sourcework
Academic Writing from Sources

SECOND EDITION

Nancy E. Dollahite
Portland State University

Julie Haun
Portland State University

NATIONAL
GEOGRAPHIC
LEARNING

CENGAGE
Learning·

Australia · Brazil · Japan · Korea · Mexico · Singapore · Spain · United Kingdom · United States

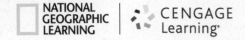

Sourcework: Academic Writing from Sources, Second Edition

Nancy E. Dollahite, Julie Haun

Publisher: Sherrise Roehr

Managing Development Editor: John Hicks

Acquisitions Editor: Thomas Jefferies

Director of U.S. Marketing: Jim McDonough

Marketing Manager: Caitlin Driscoll

Manufacturing Manager: Marcia Locke

Sr. Manufacturing Buyer: Mary Beth Hennebury

Director of Content and Media Production:
    Michael Burggren

Sr. Content Project Manager: Maryellen Killeen

Cover Design: Muse Group, Inc.

Cover Image: iStock

Composition: PreMediaGlobal, Inc.

Interior Design: Muse Group, Inc

Library of Congress Control Number: 2011922722

ISBN-13: 978-1-111-35209-7

ISBN-10: 1-111-35209-7

National Geographic Learning
20 Channel Center Street
Boston, MA 02210
USA

Cengage Learning is a leading provider of customized learning solutions with office locations around the globe, including Singapore, the United Kingdom, Australia, Mexico, Brazil, and Japan.

Cengage Learning products are represented in Canada by Nelson Education, Ltd.

Visit National Geographic Learning online at **ngl.cengage.com**

Visit our corporate website at **www.cengage.com**

Printed in the United States of America
5 6 7 18 17 16 15

Contents

Boundaries Between Humans and Machines

Questions for Writing About the Impact of Technology

More Questions for Writing About the Impact of Technology

Appendices

Credits

Acknowledgments

This book developed out of our work with writing classes in the Intensive English Language Program at Portland State University (PSU) and, thus, depends in large part on those friends, colleagues, and students who worked with us.

We thank our colleagues at PSU and elsewhere who generously shared their time and expertise in various ways and field-tested much of this material in partial form. Thanks also to our students who enthusiastically gave us feedback and allowed us to use their writing.

We have been fortunate to have the support of our development editor Kathleen M. Smith, of Sally Giangrande and Rebecca Klevberg of Content*Ed Publishing Solutions, LLC, and of Tom Jefferies and Caitlin Rakay of Cengage Learning.

Most of all, to our family and friends who cheerfully relinquished time and offered moral support that we might get the writing done, we express our deepest appreciation.

While we received help from many, we ourselves are, of course, responsible for any inaccuracies in *Sourcework*.

Preface

Introduction

Sourcework: Academic Writing from Sources applies process-approach writing to the academic setting to take students beyond writing based on personal experience. This is a guide for students writing academic papers for mainstream university courses, in which students must use sources to develop and support their ideas. *Sourcework* is designed for upper-intermediate to advanced students who have had exposure to basic rhetorical styles and have experience writing essays with a thesis statement and supporting points.

Statement of Purpose

An advanced ESL writing course is a lot of work. Students have a limited time to learn the writing skills vital to their success as university students. Teachers want to focus their energy on providing support for their students and do not want to spend time tracking down source material or creating class activities. *Sourcework* provides solutions to several critical challenges faced by ESL students and their teachers in advanced writing courses.

Students lack content knowledge to develop and support their ideas.
By including a rich and cohesive set of readings for use as sources in their writing, *Sourcework* gives students the background knowledge they need to produce the complex and sophisticated pieces of writing that will be expected of them in university courses.

Students have difficulty analyzing information for use in their writing.
Sourcework's student-centered approach to reading helps students work from a position of strength. Because students are working with a common set of sources, they work together to understand and analyze the material. Furthermore, *Sourcework* offers students in-depth practice in synthesizing concepts from their readings and selecting appropriate evidence for use in their papers.

Students struggle to paraphrase information.
Sourcework provides extensive instruction in paraphrasing. The first chapter introduces two concrete and effective strategies for paraphrasing with many opportunities for students to practice their new skills. It also details common paraphrasing challenges for students with clear examples and further opportunity for practice.

Students do not know how to integrate outside information into their writing.

Sourcework offers step-by-step instruction on how to integrate evidence. Students have many opportunities to analyze examples and practice these skills. In addition, *Sourcework* presents a clear explanation of how to document evidence from sources and avoid plagiarism.

Organization of the Text

Sourcework is organized into two parts: Part One: The Writing Process and Part Two: Sources for Research. Reflecting the process approach, Part One takes the student through the experience of writing an academic essay, step by step, drawing on the readings in Part Two as sources for the essay. A final chapter in Part One guides the learner through choosing a writing topic and finding supporting sources for an independent research project. The writing process can be repeated several times in a term using a variety of themes or sub-themes.

Content of Chapters in Part One: The Writing Process

Chapter Introduction

This summarizes the chapter including what the student will practice and accomplish by the end of the chapter.

Writing Concepts

Each chapter presents two to four overarching concepts that underlie the steps in the writing process. Examples derived from authentic student writing are included to illustrate each of the concepts.

NowYouTry

This 10-minute activity is done immediately after the presentation of a writing concept and is intended to serve as a quick comprehension check for teachers and students.

Activities

Several more complex activities are included after each writing concept. These help students practice several related skills before applying these concepts to their own writing. Teachers may choose from among the activities to suit their students' needs.

Building Your Paper (Chapters 2-6)

These assignments are designed so that students apply newly learned writing concepts to their own research paper. The Building Your Paper assignments work cumulatively through Chapters 2 to 5 to help students produce a research paper.

Content of Themes in Part Two: Sources for Research

Table of Contents: Each theme has a table of contents that lists the articles for that theme.

Getting Started 1 and 2: These short activities that students can do in class help them begin thinking about their theme.

Introduction to the Theme: The introduction provides an overview of the unit and describes the two sub-themes for the unit.

Articles: Each theme includes an article that frames the theme and three articles for each sub-theme. The articles for each sub-theme are designed to work together as sources of information for students as they write their research papers.

Questions for Writing: Writing assignments about each sub-theme and writing assignments that require additional research are included at the end of each theme.

Features Unique to *Sourcework*

1. Inclusion of a rich and cohesive set of university-level readings organized thematically
   - gives students the background knowledge they need to produce complex and sophisticated pieces of writing that will be expected of them in university courses;
   - provides a basis for developing critical thinking skills through discussion and writing;
   - saves hours of teacher preparation time.

2. Flexibility for teachers and students. The writing process instructions and practice exercises in Part One can be adapted for use with any source articles and any writing topic in Part Two.

3. A student-centered approach. The strategies in Chapters 1–5 give students confidence in their ability to think and write, and they provide a concrete set of tools to use in their university courses.

4. *Sourcework* offers repeated, in-depth practice in how to use sources in academic writing through explicit instruction, examples from actual student writing, and a variety of in-class and homework activities
   - Strategies for paraphrasing and summarizing effectively
   - Methods for synthesizing information from multiple sources
   - Techniques to select appropriate evidence
   - Simple formulas for integrating evidence into students' own writing and how to document it

5. Website support. *Sourcework* has a wealth of student and instruction resources on the companion website that support teaching and reinforce learning. These resources include an answer key, teaching notes, grading rubrics, and student downloads.

New to this Edition
Updated source articles in Part Two

Part Two now includes three themes: Risking Change, Globalization, and Technology. Each theme offers two threads providing teachers with six potential writing topics to choose from. Articles in the first thread are shorter and less complex while those in the second thread are more challenging. Favorite articles from the first edition have been folded into the new themes, and new articles have been selected with student interest, readability, and topic cohesion in mind.

Lexical and grammatical instruction specifically targeted to academic writing

Drawing on current research in corpus linguistics and discourse analysis in academic writing, this second edition of *Sourcework* includes more explicit instruction on the use of lexical and grammatical features that contribute to unity and cohesion in writing. Activities provide opportunities for students to notice these lexical and grammatical features of the articles they are reading in Part Two.

To the teacher: Guide for using *Sourcework* in the writing class

A useful guide for teachers new to *Sourcework* that provides explanation on how to use Part One and Part Two effectively in the writing class.

Updated information on documentation

This section is revised to reflect changes in documentation including expanded discussion of documentation rules for electronic sources.

TO THE TEACHER: HOW TO USE *SOURCEWORK*

A central goal of *Sourcework* is to build a "community of learners." That is, when students work together to explore and write about a common subject over the course of several weeks, they develop a shared sense of curiosity about the topic, a desire to help each other overcome difficulties encountered as they write, and a greater willingness to take risks in their writing because they are working in a supportive environment.

To achieve this goal, *Sourcework* is designed for students to work together using the writing process and activities in Part One: The Writing Process to create a research paper based on sources chosen from a theme in Part Two: Sources for Research. Because the Part One activities are based on the writing process, rather than on any specific source, they can be repeated with subsequent research papers using a different theme from Part Two or using sources students find themselves.

How do Part One and Part Two work together?

Part One guides students through the process of reading and discussing the articles they will use as sources for their research paper and then writing the paper itself. Part Two is a collection articles students will use as sources for their paper. The articles are organized around three themes. Each theme has one or two framing articles, which set forth some key issues about the topic, and two sub-themes, one with less complex sources and one with more difficult sources.

You choose the sub-theme in Part Two, either with or without input from your class, and several articles from the sub-theme that you find appropriate and interesting for you and your students. Students read and discuss the articles you have chosen and write their papers using those articles as sources for their research. To do this, they follow the steps in the writing process, which correspond to the first five chapters in Part One: Explore, Focus, Organize, Create, and Refine. This writing process is described visually in the chart on page 2.

How many research papers do students write using *Sourcework*?

Once students have completed a guided research paper, they can repeat the same writing process, working through Chapters 1–5 again, with another research paper. Many of the same activities can be used again because, as mentioned above, they are based on the writing process itself and not on any specific article. The second time around, you may choose to:

- continue with the same theme from Part Two but focus on a different sub-theme.
- select a new theme from Part Two.
- have students select their own topic and find their own sources. Chapter 6 will help them get started on an independent research paper.

Writing Research Paper #1

To work through this book, we recommend the following sequence:

CHAPTER 1   EXPLORE – Initial reading, discussion, and writing about topics

1. Choose one of the themes in Part Two to focus on. Decide on several of the articles in that theme to use as sources. You can involve students in these decisions or make them yourself.

2. Begin by Reflecting about the theme with students (see page 4).

3. Spend some time in class examining each of the articles you have chosen. Note that, for some articles, you will spend more time and do more practice than for others.

Do an Open Reading of each article:

- Assign homework for students to do an Open Reading of the article (see page 4).

- In class, complete one of the activities in Activities to Do After Open Reading on page 5. These activities will give students their first chance to compare their understanding of the article with others' understanding and to learn from each other.

4. Follow the Open Reading of each article by doing one or more of these activities with the same article:

   a) Paraphrasing

   - Present Paraphrasing on pages 6–7 and just one Paraphrasing Technique on pages 7–10. In working with another article, you can present another paraphrasing technique, or maybe you will choose not to present another technique and will just focus on one.

   - Do one or more of the Activities to Practice Paraphrasing on pages 11–13, using excerpts from the article students read for homework. In this way, you will be working with a reading that students are already familiar with, and the difficult task of paraphrasing will make more sense to them.

   b) Responding

   - Present Responding to Writing on pages 14–18.

   - Do one or more of the Activities to Practice Writing Responses on pages 18–19.

   - Assign students to write a response to the homework article.

   c) Summarizing

   - Present Summarizing on pages 19–28.

   - Do one or more of the Activities to Practice Summarizing on pages 28–29.

   - Assign students to write a summary of the homework article.

CHAPTER 2   FOCUS – Using a research question to create a rough outline

After you have worked together with all the articles you want students to use as sources, begin Chapter 2: Focus. As a research question for this chapter, you can use one of the Questions for Writing at the end of the theme you have chosen or follow the suggestions in Chapter 2 for finding a unique research question.

CHAPTERS 3, 4, 5   ORGANIZE – CREATE – REFINE – Writing the paper

Guide students through the process of writing their individual guided research papers, (probably only three to five pages long) by working through Chapters 2–5. Because they have discussed the articles, students begin their research paper with a shared knowledge of the ideas so they can help each other in each step of the writing process. However, because each person has his or her own interpretation of the ideas, each student paper will be unique.

Writing Research Paper #2: Repeat the Process

Repeat the same writing process with a new writing assignment. To do this, you will work through Chapters 1–5 again, but, because you and the students have completed the process once, it will go more quickly and smoothly. As you will notice, most practice activities can be repeated with different content, using different source articles. To further enhance the process in later rounds, the optional sections can be skipped the first time through but used to deepen students' understanding as they work on later papers. The second time around, you may choose to:

• continue with the same theme but focus on a different sub-theme within it.

• select a new theme from Part Two.

Writing an Independent Research Paper

CHAPTER 6   INDEPENDENT RESEARCH

After students have completed one or more guided papers, you may decide to have them select their own topics and find their own sources. Chapter 6 will help them get started on an independent research paper.

Writing several guided research papers, with frequent feedback from you and their classmates, will help students become familiar with the process of writing an academic essay based on sources. They will be ready to be independent writers as they go on to pursue their other academic and professional goals.

PART ONE
The Writing Process

INTRODUCTION TO PART ONE

When we write at the university level, we are entering into a conversation with others about a topic. We write not only to explain our own ideas, but also to discuss how our ideas fit into the larger context of others who have written on the topic. In this book, you will become familiar with the process of writing an academic essay for your university classes. Your first paper will be a guided research paper using information from some of the articles in Part Two: Sources for Research.

You will begin in Chapter 1 by reading one article, discussing it with your classmates, and completing short writing assignments about it. Then, you will read one or two more articles and process them in a similar way. After you have spent some time working with several articles, you will focus on one aspect of a topic you have been reading about and discussing. You will then write a short research paper, following the writing process through Chapters 2–5.

In later assignments, you will follow the same basic process of reading, discussing, and thinking about your topic. This time you may write a longer research paper, either using more articles from Part Two or using Chapter 6 in this book to help you find your own articles to use as sources.

After you have written several guided research papers, you will adapt the process of research writing to your own needs as you continue your academic work.

To see how this research writing process looks in a visual way, turn to the chart on the next page.

The Writing Process

CHAPTER 1 Page 3	**Explore** The writing process begins by exploring your topic. Actually, this first step involves more reading, thinking, and discussing than actual writing. While you explore, you are building an understanding of the ideas and issues related to the topic you will eventually write about.
CHAPTER 2 Page 30	**Focus** In this step, you decide on a focus, or a specific part of your topic, to discuss in your research paper. You read each source article again to find ideas that will help you develop and explain your main points.
CHAPTER 3 Page 45	**Organize** Once you have a clear focus for your essay and have collected supporting information from sources, you can begin organizing your ideas. You write your thesis and make a detailed outline that maps out how you will organize your ideas in the body of your essay.
CHAPTER 4 Page 71	**Create** Now you are ready to write your first full draft, following the outline you developed in Chapter 3. This step includes combining information from sources with your own ideas to create a coherent essay.
CHAPTER 5 Page 100	**Refine** In this final step, you consider your audience. You edit and shape your writing so that it is smooth, clear, and easy for your readers to understand.
CHAPTER 6 Page 139	**Independent Research** For your next paper, you may choose a topic that is *not* included in Part Two of *Sourcework*. In that case, you will need to research and evaluate your own sources. Once you have found and explored your sources (using Chapter 1), you will be ready to start the writing process of your new paper, beginning again with the Focus step in Chapter 2.

CHAPTER 1

BUILDING A PAPER:
Explore

Writing often begins, not with a pen on paper or fingers on a computer keyboard, but with thinking, talking, and reading about a topic. Although we, as writers, are impatient to get on with the actual writing, the preparatory work we do exploring and evaluating themes, topics, and sources actually saves time and effort later.

When we read and consider what others have said about a topic, we are essentially having a conversation with experts in the field. We learn about the issues involved, get acquainted with the vocabulary used, and develop our own opinions about the subject. When we write our own paper, we use some of these ideas from the sources as evidence to support the points we want to make. Learning about what others have to say about your writing topic and forming your own thoughts about the topic are the two goals of this chapter.

This chapter describes an approach to use when you read a source for the first time.

- Reflecting
- Open Reading
- Paraphrasing
- Responding
- Summarizing

You will use one or more of these strategies with each article you read for your research paper. By the end of this chapter, you will have learned something about what others have to say about your topic and formed your own thoughts about it as well.

REFLECTING

- Consider what you know and what questions you have about the theme from Part Two that your class has chosen or is working on. What do you already know about the topic?

- Do the Getting Started 1 activity on the introductory page about your topic.

- Write a list of questions about your topic.

OPEN READING

Next, begin exploring your theme by doing an **open reading** of one of the articles in Part Two. This reading is done quickly. Your goal is to develop an understanding of the ideas, issues, and terminology related to the topic you have chosen. You do not need to memorize the information or even understand every sentence in the article. Remember, your goal is to explore ideas. Choose from the following three techniques to help you think about ideas in the article as you read.

Three Techniques for Open Reading

1. **Focus on ideas that interest you.**
   - Highlight sections that capture your interest and make you pause and think.
   - Highlight sections that relate to your experiences or to ideas you have seen elsewhere.

2. **Write questions and comments in the margins.**
   - Note words or sentences that you don't understand.
   - Note examples or explanations that are unclear.
   - Write your reactions such as "I don't believe this!" or "This is exactly what happened to me" or "This idea is the same as what I already know or have read."

3. **Skim the article.**
   - Read first and last paragraphs.
   - Look for subtitles.
   - Look for key words and repeated words.
   - Develop a general sense of the topic.
   - Then, read through the entire article.

ACTIVITIES TO DO AFTER OPEN READING

ACTIVITY **1** Discussing an Interesting Idea

A. Do the following on your own.

1. Select one idea from the article you read that you think is interesting. Copy the sentences about that idea below.

_____

_____

2. What do you think the sentences mean?

_____

_____

3. Why does this idea interest you? What does it make you think about?

_____

_____

B. Now you are ready to share your ideas with a partner, a group, or the class.

1. Read the sentences you copied aloud to the others in your group. Explain what you think the passage means. Discuss why the idea is interesting to you.

2. As you listen to each other share ideas, ask questions when you don't understand something and comment on group members' ideas that also interest you.

ACTIVITY **2** Writing Questions

With a small group, return to the questions you generated in Reflecting about your topic and during your Open Reading.

1. Do you have other questions to add?

2. Can you begin answering some of the questions?

3. Share your questions and answers with a group.

ACTIVITY **3** Freewriting

Freewrite for five to ten minutes using these questions as a guide.

1. What ideas in the article get your attention?

2. What have you learned so far about your topic?

3. What other questions come to mind?

Share your writing with your partner or small group.

PARAPHRASING

When we describe something we have heard, we often repeat the same idea but use different words. For example, if you hear the TV announcer say, "There is an 80 percent chance of rain tomorrow," you may tell a friend, "It will probably rain tomorrow." This last statement is a paraphrase. A *paraphrase* is a restatement of another person's ideas using our own words.

You can use paraphrasing in writing as well. Repeating the author's ideas in your own words shows that you truly comprehend the original idea.

The paraphrasing skills that you learn now as you explore your theme will also be useful later when you integrate ideas from the articles into your paper. Chapter 4 discusses how to use information from articles appropriately in academic writing.

 # Three Criteria for a Good Paraphrase

1. **A good paraphrase has the same meaning as the original.**
   - All main ideas included
   - No new ideas added

2. **A good paraphrase is different enough from the original to be considered your own writing.**
   - Uses no more than four or five words in a row from the original source
   - Changes grammar and vocabulary as much as possible

3. **A good paraphrase refers directly to (or cites) the original source.**
   - Include the name of the author and/or the name of the source (You will study citing and documenting sources in Chapter 5.)

PARAPHRASE EXAMPLES

Original:	Genuine multitasking, too, has been exposed as a myth, not just by laboratory studies but by the familiar sight of an S.U.V. undulating between lanes as the driver cuts deals on his cellphone.
	—*Pinker, Steven, "Mind Over Mass Media," June 10, 2010*
Paraphrase 1:	Pinker (2010) writes that people can't really do more than one thing at a time; we can see this from scientific research projects and also from just watching a car moving unpredictably down the highway while the driver is talking on a cell phone.
Paraphrase 2:	Pinker (2010) says that both lab research and actual experience show that people are incapable of doing several things at once. As an example of this act, he mentions the frequent sight of a person driving dangerously while using a cell phone.

NOW YOU TRY

Here is an original sentence and two paraphrases of it. One of the paraphrases is well done, but the other does not meet all the criteria for a good paraphrase. Decide which of the two paraphrases is weak. Identify which of the criteria is missing.

Original: A global village was upon us that more and more resembled an American buffet table – even if chilis, chutney and kimchee were added to the mix.

—*Rifkin, Ira, Spiritual Perspectives on Globalization, 2003*

Paraphrase 1:   We came to a big table with food from many different countries, but it was really a lot like an American meal.

Does the paraphrase meet all three criteria?   Yes   No   (circle one)
If no, what is the problem? _lack in citation_

_____

Paraphrase 2:   In this article, Rifkin (2003) says that the whole world seemed increasingly like the United States, although it also included contributions from many other cultures.

Does the paraphrase meet all three criteria?   Yes   No   (circle one)
If no, what is the problem? _____

_____

 # Two Techniques for Paraphrasing

Below are two ways to approach paraphrasing:
- tell-a-friend method
- chunking method

TELL-A-FRIEND METHOD

One effective way to paraphrase is to focus on the meaning of the passage and find a completely new way to explain it. The tell-a-friend method works well in this situation.

1. Read the original and concentrate on what it means.

2. Cover the original so that you cannot see it.

3. Imagine you are talking to a good friend. How would you explain this idea to your friend? Write down your explanation.

4. Go back and read the original again to see if it means the same as your paraphrase.

EXAMPLE

Original:	Leadership by birth order apparently holds for both genders. Studies have found that female executives are much more likely to be firstborns than later-borns.
	—*Koselka, Rita and Shook, Carrie, "Born to Rebel? Or Born to Conserve?" 1997*
Paraphrase:	Not only firstborn men, but also firstborn women are more likely to be executives than people who are later born (Koselka & Shook, 1997).

- Notice that while the key ideas from the original are included in the paraphrase, the structure of the paraphrase is very different.

NOW YOU TRY

Using the proverbs below, practice the tell-a-friend method of paraphrasing.

Proverb: Don't cry over spilled milk.

Paraphrase: When something bad happens that you can't control, it doesn't help to get upset.

1. With a partner, choose one of the proverbs below and use the tell-a-friend method to write a paraphrase of it.
   - All work and no play make Jack a dull boy.
   - All that glitters is not gold.
   - The squeaky wheel gets the oil.

   Write your paraphrase here. _When something start being bad, it_
   need to be fixed.

2. Find a new partner and tell that person your paraphrase. Have your partner guess which proverb you're paraphrasing.

CHUNKING METHOD

Another way to paraphrase is to divide the original into phrases, or "chunks," and concentrate on explaining the meaning of each chunk. A chunk is a group of words that expresses a key idea in the passage you are working with. Chunks are often noun, adjective, or adverb clauses. This method can be especially helpful when you are working with longer passages. Here's how *chunking* works.

1. Read the original passage several times to develop a basic understanding of the ideas.

2. Divide the passage into chunks by underlining the main ideas. As you divide the passage, focus on phrases rather than on individual words.

3. Explain each chunk using your own words.

4. Combine these explanations into one or more sentences to create a paraphrase. As you combine these chunks, you will need to think about how the ideas are related to each other. It is okay to rearrange these chunks into a new order for your paraphrase.

In the two examples below, the original sentences are divided into chunks. Each chunk is then explained in a new way. Finally, the chunks are combined to form a paraphrase.

EXAMPLE 1

Original:

It's estimated that hunger and malnutrition could be eliminated globally
Chunk #1

for less than is spent on pet food in Europe and the US; universal literacy
Chunk #2

could be achieved for one-third of what is spent annually on perfumes.
Chunk #3   **Chunk #4**

—Knickerbocker, Brad, "If Poor Get Richer, Does World See Progress?"
The Christian Science Monitor, Jan. 22, 2004

Explanation
of chunks:

starvation.

1. Problems of famine could be solved worldwide
2. For less money than it costs people to feed their pets in the US and Europe
3. Everyone could learn to read and write
4. For about 33 percent of the amount that people spend on perfume every year

Paraphrase:

Knickerbocker (2004) notes that problems of famine could be solved worldwide
Chunk #1

for less money than it costs people to feed their pets in the US and Europe,
Chunk #2

and everyone could learn to read and write for about 33% of the amount
Chunk #3

that people spend on perfume every year.
Chunk #4

Example 2 shows a paraphrase in which the chunks have been arranged in an order that is different from the original.

EXAMPLE 2

Original:

There is an element of sacrifice and obligation: women are expected to make
Chunk #1

many things secondary once the husband comes along, to devote their
Chunk #2

energies to him and his house and the building of another family Unit.
Chunk #3

—Wark, Penny, "What Does Life Tell Us About Love?" 2003

Explanation of chunks:	**1.** Women must give up time and energy for themselves
	2. After women get married
	3. Women are expected to focus on taking care of their husband, home, and children

Paraphrase: After they get married, women must give up time and energy for themselves
              <u>Chunk #2</u>   <u>Chunk #1</u>

              because they are expected to focus on taking care of their husband, home,
                                          Chunk #3

              and children (Wark, 2003).

NOW YOU TRY

Use the chunking method to paraphrase this sentence.

Original: Often procrastination stems from a real or imagined fear or worry that is focused not so much on the thing you are avoiding, but its potential consequences.

              —*Moore, Rebecca; Baker, Barbara; Packer, Arnold, "Coping With Procrastination" 1997*

1. How would you divide this sentence into smaller chunks? Underline each chunk. As you divide the sentence into chunks, remember to focus on phrases rather than on single words.

2. Explain the meaning of each chunk using your own words.

   a. _____

   b. _____

   c. _____

3. Using your explanations, write a paraphrase of the original sentence. It is okay to arrange the chunks in a different order than they appear in the original sentence. As you put the chunks together, remember to consider how they are related to each other.

   _____

   _____

A third paraphrasing method that involves changes in grammar, word order, and vocabulary is available on the *Sourcework* website at **http://elt.heinle.com/sourcework.** Look for **Grammar Toolbox Method.**

ACTIVITIES TO PRACTICE PARAPHRASING

ACTIVITY **1** Identifying Problems in Paraphrases

Below are several paraphrases that have been created using the chunking method. By yourself or with a partner, read the original sentences and then evaluate the paraphrases using the criteria for a good paraphrase on page 6. Circle *OK* or *Not OK* and give an explanation.

1. *Original:*   The United States leads the world in its belief in romantic love—86 percent

Chunk #1   Chunk #2   Chunk #3   Chunk #4   Chunk #5

of American college students say they would not marry without love.

Chunk #6   Chunk #7   Chunk #8

—*Levine, Robert, "Is Love a Luxury?" 1993*

Paraphrase 1:   America is ahead in the world in its faith in dreamy love—three quarters of US students in college declared they don't want to marry without being in love (Levine, 1993).

OK   ~~Not OK~~

Explanation ① More than three quarters of ② romance.

Paraphrase 2:   Romantic love is valued in the United States more than anywhere else in the world; more than three quarters of US college students say they will not marry unless they love their partner (Levine, 1993).

OK   Not OK

Explanation _____

2. *Original:*   Countries are likely to indulge in romance if they are

Chunk #1

wealthy and value individualism over the community.

Chunk #2   Chunk #3

—*Levine, Robert, "Is Love a Luxury?" 1993*

Paraphrase 1:   Rich, individual countries are more likely to think love is important (Levine, 1993).

OK   Not OK

Explanation _____

Paraphrase 2:   Countries that are rich and value individualism are more likely to believe in romantic love (Levine, 1993).

(OK)   Not OK

Explanation _____

_____

3. *Original:*   <u>Globalization so often seems to threaten</u> <u>the identity of the individual,</u>
                      Chunk #1   **Chunk #2**

   <u>by subjecting us to someone else's rules.</u>
                      Chunk #3

   —Ma, Yo-Yo, "Paths of Globalization: From the Berbers to Bach,"
   New Perspectives Quarterly, Spring 2008

Paraphrase 1:   Ma (2008) comments that globalization frequently appears to challenge a person's sense of who he or she is because it makes us follow decisions made by others whom we don't know.

(OK)   Not OK

Explanation _____

_____

Paraphrase 2:   Ma (2008) says that globalization usually terrorizes people by enslaving them in rules that someone else has written.

OK   (Not OK)

Explanation ___*terrorizes are to much*_____

_____

ACTIVITY ❷ Chunking Practice

Select a longer passage (no more than three full sentences) from one of the articles you are reading from Part Two. Use the chunking method to paraphrase this passage. You may work alone, with a partner, or in a group. Share your paraphrasing process with a small group of the class.

1. Read the original passage.

2. Show how you divided the passage into chunks. Discuss why you divided the passage as you did.

3. Explain your paraphrase of each chunk.

4. Show your final and complete paraphrase. Discuss the choices you made as you arranged the ideas in your final paraphrase.

5. Ask for feedback on your paraphrase. Does the paraphrase have the same meaning as the original? Is it written in your own words? Is it grammatically correct?

ACTIVITY ❸ Paraphrasing Proverbs

1. Working in a small group, think of a proverb familiar to you.

2. Take a few minutes for each group member to write a paraphrase of the proverb.

3. Read each person's paraphrase aloud and discuss each of the paraphrases using the following criteria:
   - It is close in meaning to the proverb.
   - No new ideas are added.
   - Important ideas are not deleted.

ACTIVITY ❹ Finding the Paraphrase

1. With a small group, select two or three sentences from an article in Part Two that everyone in the class has already read.

2. Using the tell-a-friend method, the chunking method, or a combination of the two, rewrite the passage you have selected.

3. Evaluate your paraphrase, according to the criteria for a good paraphrase on page 6.

4. Trade your paraphrases with another group.

5. Read the other group's paraphrases and see if you can identify the original passage in the article.

ACTIVITY ❺ Guessing the Paraphrase

1. Work in groups of three. Ask one member of each group to leave the room.

2. The remaining group members read a sentence or short excerpt from an article in Part Two that you have already read.

3. Cover the passage and discuss the meaning of what you have read.

4. Write a paraphrase of the passage.

5. Ask the group member who left the room to return. That person reads your paraphrase and identifies the original passage in the article.

6. Write your group's paraphrase on the board. Then, discuss each group's paraphrase as a class, using the criteria for a good paraphrase on page 6.

RESPONDING TO WRITING

As we read to explore the ideas of other writers on our topic, we may find that we agree or disagree with an author's ideas, or an idea from an article may remind us of our own experiences. We may also find a particular idea interesting because it helps us see the world in a new way.

Teachers are often interested not only in your understanding of an article, but also in your reactions to it. Thus, as a university student, you may be asked to write responses to the material you are reading for a class.

When you write a response, you are having a short conversation with the author, explaining what his ideas mean to you. Also, writing a response gives you a chance to practice paraphrasing, a skill you will need often as you integrate evidence into your research paper.

 ## Three Characteristics of a Response

1. **Responses are subjective.** This means you explain *your* opinion, perception, or insight about an idea or ideas in the article.
2. **Responses vary in content.** Here are several types of responses. You will probably think of other ways to respond on your own:
   - **Personal Experience**
     Write about an idea in the article that matches your own experience or reminds you of something you or someone you know has experienced.
   - **Application**
     Write about something that illustrates an idea in the article. This might be something you have read or heard that applies to or supports what the author has written.
   - **Agree/Disagree**
     Write about a point the author makes that you strongly agree or disagree with. In your response include an explanation of why you think this way.
3. **Responses vary in length.** The length depends on such factors as the requirements of your assignment and the length of the original source.

Techniques for Thinking About a Response

1. **Have a written conversation with the writer.**
   To write a response, begin by reading your source again as if you were talking to the writer. As you read, jot down notes about places where you would interrupt the writer to give your opinion, ask a question, or relate a similar idea or experience you have had.

2. **Look over your notes and choose one or two ideas you want to pursue further.**

3. **Explain your response to the writer's idea.**

   Once you have identified the specific idea you plan to discuss and provided an explanation of what this means in your own words (a paraphrase), you can begin to discuss your reaction to this idea using one of the approaches suggested in Three Characteristics of a Response on page 14.

The following are student examples of the three approaches to responding just described. Study each example and do the Now You Try exercise that follows.

EXAMPLE 1

A Response Using Personal Experience Approach

In her article "Closing the Gap," Mary Piper writes, "My life is richer, too, because of the time that I've spent with my elders. Over the past three years I've interviewed my five aunts, listened to family stories, looked at pictures and eaten home-cooked meals. As a result, I better understand my own parents and our country's history." The author's point is that our life becomes more meaningful when we take time to listen to older people's stories of their experiences because we can begin to understand the history of our family and country.

In my experience, I heard from my grandfather about how my great grandmother began a business making and selling clothing after my great grandfather died. My great grandmother was a good seamstress and many people in the town wanted to buy her clothes. She hired other people to help her sew and built her shop into a successful business. Learning about my great grandmother's strength and business ability has inspired me to study business in college. I'd like to someday run my own business just as my great grandmother did and also to encourage other women In my country. As Piper wrote, listening to my grandfather has been a way to give more meaning to my own life.

NOW YOU TRY

1. Underline the author and article title in the introduction to the response above.

2. Put a vertical slash at the beginning and end of the quote from the article.

3. Circle the student's explanation of the idea that she is interested in from the article.

EXAMPLE 2

A Response Using Application Approach

One idea from the article that I'd like to discuss is Sudo's statement in "Larger Than Life" about a hero's focus on helping other people even when personal risk is involved. Sudo writes, " 'In fact, the one trait of heroes that transcends all cultural boundaries,' Lesy says, 'is the willingness to risk one's life for the good of others.' " Humans are naturally selfish. Most people live their entire lives thinking only about how to improve their own situations. However, for our society to function, we need people who are willing to consider the world beyond their own lives. Cooperation among people is the only solution to many problems such as war, environmental destruction, and poverty. Unfortunately, few people are willing to solve these problems because there is no material reward and sometimes they involve personal risk.

Martin Luther King is a hero because he was willing to lead a fight against racial discrimination. He did not lead this movement to improve his own wealth or reputation. The only reason he devoted his life to civil rights was because he knew that the discrimination blacks experienced was wrong. We would not have improved racial equality today without him. His willingness to risk his own life for the good of others has encouraged many ordinary people to jump into other social, environmental, and political causes. His sacrifice was enhanced by the sacrifices and social movements that followed his own.

NOW YOU TRY

1. Underline the author's name and title of the article in the response introduction above.

2. Put a vertical slash at the beginning and end of the quote from the article.

3. Circle the student's explanation of the idea from the article that he is interested in.

4. This student gives an example of his point about heroes. Where does his example begin? Mark this place with an *X*.

EXAMPLE 3

A Response Using Agree/Disagree Approach

One important idea from "Going Over the Top" is that a need for personal challenge is a significant reason for the popularity of extreme sports. Bower writes, "Challenging yourself to go to the edge, say extreme sports enthusiasts, triggers an almost addictive sense of accomplishment and power." He also writes, "Meeting challenges and realizing goals can also yield a greater appreciation for living." In other words, putting yourself in a high risk situation and overcoming your fear and your limitations can make you appreciate yourself and your life.

While I agree with his general point, I need to ask why extreme sports? You can challenge yourself through many other things. Playing basketball can be challenging too, if you are really serious about it. You can find challenge by saying something to your boss that you couldn't say before. You can also start a new business instead of complaining about your old job. Why should people endanger their lives to feel their power and appreciate their lives? I like peaceful days, but I could also get bored if I have nothing to challenge me. Challenging myself broadens my possibilities. It is exciting to me, so I can relate to extreme sports to some extent. But I will take another path which could be as wild as extreme sports, but less dangerous physically.

NOW YOU TRY

1. Underline the name of the author and the article title in the response above.

2. Put a vertical slash at the beginning and end of the quotes from the article.

3. Circle the student's explanation of this quote. What words does the student use to introduce her explanation?

_____

4. Where does the student begin to discuss how she disagrees with the author? Mark this place with an *X*.

 # Two Steps for Writing a Response

1. **Write an introduction that includes the author and title, and the idea you plan to discuss.**

2. **Write your response or reaction to a part of the article.**

INTRODUCING YOUR RESPONSE

In your introduction include the following:

- The name of the author and the title of the article
- A paraphrase of the specific point from the article that you plan to discuss. You may also want to include a quote of the idea you are discussing.

You may choose to use one of the following two formats.

Format 1: Including the Quote, Then Paraphrasing It
In (name of article), (name of author) writes, (quote of sentence or sentences you plan to discuss). In other words . . . (paraphrase of this idea).

> **EXAMPLE**
>
> In "The Case for Torture," Michael Levin writes, "There are situations in which torture is not merely permissible but morally mandatory." In other words, he says that torturing people is sometimes acceptable and even necessary.

Format 2: Paraphrasing Only
One interesting idea from (name of article) by (name of author) is . . . (paraphrase of the ideas you plan to discuss).

> **EXAMPLE**
>
> One interesting idea from "The Case for Torture" by Michael Levin is that torturing people is sometimes acceptable and even necessary.

EXPLAINING YOUR RESPONSE TO THE IDEA

Once you have identified the specific idea you plan to discuss and provided an explanation of what this means in your own words (a paraphrase), you can begin to discuss your reaction to this idea using one of the approaches suggested in Three Characteristics of a Response on page 14.

NOW YOU TRY

Choose one of the two response formats and write an introduction using the information below.

Name of article: "The Friendship of Boys"

Name of author: Mike Barns

Quote: "When boys compete with each other, it can be a form of bonding."

Paraphrase: Some boys develop friendship through competitive activities.

Introduction:

_____

_____

_____

ACTIVITIES TO PRACTICE WRITING RESPONSES

ACTIVITY **1** Discussing Your Reaction

1. Read the short article "Coping with Procrastination" on page 20.

2. In a small group or with the class, discuss your response to the article. Here are some questions to get you started.
   - Is there an idea in the article that reminds you of something you have experienced? Have you put off something for one of the reasons the authors mention?
   - Can you think of an example of how someone has applied one of the solutions to procrastination mentioned in the article?
   - Is there an idea from the article that you agree or disagree with? For example, you might choose one of the reasons for putting things off and explain why you agree that it is a powerful reason for people to procrastinate.

ACTIVITY **2** Responding to One Interesting Idea

1. Choose an article you have read from Part Two. Select one or two sentences that you find interesting.

2. Write a paraphrase of the sentences.

3. Do the following with a partner:
   - Read the original sentences.
   - Use your paraphrase to explain what you think the sentences mean.

- Discuss your reaction to this idea. If you have had an experience that is related to the idea, tell your partner the story. If you can think of a good example to illustrate an idea, describe your example. If you agree or disagree, explain why.

4. For more practice, you may repeat step 3 with several partners. Each time you explain the author's idea and your response to it, the process will become easier and your ideas will become clearer.

ACTIVITY ❸ Analyzing Articles

1. Choose two or three articles that deal with the same theme you have already read in Part Two.

2. Look for an idea that is repeated in more than one article. Highlight or write on a separate piece of paper all the sentences from each article that discuss this idea.

3. Discuss with your partner or a small group how this idea is treated in each article. Is it defined? Is an example given? Does the author express an opinion?

4. Orally summarize how the different articles discuss this idea. Present your ideas to the class.

ACTIVITY ❹ Writing a Response

Write a response to one of the articles you have been exploring in Part Two. As you write your response, remember the following:

- Responses are subjective. They explain your reaction to the ideas in the article.
- Response introductions include the name of the author and/or the title of the article.
- The introduction to your response should identify the specific idea, either quoted or paraphrased, that you plan to discuss.

SUMMARIZING

Summarizing, like paraphrasing, is your explanation of another person's ideas. One of your jobs as a writer is to place your ideas within the context of other writers and thinkers on your topic. Summarizing is a useful tool for this job. You can summarize an article of many pages or even an entire book in just a few short sentences or paragraphs. Teachers may also assign you to write a summary to check whether you understand the material you have read. We often use summaries in both speaking and writing to tell listeners or readers our ideas quickly and clearly. In academic writing, a summary of someone else's text has four important elements.

Four Criteria for a Good Summary

1. **A good summary acknowledges the original author.**
   - It refers to the writer and/or the title of the work in a formal way.
   - It presents the writer's ideas objectively, without your interpretation or opinion.

2. **A good summary contains only the most important information.**
   - The topic (the general subject of the article)
   - The main point that the author makes about that topic (the *thesis*)
   - The key ideas that support or explain the thesis

3. **A good summary is much shorter than the original writing.**
   - A one-sentence summary describes only the author's thesis, or the main idea.
   - A fuller summary explains both the thesis and the main supporting points.

4. **A good summary paraphrases any information taken from the original writing.**
   - Paraphrasing shows that you understand what the author is saying.

Below is an article about why people procrastinate. Following the article there are two summary examples. The first is a one-sentence summary that explains the authors' thesis. The second is a longer, complete summary that includes both the thesis and the main supporting points of the article.

"Coping with Procrastination"

Rebecca Moore, Barbara Baker, and Arnold Packer
College Success, 1997

Any discussion of time management would not be complete without an examination of the most well-intentioned person's worst enemy—procrastination. The dictionary (*Webster's New Collegiate*) defines *procrastination* as "the act of putting off intentionally and habitually the doing of something that should be done." Interestingly, most
5 procrastinators do not feel that they are acting intentionally. On the contrary, they feel that they fully *intend* to do whatever it is, but they simply cannot, will not, or— bottom line—they *do not* do it. Procrastinators usually have good reasons for their procrastination (some would call them excuses): "didn't have time," "didn't feel well," "couldn't figure out what to do," "couldn't find what I needed," "the weather was too
10 bad"—the list is never-ending.

Even procrastinators themselves know that the surface reasons for their procrastination are, for the most part, not valid. When procrastination becomes extreme, it is a self-destructive course, and, yet, people feel that they are powerless to

stop it. This perception can become reality if the underlying cause is not uncovered.
15 Experts have identified some of the serious underlying causes of procrastination.
Think about them the next time you find yourself struck by this problem.

Often procrastination stems from a real or imagined fear or worry that is focused
not so much on the thing you are avoiding but its potential consequences. For
instance, your procrastination over preparing for an oral presentation could be based
20 on your fear that no matter how well prepared you are, you will be overcome by nerves
and forget whatever you are prepared to say. Every time you think about working on
the speech, you become so worried about doing "a bad job" that you have to put the
whole thing out of your mind to calm down. You decide that you will feel calmer about
it tomorrow and will be in a much better frame to tackle it. Tomorrow the scenario gets
25 repeated. The best way to relieve your anxiety would be to dig in and prepare well so
that you can't possibly do poorly.

Being a perfectionist is one of the main traits that spawns fear and anxiety. Whose
expectations are we afraid of not meeting? Often it is our own harsh judgment of
ourselves that creates the problem. We set standards that are too high and then
30 judge ourselves too critically. When you picture yourself speaking before a group,
are you thinking about how nervous the other students will be as well, or are you
comparing your speaking abilities to the anchorperson on the six o'clock news?
A more calming thought is to recall how athletes measure improvements in their
performances by tracking and trying to improve on their own "personal best."
35 Champions have to work on beating themselves in order to become capable of
competing against their opponents. Concentrating on improving your own past
performance, and thinking of specific ways to do so, relieves performance anxiety.

On the surface this would seem to be the reason for all procrastination, and the
obvious answer is for the procrastinator to find a way to "get motivated." There are
40 situations where lack of motivation is an indicator that you have taken a wrong turn.
When you seriously do not want to do the things you need to do, you may need to
reevaluate your situation. Did you decide to get a degree in Information Systems
because everyone says that's where the high paying jobs are going to be, when you
really want to be a social worker or a travel agent? If so, when you find yourself shooting
45 hoops or watching television when you should be putting in time at the computer
lab, it may be time to re-examine your decision. Setting out to accomplish something
difficult when your heart isn't in it is often the root cause of self-destructive behavior.

Often procrastination is due to an inability to concentrate or a feeling of being
overwhelmed and indecisive. While everyone experiences these feelings during a
50 particularly stressful day or week, a continuation of these feelings could indicate that
you are in a state of burnout. Burnout is a serious problem that occurs when you have
overextended yourself for too long a period of time. It is especially likely to occur if you
are pushing yourself both physically and mentally. By failing to pace yourself, you will
"hit the wall," like a long distance runner who runs too fast at the beginning of the race.
55 Overworking yourself for too long without mental and physical relaxation is a sure way
to run out of steam. Learning to balance your time and set realistic expectations for
yourself will prevent burnout.

Sometimes you put off doing something because you literally don't know how to
do it. This may be hard to admit to yourself, so you may make other excuses. When

60 you can't get started on something, consider the possibility that you need help. For example, if you get approval from your favorite instructor for a term paper topic that requires collecting data and creating graphics, you can be stymied if you don't have the necessary skills and tools to do the work and do it well. Does the collection and analysis of the data require the use of a software program that you don't have and

65 cannot afford to buy? Sometimes it is difficult to ask for help and sometimes it is even hard to recognize that you need help. When you feel stymied, ask yourself, "Do I need help?" Do you need information but haven't a clue as to where to go to get it? Have you committed to doing something that is really beyond your level of skills? Being able to own up to personal limitations and seek out support and

70 resources where needed is a skill used every day by highly successful people.

EXAMPLE: ONE-SENTENCE SUMMARY

In "Coping with Procrastination," Moore, Baker, and Packer discuss the fundamental reasons why people put off doing things and how to overcome these issues.

- A one-sentence summary includes only the author's thesis, plus the name of the author and/or the title of the article.

EXAMPLE: FULL SUMMARY

In their article "Coping with Procrastination," Moore, Baker, and Packer suggest that, in order to change the habit of procrastination, it is essential to look below the surface for the real reasons why one puts off doing things. Worry about bad results can cause procrastination, but a better way to approach the task you dread is to be very sure you are so ready that nothing bad can happen. If a person expects nothing less than perfection from himself, he will fear failure and simply not begin the task. A suggestion for dealing with this is to copy athletes who strive to achieve their own best effort rather than comparing themselves with the champion in their field. Sometimes motivation is the problem; a person may feel trapped by a bad decision that no longer matches his desires. Re-examining one's goals may help. Burnout, or exhaustion from pushing oneself too hard for too long, can lead to procrastination. In this situation, it is essential to set doable goals. Finally, a person may avoid doing a task because of a real lack of knowledge or experience about the job at hand. Seeking assistance from others can make the task less forbidding.

- A full summary includes the name of the author and/or the title of the article, the author's thesis, and the main ideas that support it.

Three Techniques for Identifying Main Ideas for a Summary

One of the challenges of summarizing is that we must choose which information to include, keeping in mind the principles of being complete and objective. You can choose one of the three techniques that follow to help you identify the main ideas in an article.

TECHNIQUE 1: UNDERLINING KEY IDEAS

1. Read the article completely several times to develop a basic understanding of the ideas presented.

2. With a highlighting pen, mark each idea in the article that you believe is important.

   - Often, although not always, you will find that each paragraph has a key sentence. It is often the first or last sentence in a paragraph.

   - Look for key words that are repeated throughout the article. These repeated words and phrases will help you identify main ideas.

   - If you find that you have highlighted most or all of the sentences in a paragraph, you may be highlighting supporting details rather than main ideas.

   - If so, go back and underline only the main ideas in the sentences that you highlighted.

3. When you finish highlighting, read each sentence again to ensure you understand it.

4. Use either the tell-a-friend or chunking method to paraphrase each sentence you highlighted.

5. You can use these paraphrased ideas in your summary.

NOW YOU TRY

Re-read the article "Coping with Procrastination." As you read, underline the one or two sentences from each paragraph that you believe are the most important points. Check the sentences you have chosen against the full summary of the article on page 22.

TECHNIQUE 2: DIVIDING AND DESCRIBING

1. With a pen in hand, read the entire article, "Coping with Procrastination." Each time you sense that the topic is shifting, draw a vertical line where you think the shift begins.

   - Don't analyze how the topic is changing. Let your intuition do the work.

   - Throughout the article, draw a line each time you feel the topic shifts.

2. By drawing these lines you have created sections. In a longer article, you will discover that paragraphs are grouped together according to common topics.

   - Analyze the topic of each section you have created.

   - Write a phrase or short sentence that explains the topic of each section.

3. The topics of these groups of paragraphs are usually the author's main supporting points. Examining how many paragraphs an author uses to discuss a single idea can help you decide which information is most important and should be included in your summary.

4. Use your list of phrases describing the sections to write your summary.

NOW YOU TRY

In the copy of the article "Coping with Procrastination" on the website at **http://elt.heinle.com/sourcework**, a line has been drawn each time the topic shifts. In the first two sections, a short phrase describing the topic has been given. Write a short phrase or sentence describing the topic of the other three sections of the article.

TECHNIQUE 3: SUMMARY GRID

Sometimes it is helpful to lay out your notes in a visual way. Using a grid is one way to help organize the information in an article.

1. Use a grid to take notes on each paragraph or section of several paragraphs.

   • Writing main ideas and supporting details in separate columns is a good way to help distinguish between the two.

2. Use your notes to create a summary of your article.

   • Remember, a summary focuses on main ideas. Details are usually not included in summaries. In some cases, a specific example from the article might be included.

3. Here is an example of a summary grid created by a student after reading an article on the negative aspects of drinking bottled water.

Example Summary Grid

Paragraph(s)	Main Idea	Some Supporting Details
1	• Bottled water may not be any safer than tap water.	
2–3	• Bottled water manufacturers don't have to disclose the source of their water.	• Yosemite brand comes from a Los Angeles suburb. • Everest brand comes from Texas.
4	• The EPA requires fewer contamination tests for bottled water than city water.	• The FDA only tests once a year, or if there is a complaint.
5	• Plastic bottles are a source of water contamination.	• Bacteria develop in bottles. • Chemicals leach from plastic material.

Use the grid below to take notes on each paragraph of the article "Coping with Procrastination."

Summary Grid

Paragraph(s)	Main Idea	Some Supporting Details

 To print out a copy of this grid, go to the *Sourcework* website at **http://elt.heinle.com/sourcework.**

Two Steps for Writing a Summary

1. **Write an introductory sentence or two that includes three pieces of information:**
   - The title of the article or source
   - The name of the author(s)
   - The author's thesis, or main idea

2. **Write the body that describes the main ideas in the original source. This may be one or more paragraphs, depending on the length of the original writing.**

INTRODUCING YOUR SUMMARY

You can choose how you want to arrange the information in your introduction. Below are two possible formats.

Format 1: One Sentence
In (title of article), (author's name) writes/discusses (article thesis).

In "Mind Over Mass Media," Pinker (2010) writes that both lab research and actual experience show that people are incapable of doing several things at once; as an example of this fact, he mentions the frequent sight of a person driving dangerously while using a cell phone.

NOTE: This format appears in the one-sentence example summary on page 22.

Format 2: Two Sentences

(Name of author) writes about (article topic) in (his/her/their) article, (name of article). The second sentence of the summary introduction describes the thesis.

EXAMPLE

Pinker (2010) writes about the fallacy of multitasking in his article "Mind Over Mass Media." He says that both lab research and actual experience show that people are incapable of doing several things at once; as an example, he mentions the frequent sight of a person driving dangerously while using a cell phone.

NOW YOU TRY

Using Format 2, write an introduction for a summary of "Coping with Procrastination."

_____

_____

_____

DESCRIBING THE MAIN IDEAS

After you introduce the author, title, and main idea or thesis of the original, use the notes you made with one of the Techniques for Identifying Main Ideas for a Summary on page 23 to write the body of your summary.

Combining a Summary and a Response

Sometimes you might want to combine a summary with a response as a means of exploring sources for your research paper. In this case, your summary appears first and your response is second. Your summary may be a one-sentence summary or a fuller summary, depending on your assignment. Your response may focus on just one or two ideas or it may discuss the entire article.

1. **Write an introduction that summarizes the article and tells the reader which ideas you plan to discuss.**

   • The name of the author and the title of the source

   • A summary of the article

   • A statement of the idea or ideas you will respond to

2. **Write your response, or reaction, to the ideas in the article. This includes paraphrases of specific ideas you will discuss.**

- Your response to one or more ideas from the article
- Paraphrases of each idea as you discuss it

SUMMARY AND RESPONSE EXAMPLE

author ——————— Susan Scarf Merrell (1995) writes about birth order in her book *The Accidental Bond*. She explains whether it is true or a myth that birth order can predict a person's future. Even though many people think that birth order defines a person's life, other important factors such as culture, gender, and social and economic status affect a person's achievement. Two important issues from the book that I would like to discuss are Merrell's statements about gender and culture. For me, they are connected to each other.

The first issue is about gender. Merrell (1995) indicates that if the firstborn in the family is a girl, she has different experiences than her brothers. I agree with her because her statement applies in my own culture. Even though Mexican culture about "machismo" is changing, it still exists in our society. By the term "machismo," I mean that men are considered more important than women. In some Mexican families the gender of the firstborn is very important. If the firstborn is a boy, he will receive more benefits or advantages than a girl. Also, he will receive more privileges and he will have access to more things. For example, in my father's family my father was the firstborn, so he had the opportunity to study in Mexico City from the time he was 12 years old (the family used to live in a little town far from Mexico City). However, his sisters had to wait to study outside the town until they were more than 18 years old. They went to live in a city close to their parents' house so their parents could visit them every weekend.

The next important idea is about culture. Merrell (1995) indicates that if a firstborn in a wealthy family is a boy, he receives the economic and powerful benefits of his family. In the "machismo" culture the primogeniture is supposed to inherit control of the family's business and money. Therefore, for the family, it is very important that the firstborn is a man because they think that a man has more intelligence or capacity than a woman. For instance, a very famous Mexican family from the North of the country, which owns a big company, had as firstborn a girl, but they did not give her control of the business. They gave her a comfortable and nice life as a member of the family. However, the second born was a boy, and he has in his hands the control of the business because he is a man. Currently, he is the president of his family's business.

In conclusion, in these cases, gender and culture affect a person's development more than birth order. Therefore, it is only a myth. Merrell's thesis is interesting and I agree with her. It is important to remember that factors such as culture, gender, social and economical status influence the development of a person.

NOW YOU TRY

Work with a partner to label the following parts in the summary and response example on birth order.

1. Author of book discussed in summary (This one has been done for you.)

2. Title of the source (a book)

3. Summary of the source

4. Two ideas in the book that the writer will respond to

5. Paraphrase of first idea writer will respond to

6. Writer's explanation of her response

7. Paraphrase of second idea writer will respond to

8. Explanation of her response to second idea

9. Conclusion

ACTIVITIES TO PRACTICE SUMMARIZING

ACTIVITY **1** Sharing Ideas for a Summary

Do this activity when everyone in the class is reading the same article in Part Two for possible use in your guided research paper.

1. For homework, read the assigned article from Part Two. As you read, underline what you believe are the key ideas or complete a summary grid (review the example grid on page 24). Bring your underlined article or summary grid to class for discussion.

2. In a small group, work through the article paragraph by paragraph and discuss which ideas you have selected and why.

3. Share your list with the class.

4. If there is time, work with your group to write a summary using the ideas from your list.

ACTIVITY **2** Dividing and Describing

1. Working by yourself, read through an article from Part Two and draw a vertical line at each point where you feel the topic shifts.

2. In a small group with others who have read the same article, share where you have drawn lines and discuss why you think your divisions make sense.

3. Try to come to an agreement with your group about where the topic shifts and how the article should be divided.

4. With your group, describe the main idea of each section of the article in one or two sentences.

5. Share your divisions and descriptions with the rest of the class.

6. As a class or in your small group, use your descriptions to write a summary of the article.

ACTIVITY **3** Writing a Summary

- Write a summary, or a summary and response, of an article that you have been reading in Part Two. Use one of the strategies described in class to help you identify the main ideas of your article.

- The summary introduction should include the name of the author, title of the source and the author's thesis.

- Remember that a summary contains only the most important information and is shorter than the original.

CHAPTER 2

BUILDING A PAPER:
Focus

After exploring the theme in a broad sense, you are ready to write a research paper about one specific aspect of the theme. Here you will begin to develop your unique point of view about the topic. Your teacher will assign a question for writing from the end of the theme you have been reading about in Part Two, or you will work with your classmates to develop a research question.

This question will be your guide as you go forward with your paper. With your research question in front of you, read your sources in Part Two again, but in a different way than you did in Chapter 1. This time, make notes only about the parts of the source that help to answer your research question. As you read each source and take notes, you'll start to accumulate useful ideas that will contribute to the content of your paper.

When you review these notes, look for patterns of similar or related ideas. Then, organize these concepts into a rough outline of the potential supporting points for your paper.

In this chapter you will practice the following:

- Using a research question

- Doing a focused reading and taking notes

- Creating a rough outline of your research paper

By the end of this chapter you will have used a research question as a guide in taking notes on articles from Part Two. You will also have organized your notes into a rough outline for the paper you'll write.

USING A RESEARCH QUESTION

To explore your topic in Chapter 1, you did an open reading of several articles from one of the themes in Part Two. In this next step of the writing process, you will do a second reading of the same articles. As you read your sources again, you will look for information about a specific aspect of your topic, using a research question to guide you. A research question is a tool that enables you to read your sources more efficiently by providing you with a specific focus. The research question helps you decide which information might be useful for your research paper, that is, which information can help to answer your research question, and which information will not be relevant.

 # Elements of a Research Question

A research question includes two parts:

1. **The topic for your paper, usually in the form of a noun or noun phrase**

2. **The focus, which suggests what you will say about the topic and tells you what kind of information to look for as you read**

EXAMPLE: SAMPLE RESEARCH QUESTION

Why do people become addicted to alcohol?

- The general topic of this question is the noun phrase "addicted to alcohol," and the focus is about why people become addicted—causes of addiction.

Using this sample research question, you would look in your sources for information about the causes of addiction. You would disregard any information about the effects of drinking alcohol or about types of alcohol addiction, since the focus of the question does not mention these ideas.

TYPES OF FOCUS

The focus of a research question points you toward the specific aspect of your topic that you are going to explore further through your reading. Your focus may be one of several types.

Cause

This kind of question asks you to explain the causes or reasons for something. See the example about why people become addicted to alcohol.

Effect

Writing about the consequences or effects of an event or action is another common focus of academic writing, as in this research question.

What are the negative consequences of alcohol addiction?

- The writer using this research question will read sources looking for effects of alcohol addiction.

Comparison

Your research question might ask you to compare two or more concepts.

How are attitudes toward drinking alcohol similar or different in the United States and Japan?

- The focus for this question is comparing attitudes in the two countries. As the writer reads through sources, he will search for information that describes the attitudes towards drinking in the two countries.

Definition

Some research questions ask for an in-depth definition of a topic.

What are the signs of alcohol addiction?

- Here the focus is on explaining what alcoholism is, so the writer will read sources and note any information that helps define alcoholism.

Classification

Other research questions are about ways of classifying a topic.

What are the different patterns of alcohol use?

- The focus in this paper will be how people use alcohol. The evidence the writer looks for in reading sources will be about various ways people incorporate alcohol into their lives.

Problem and Solution

A research question may present a problem and point toward solutions.

How can a person who is an alcoholic stop drinking?

- With this focus about the problem of how to stop using alcohol, the writer will read for information about ways to solve the problem of addiction.

Process

A research question may ask how something is done or how something happens.

How does an individual become addicted to alcohol?

- Using this focus on how the addiction develops, the writer will search for information about the steps in becoming addicted to alcohol.

Argument

Some research questions may be in a *yes/no* format and ask you to explain an opinion.

Should the legal age for drinking be lowered from 21 to 18?

- In this case, the focus is an opinion and why that opinion is right. The writer using this research question will decide his opinion about the question and look for information about why that opinion is correct.

Again, notice that a research question helps you look for certain specific information and discard other information. In the argument question, for example, you would look for information to support your opinion, and you would ignore information that discusses causes or effects of alcoholism or any other focus. In this way, as you read through sources, the research question helps you select only the information that will be useful in writing your paper.

NOW YOU TRY

For each research question, identify the topic and the type of focus: cause, effect, comparison, definition, classification, problem and solution, process, or argument. Then, describe the kind of information to look for in sources to answer the question.

1. How does early homeschooling affect students' later academic performance?

   Topic _____

   Type of focus _____

   Kind of information to look for _____

2. Should assisted suicide be legal?

   Topic _____

   Type of focus _____

   Kind of information to look for _____

3. How do the public school systems in the United States and Canada compare with each other?

   Topic _____

   Type of focus _____

   Kind of information to look for _____

RESEARCH QUESTIONS WITH MORE THAN ONE FOCUS

Sometimes a research question combines more than one focus idea. In this case you need to identify each focus and consider how all the focus ideas relate to each other.

EXAMPLE 1

Research Question: In what ways can understanding the causes of alcohol addiction help a person stop drinking?

- This research question includes two focuses:

  1. the causes of alcohol addiction (cause)

  2. the methods for stopping addiction (process)

- The writer must also discuss how methods for stopping relate to causes of drinking.

EXAMPLE 2

Research Question: How does the value of individualism influence people's expectations of marriage?

- This research question has two focuses:

  1. the definition of the concept of individualism (definition)

  2. the effects of individualism on ideas about marriage (effect)

NOW YOU TRY

For each research question, write the topic and the type of focus: cause, effect, comparison, definition, classification, problem and solution, process, or argument. Then, describe what kind of information to look for in order to answer the question. Remember there is more than one focus in each research question.

1. How does blues music reflect the values of US culture?

Topic _____

Types of focus _____

Kind of information to look for _____

2. What are the different kinds of yoga and how do they compare in methods and health benefits?

Topic _____

Types of focus _____

Kind of information to look for _____

BUILDING YOUR PAPER

Identify the Focus of Your Research Question

Look at your research question again for the paper you are building and identify the topic and the focus.

- Recall that the topic of the research question is usually a noun or noun phrase. The focus suggests what you will say about that topic.

- Remember that your research question may have more than one focus.

OPTIONAL

Creating a Research Question

If your teacher does not give you a research question, it is worthwhile to create your own because using it will save you time and help you read sources more effectively. This is your chance to find some aspect of your topic that is really interesting to you. You can create a research question from the notes you took during your open reading of sources in Chapter 1.

TWO WAYS TO CREATE A RESEARCH QUESTION

1. Consider the ideas you shared with classmates or wrote about after you did your open reading in Chapter 1. For example, in a discussion on heroism, one student shared her thoughts with her classmates on the following quote from "Eve's Daughters," in Part Two on page 162.

   "The hero has an original perspective that distinguishes her from others who settle for agreement and conformity or are too beaten down to ask necessary questions. The relationship between the hero and the established order of things is fluid; she insists on her freedom to perceive, within the context of things-as-they-are, the way things *could* be."—*Polster, Miriam, 2001*

   Talking about this quote led to a more general discussion of the definition of a hero. This student eventually developed the following research question:

   What is a hero?

2. Look at some of the sections you highlighted in your sources during your open reading. These ideas can turn into more general questions. For example, in an article on cell phone addiction, a student highlighted the following sentences:

   "'Although experts have pinpointed these problems in frequent cell phone users, studies have yet to show if a bad cell phone habit constitutes an actual addiction. Yet as with traditional addictions, excessive cell phone use is associated with certain hallmark patterns of behavior, including using something to feel good, building up a tolerance and needing it more and more over time to get the same feeling, and going through withdrawal if deprived of it,' Merlo said."

—*Birdwell, April Frawley, Health, Research Technology, 2007.*

After thinking about this quote, the student developed her research question:

How do cell phones affect people in a harmful way?

NOW YOU TRY

Write one or two possible research questions based on this excerpt from "If Poor Get Richer, Does World See Progress?" in Part Two, Globalization on page 185.

"Rising consumption has helped meet basic needs and create jobs," says Christopher Flavin, president of the Worldwatch Institute, a Washington, D.C., think tank. "But as we enter a new century, this unprecedented consumer appetite is undermining the natural systems we all depend on and making it even harder for the world's poor to meet their basic needs."

—*Knickerbocker, Brad, 2004*

Research Questions:

_____

_____

_____

BUILDING YOUR PAPER

Create a Research Question

If your teacher has not given you a research question, create one now. In developing your research question, you may want to:

- go back to Chapter 1 and use an idea from the discussion and writing activities that you did after your open reading of the articles on your theme in Part Two.

- consider the general description, expectations, and limitations of the research paper assignment, if your teacher has given you one.

After you have written your research question, identify the topic and the focus.

FOCUSED READING AND TAKING NOTES

With your research question as a guide, you can begin to decide which information from the articles will be useful for the research paper you are building. To use your research question effectively, you need to be clear about its focus, or what it is asking you to look for in your reading.

 # Focused Reading Guidelines

With the topic and focus of your research question clearly in mind, you are ready to do a focused reading of the articles on your theme in Part Two. Do the following as you read through your sources.

1. **Read quickly.**

2. **Highlight any information that looks like it might answer your research question.** Use a different color marker than you used for open reading.

3. **Don't analyze what you highlight. Just mark anything that seems useful.**

4. **Notice that some sources will be covered with highlights while others will have only a few marked areas.** However, it is not the quantity of information that makes a source valuable, but whether the information actually relates to your research question.

5. **Go back and re-read only the information you just highlighted.** Look up any confusing words, and then read those sections again until you understand them.

6. **Choose a way to keep track of what you have highlighted.** These notes are the information you will use as supporting evidence in your paper.

NOW YOU TRY

To understand how a research question can guide and focus your reading, do two focused readings of "Coping with Procrastination" on page 20, using different research questions.

1. Use a colored marker to highlight any information that you think will help answer the question *Why do people procrastinate?*

2. Read the article a second time. This time look for information to answer the question *How can people overcome procrastination?* Use a different color marker to highlight useful information.

3. Share the information you highlighted for each question. Is it the same as or different from what your classmates highlighted?

NOTE-TAKING METHODS

With many sources to read and evaluate, you need a way to keep track of the material you may use in your research paper. You need to record where you have looked, what you have found, and how to find each piece of information again. In short, you need a system for taking notes. There are many ways to keep and organize information. Choose a system that's useful for you and that you will use every time you do research for your paper.

It's not a good idea to neglect taking notes on an article "just this one time" because you are in a hurry or because you plan to come back to it later and read it in more detail. You will save yourself time and frustration if you take notes on everything you think may be of even the slightest use. You can always throw away any notes you don't use. You can't always retrace your steps and find the same quote again if you haven't kept track of it. Below are four common methods for taking notes.

Using Your Highlighted Sources

For a short paper, or if you are reading only two or three sources, you may be able to simply use as your notes the parts that you highlighted during your focused reading.

The advantage of this system is that you've already done the work—the notes are right there in the articles you've read. The drawbacks are that you can't move the notes around to group similar ideas together, and you still have to paraphrase the ideas in order to use them in your writing.

Taking Notes on a Computer

1. Type your research question at the top of the page.
2. Type the source information under the research question: the title of the article, the author, the publication where the article appeared, the date it appeared, and the page numbers.
3. Type any sentences from the article that you think can help provide an answer to your research question.
4. Next to each piece of information, type comments about how you might use this information in your paper.

The advantage of this system is that you begin to develop material that is directly related to your paper. This method allows you to focus on useful source information without being distracted by other information in the article. The disadvantage is that you must have access to a computer when you are doing your focused reading.

Writing Margin Notes

At this stage in the writing process, some writers prefer to simply refer to the text they highlighted during their focused reading rather than create a separate set of notes. In addition to the highlights, you can write comments in the margins of the article next to highlighted information.

The advantage of this system is that it is quick and easy. The disadvantage is that you must photocopy all your sources and have them with you whenever you work on your paper. In addition, you will not be able to move these notes around as you begin to sort and organize them in later stages of the writing process.

Using Note Cards

1. Use a separate card for each sentence or group of sentences from the source article that might help you answer your research question.

2. Write the title, author, date of publication, and page number of the source on the card.

3. In addition to the quote from the article, write notes to yourself about how you might use this information.

The advantage of this method is that you can easily reorganize the information by rearranging the cards. However, taking notes this way is time-consuming, and the stack of note cards can be awkward to carry.

The key point is to take some time at this focus stage of your research process to devise a way to take notes that works for you. Your method should be easy, accurate, and comfortable enough that you will follow it for taking notes on all your sources.

ACTIVITIES TO PRACTICE TAKING NOTES

ACTIVITY **1** Sharing Highlighted Information

Do this in a small group with others who have the same research question.

1. For homework, do a focused reading of at least one source in Part Two that you are reading for your research paper. Bring your highlighted article to class.

2. In small groups, share three pieces of information you highlighted. Discuss how this information could be used to help answer the research question.

3. If the whole class is working on the same research question, share up to four pieces of information that your group believes would be most useful in answering the research question. There will probably be more than four pieces of useful information, but limit yourself to four.

ACTIVITY **2** Explaining Information from Sources

Do this with several classmates who are working with different research questions and/or different sources of information from Part Two.

1. Complete a focused reading on at least three sources in Part Two.

2. In a small group or with a partner, share your research question and then explain some of the information you found to help you answer the research question.

3. Use your own words when discussing the information from your sources; in this way, you will begin to develop a greater level of comfort in using and writing about the ideas in a source. The more you practice talking about this information, the easier it will be to write similar explanations when you begin your paper.

BUILDING YOUR PAPER

Read and Take Notes on Your Sources

1. Using your research question as a guide, complete a focused reading of the articles in Part Two that you plan to use. Remember to highlight any information that may help to answer your research question.

2. Write a set of notes for each source you selected. You can write your notes on a computer, in the margins of the articles, or on note cards.

CREATING A ROUGH OUTLINE

Up to now, you have explored and focused on your subject in a broad way: reading and discussing sources, paraphrasing passages in order to understand them better, writing your opinions about the topic, and taking notes on your reading. At this point, you may feel that you have so much information that it is confusing. But think of this stage as "necessary chaos," when lots of ideas are in the air just before the "dust clears" and you see a clear image of what you want to say.

In fact, with the ideas you are thinking about and the notes from your focused reading, you already have much of the substance of your paper. The next step is to figure out how your ideas fit together. A useful way of doing this is to create a rough outline. This way of organizing your thinking will help you write your paper.

 ## Elements of a Rough Outline

1. **It begins with your research question.**
2. **It identifies the focus of the research question.**
3. **It lists several, usually two to five, categories of answers to your research question.**

EXAMPLE: ROUGH OUTLINE

Research Question: Why do people become addicted to alcohol?

Focus of Research
Question: Causes

Answers to Research
Question: **1.** Emotional distress
2. Social pressure
3. Genetic predisposition

To create this rough outline, the writer used the Sample Research Question on page 31. She identified the focus of her research question as "causes" and did a focused reading of her sources about the causes of alcohol addiction, taking notes as she read. Then, she analyzed the notes from her reading and grouped similar ideas together. She identified three main categories of answers to her research question, or three main types of causes of alcohol addiction, and created the outline from these.

To create your rough outline, look again at the focus of your research question. This focus will guide the way you analyze your notes and, eventually, how you organize the ideas from your notes into a rough outline. Look through the notes you took during your focused reading and group similar ideas together. You will see a pattern emerge, and the answers to your research question will fall into several categories. Find a word or phrase to describe each category and list the categories as points in your rough outline.

As you refine this short outline into a more detailed outline and draft your research paper, you may change how you describe these supporting points, what information you include in each point, or the points themselves. But your rough outline is a useful first step in analyzing and organizing your ideas.

Following are a few techniques to choose from to help you group your notes into categories of similar ideas or supporting points for your research paper.

 # Three Techniques for Analyzing Notes for a Rough Outline

TECHNIQUE 1: BRAINSTORMING A LIST

To use this technique you need to have your notes written on a piece of paper separate from the source article, or on note cards.

1. Read all your notes quickly to refresh your memory and then put them aside.

2. On a fresh piece of paper, or on your computer, write your research question.

3. Without looking at your notes, brainstorm a list of words and phrases from your notes that come to mind as you consider the answer to your research question. Write quickly without analyzing or judging the ideas.

4. Return to your notes and check to see if you have missed any ideas during your brainstorm.

5. Read over your list to see which words or phrases seem to go together. Label each group of words that go together with a different number. Work quickly, letting your intuition do the work. Don't stop to figure out how the words in each group are related.

For example, in a brainstorm about the characteristics of a successful city, a group of students created the list that follows and numbered the related ideas.

EXAMPLE

Research
Question: What makes a successful city?

Strong neighborhoods 1	Natural beauty 3
Good economy 2	Safe 2
Cultural amenities 3	Dynamism 3
Arts community 3	Diverse industry 2
Major league sports team 3	Flexibility 2
Volunteerism 1	Opportunities for variety
Interesting places to go 3	of people 2
Easy to get around 3	Good citizens 1
Affordable housing 1	Strong leadership 1
Good air and water quality 3	Attractive urban design 3
Strong sense of itself 1	Good colleges 2
Good schools 1	Low crime 1

6. Once you have created and numbered a list, look for ways to describe the different groups of ideas. Ask yourself: What do all the ideas with the same number have in common?

Using the list above, the students decided that all the items numbered "1" were about social structure; all "2s," about the economy; and all "3s," about the environment. They then created a rough outline using these categories.

Sample Rough Outline

Research Question: What makes a successful city?

Focus of Research
        Question: Definition

Answers to Research
Question: **1.** Strong social structure
2. Solid economy
3. Good physical and cultural environment

TECHNIQUE 2: SORTING YOUR NOTES

1. Read your notes and put a check mark next to each piece of information that you find particularly useful in answering your research question. Try for 15 to 30 check marks.

2. If your notes are on a single piece of paper, cut them apart so that each piece of information is on a separate strip. If your notes are on note cards, you already have your separate pieces of paper.

3. Put all the notes that seem to belong together into the same pile. Don't spend time analyzing how they are related; just work intuitively. You will probably find that some ideas don't fit easily into any category, so you may decide to omit them. You may also notice that some categories have many ideas and others have very few.

4. Now analyze what connects the ideas in each pile and give each pile a category name—a descriptive word or phrase, as the students did in the list about a successful city on page 42. These categories will become the main supporting points in your rough outline.

TECHNIQUE 3: COLOR CODING

1. Assemble all your reading notes and several different colored highlighting pens.

2. Read all your notes quickly and decide on some categories for the different kinds of information. Between three and eight categories is usually a good number.

3. Assign a different color to each category and make a key showing which color represents which idea.

4. Highlight all the notes in a category with the same color.

5. Name each category and use these categories as the main supporting points in your rough outline.

ACTIVITIES TO PRACTICE ORGANIZING YOUR NOTES

ACTIVITY **1** Brainstorming a List from Your Notes

1. With a group of classmates who are working on the same research question, brainstorm a list of ideas from your notes that will answer the question. One person should be the secretary while the others suggest ideas.

2. Write your list on the board for the whole class.

3. With your class, look at each list and begin to categorize the ideas into groups, numbering each group.

4. In your small groups, write a phrase or sentence that describes each category of ideas. Share these descriptions with the class.

ACTIVITY **2** Sorting Your Notes

Do this activity with a partner or group using the same research question as you.

1. For homework, create a set of strips from your notes following steps 1 and 2 in Technique 2: Sorting Your Notes on page 43. Bring these strips to class. As an alternative, your teacher may complete this step and provide each group with a set of strips.

2. In your group, read each strip. Make sure you understand each separate idea. Throw out any duplicate information.

3. With your group, begin to sort the strips into piles.

4. Once the strips are sorted, analyze the common idea in each pile of notes. Develop a category name—a descriptive word or phrase—that describes each pile.

5. Share your categories with the class and ask for feedback about whether the notes in each category fit the category name.

ACTIVITY **3** Color Coding Your Notes

1. For homework, color code your own focused reading notes from an article in Part Two.

2. With a partner, compare how you've labeled your notes.
   • Do some sources have ideas that are similar?
   • Which point(s) seems to have the most supporting information?
   • Do any points have only one piece of supporting information?

3. Create a category name—a descriptive word or phrase—for the ideas in each color.
   • Do you have any questions about how some of the information in your sources relates to these categories?

BUILDING YOUR PAPER

Create a Rough Outline

Create a rough outline for your research paper that includes your research question and a list of potential supporting points from your notes.

• Remember that *brainstorming a list, sorting your notes,* and *color coding* are three useful ways to identify key ideas for your paper.

CHAPTER 3

BUILDING A PAPER:
Organize

Sooner or later you have to write the first sentence of your research paper. It might seem like the most difficult sentence of all because you are facing a blank page.

However, now that you've explored and analyzed so much information—facts from and opinions about articles in Part Two and thoughts of your own about the topic—your paper may be blank, but your mind certainly isn't. Several things you have already written will help you with that first important sentence.

Look at your research question and rough outline that you created in Chapter 2 and you will find that, together, they lead to a thesis statement: that single sentence that, all by itself, gives the central idea for your paper. Once you have a thesis statement, you can use it to help organize the rest of your paper.

In this chapter you will mostly use notes you took while reading articles from Part Two. As you read your notes, you will look for information, or evidence, that you can use to explain the ideas in your paper.

In this chapter you will practice the following:

- Writing a thesis statement

- Expanding your rough outline with evidence

- Creating a detailed outline

By the end of this chapter, you will have written your thesis statement, chosen the most useful evidence to support your ideas, and organized your evidence into an outline that is easy to use when you write your paper.

WRITING A THESIS STATEMENT

Your rough outline from Chapter 2 reflects the focus of your research question and provides some general ideas about how to answer it. The next step is to plan your answer to your research question in more detail.

The short, concise answer to your research question is your thesis statement. Although it's only one sentence long, your thesis statement is one of the most important sentences in your essay because it tells the reader what the rest of your paper will say. Therefore, it is worthwhile to take some time to write your thesis and consider each element that will make it as clear as possible.

Articulating your thesis, or the main thing you want to say, right at the start will help in two ways:

- You will find out at the beginning whether you have a clear and workable idea.

- You will be able to use the thesis statement as a guide while writing the essay.

The thesis statement you develop in this chapter will be your **working thesis.** This means it's still tentative. Further along in the writing process, you may discover that you need to revise your thesis statement because of additional information you find or a new direction your research takes.

 # Four Characteristics of an Effective Thesis Statement

1. **It states your topic and focus, which answer your research question.**

2. **It gives an overview of your supporting points, which are logically connected to your focus.**

3. **It gives enough information without too much detail.**

4. **It uses correct grammar and precise vocabulary.**

EXAMPLE: Thesis Statement versus Topic

Notice that your thesis statement is different from your topic. A topic is a short phrase that states the general subject of your paper, such as:

Taking risks

A thesis statement sets up the framework for your entire essay. It tells the reader not only your topic, but also the focus, or what you plan to say about that topic, such as:

Biological need, social environment, and psychological satisfaction are three reasons why people take risks.

TOPIC AND FOCUS

A thesis statement is a concise one-sentence answer to your research question. Recall that your research question from Chapter 2 defines the topic and focus of your paper. So, as you write your thesis statement, make sure this topic and focus are both clearly stated.

EXAMPLE 1

Research Question: How are expectations of marriage in the United States and India similar or different?

- The focus of this research question is a comparison (similar or different) of the topic (expectations of marriage in two countries).

Thesis Statement: Belief in romantic love, the division of family responsibilities, and attitudes toward divorce *are three differences between American and Indian expectations of marriage.*

- The topic, "expectations of marriage," and a restatement of the focus, "three differences between American and Indian," are directly stated in the thesis.

EXAMPLE 2

Research Question: Why do people become homeless?

- The topic of this research question is homelessness, and the focus is a discussion of the causes of homelessness.

Thesis Statement: The lack of affordable housing, inadequate public assistance, and the breakdown of the family are *three causes of homelessness.*

- The topic, "homelessness," and the focus, "three causes," are directly stated in the thesis.

NOW YOU TRY

For each thesis statement below, circle the topic and underline the focus.

1. Three major factors cause teenagers to commit murder: the influence of the media, the easy availability of guns, and the lack of family contact.

2. The death penalty should be abolished for two reasons: it might kill innocent people, and it is unfairly applied to the poor and minorities.

3. Two results of promoting birth control are increased education for women and greater economic opportunity for everyone.

OVERVIEW OF SUPPORTING POINTS

In the rough outline you developed in Chapter 2, you included a list of answers to your research question that will become the major supporting points in the body of your research paper. The number of supporting points you use will depend on such factors as the amount of time and information you have and your interest.

An effective thesis statement includes this overview of your supporting points, so the reader knows what you will discuss and how your ideas are organized.

SAMPLE ROUGH OUTLINE 1

Research Question:	Why do people become homeless?
Focus of Research Question:	Causes
Answers to Research Question:	1. Lack of affordable housing
	2. Inadequate public assistance
	3. Drug and alcohol problems
	4. Breakdown of the family
	5. Mental health problems
Thesis Statement:	The lack of affordable housing, inadequate public assistance, and the breakdown of the family are three causes of homelessness.

- In this example, the writer selected three ideas from the answers to the research question to include in his thesis statement: "lack of affordable housing," "inadequate public assistance," and "breakdown of the family." These three causes are the overview of his supporting points.

- As a reader, you would expect the paper to follow the order of the supporting points as they are presented in the thesis statement.

1. First, a section that discusses the problem poor people have in finding housing they can afford.

2. Second, a discussion of the inadequate amount of money the government provides to support poor people.

3. Third, a discussion of how family breakups can lead to homelessness.

SAMPLE ROUGH OUTLINE 2

Research Question:	What are the signs of alcohol addiction?
Focus of Research Question:	Definition
Answers to Research Question:	1. An urge to drink 2. An inability to stop 3. A physical dependence 4. A need to drink more
Thesis Statement:	Alcoholism is a disease that has four symptoms: physical dependence, a need to drink more to feel its effects, a strong urge to drink, and an inability to stop drinking.

- In this example, the writer used all four signs of alcohol addiction from her rough outline. They provide the overview of her supporting points. Notice, however, that she has changed the order of the supporting points so that each idea will flow logically from one to the next in her essay.

Your overview of supporting points may change as you work. You may decide that you need to modify it after you have written the first full draft of your essay. For example, you may decide to add or delete categories or rearrange the order.

NOW YOU TRY

Look at each rough outline and research question. Then, decide whether each thesis statement is a good answer to the research question.

- Does it include an appropriate focus?
- Does it include an overview of supporting points?

Circle *OK* or *Not OK* and explain your reasons.

Rough Outline 1

Research Question:	Should marijuana be legal?
Focus of Research Question:	Argument
Answers to Research Question:	1. Damages the brain 2. Causes memory loss 3. Leads to birth defects
Thesis Statement A:	Marijuana should not be legal because it is too dangerous.

OK   Not OK

Why? _____

_____

Thesis Statement B: The use of marijuana and alcohol should be legal.

OK   Not OK

Why? _____

_____

Thesis Statement C: Using marijuana should be against the law because it damages the brain and leads to birth defects.

OK   Not OK

Why? _____

_____

Rough Outline 2

Research Question: How does junk food affect health?

Focus of Research Question: Effects

Answers to Research Question:
1. Poor nutrition
2. Weight gain
3. Inability to concentrate

Thesis Statement A: Eating junk food results in poor nutrition, weight gain, and inability to concentrate.

OK   Not OK

Why? _____

_____

Thesis Statement B: Junk food and health food are different in several ways.

OK   Not OK

Why? _____

_____

Thesis Statement C: Every culture has its own junk food.

OK   Not OK

Why? _____

_____

JUST ENOUGH INFORMATION

A good thesis statement gives just enough information to let the reader know the key points you will make about your topic. After reading your thesis statement, your reader should be able to answer the question: What is this paper going to tell me?

EXAMPLE

Thesis with too little information

> Capital punishment causes many problems.

- This thesis statement does not tell us enough. It does not tell us what problems are caused by capital punishment.

EXAMPLE

Thesis with too much information

> Capital punishment, which is practiced in many countries such as Pakistan, China, and parts of the United States, is a problem because it actually costs more than a carefully planned system of rehabilitation, often leads to the execution of innocent people when the justice system is corrupt or operates too quickly, and can cause unreasonable pain to the person being executed if methods like electrocution are used.

- This thesis statement gives more details than the reader needs at this point in the paper. For example, the reader will find out in the body paragraphs which countries use capital punishment, what problems exist in the justice system, and what methods of execution are used.

NOW YOU TRY

These three thesis statements all answer the same research question. Evaluate each and choose your answer.

Research Question: How can the negative effects of global warming be stopped?

Thesis Statement 1:   Making the United Nations into a law-enforcing agency with the power to enforce regulations about energy use, encouraging households to install insulation, forcing farmers to recycle water, developing solar power, establishing maritime laws to regulate deep-water fishing, and passing laws against logging in the Amazon are some of the ways the damaging effects of global warming can be controlled, although it is impossible to completely stop them.

This thesis statement has
>   too little information; (I do not know what this paper is about.)
>   too much information; (This is like a paragraph about the topic.)
>   enough information but not too much.

Thesis Statement 2:   It is important to find the best way to stop global warming.

This thesis statement has
>   too little information; (I do not know what this paper is about.)
>   too much information; (This is like a paragraph about the topic.)
>   enough information but not too much.

Thesis Statement 3:   Creating stricter regulations worldwide and encouraging conservation of resources are two good ways to slow the effects of global warming.

This thesis statement has
>   too little information; (I do not know what this paper is about.)
>   too much information; (This is like a paragraph about the topic.)
>   enough information but not too much.

CORRECT GRAMMAR AND PRECISE VOCABULARY

Structure, style, and vocabulary are three aspects of language to consider in writing a good thesis statement.

Structure

The topic, focus, and overview of supporting points can appear in any order in your thesis statement. The example illustrates three correct versions of the same thesis.

EXAMPLE

Topic: Vegetarianism

Focus: Reasons for becoming a vegetarian

Supporting points: Health, ethics, and ecology

Possible Thesis Statements:
- Three reasons why people become vegetarians are health, ethics, and ecology.
- Health, ethics, and ecology are three reasons why people become vegetarians.
- People become vegetarians for three reasons: health, ethics, and ecology.

Style

Thesis statements are written in third person rather than first person. Phrases such as "I'm going to talk about" or "I think" are not appropriate in a thesis.

EXAMPLE

Inappropriate Language: I'm going to talk about two reasons why video games have a negative impact on children: isolation from other people and overexposure to violence.

Appropriate Language: Two reasons why video games have a negative impact on children are isolation from other people and overexposure to violence.

Vocabulary

Because you need to include a lot of information in a thesis statement, precise vocabulary is essential. You can sometimes repeat carefully chosen vocabulary in a thesis statement throughout the research paper, providing an effective unifying thread. In particular, choosing appropriate words for the focus can help clarify and strengthen the thesis.

For a list of words and phrases associated with several common types of focus refer to Appendix B on page 220.

NOW YOU TRY

Use the vocabulary in each thesis statement in the left-hand column to identify its focus. Draw a line to connect the thesis statement with the type of focus in the right-hand column.

Thesis Statement	Type of Focus
1. High school education in Japan has two points in common with high school education in Korea: a rigorous testing system and strict expectations of classroom behavior.	Process
2. To develop a successful space program, the United States has gone through three stages of planning: research, development, and testing.	Effect
3. Although globalization produces a few negative results, it is largely a positive force in the world today for three reasons: increased opportunities for employment, higher education, and greater equality for women.	Classification
4. An effective public transportation system is based on four components: regional growth plans, available resources, community needs, and sustainability principles.	Comparison
5. Two types of video games teach children valuable skills: educational and cooperative.	Definition

Common Problems with Thesis Statements

A thesis statement is one of the most important sentences in your research paper. The purpose of a thesis statement is to help the writer to focus and the reader to predict the content of the paper.

There are five common problems writers face when creating thesis statements.

Problem 1: Lack of Focus

Weak Thesis Statement:
> The United States has a lot of crime.

- This statement does not tell whether the paper will discuss the causes of crime or its effects; contrast the amount of crime now compared with ten years ago; argue in support of certain ways to reduce crime; or present some other ideas. To improve this thesis, the writer must include a focus. Here are two possible ways to revise the thesis statement to include a focus.

Stronger Thesis Statement (focus on cause):
> The rising crime rate in the United States has caused a loss of talented young people to crime, high government costs for law enforcement, and a drop in tourism.

Stronger Thesis Statement (focus on comparison):
> Crime today is more widespread among many economic groups, more violent, and more costly to society than it was ten years ago.

Problem 2: Lack of Supporting Points

Weak Thesis Statement:
> Three types of crime have been increasing in US cities.

- By briefly describing as supporting points the types of crimes that have increased, the writer can have a more effective thesis statement that tells the reader what kinds of crime she will be discussing.

Stronger Thesis Statement:
> Three types of crime have been increasing in US cities: personal assault, car robbery, and home burglary.

- The new thesis tells us that the first part of the paper will be about increases in personal assault; the second section, increases in car robberies; and the third, increases in burglaries of homes.

Problem 3: Confusing Supporting Points

Some thesis statements have supporting points that are not logically connected to the focus of the thesis.

Weak Thesis Statement:

Many factors influence the hunting behavior of sharks: the type of shark, its age and strength, its migration patterns, people's misunderstandings about sharks' hunting behavior, and the current overfishing of sharks.

- The focus of this research paper is "factors [that] influence the hunting behavior of sharks" or causes of sharks' behavior while hunting. The following are the supporting points:

  1. the type of shark
  2. a shark's age and strength
  3. migration patterns
  4. people's misunderstandings about sharks
  5. overfishing of sharks

Notice that while points 1, 2, and 3 support the focus by explaining causes for the sharks' behavior, points 4 and 5 do not. A better thesis statement would include only the supporting points related to the focus of causes for sharks' hunting behavior.

Stronger Thesis Statement:

Many factors influence the hunting behavior of sharks: the type of shark, the age and strength of the shark, and the shark's migration pattern.

Problem 4: Too Much Information

Weak Thesis Statement:

Although some people argue that voting should be mandatory because it is a civic duty, it would increase voter turnout among poor people, and it would cause politicians to consider the needs of every citizen, compulsory voting is not a good idea because it is every citizen's right to choose to vote or not, it would not be feasible to enforce mandatory voting, and people who are forced to vote may not vote carefully.

- This statement is too long. These details are more appropriate as supporting information in the body of the paper. This thesis statement would be more effective if some of the ideas were condensed.

Stronger Thesis Statement:

Although some people argue that voting should be mandatory, there are three reasons why it should not.

Problem 5: Inappropriate Language

Weak Thesis Statement:

In this paper, I will write about why I support capital punishment and what people on the other side have to say about it.

- This thesis statement includes the opinion of the writer directly with the words "why I support." A more appropriate thesis statement for an academic paper indicates your opinion indirectly, without using "I."

Stronger Thesis Statement:
Although some people disagree with capital punishment, it is necessary for three main reasons.

- The use of "it is necessary" tells the reader that the writer thinks capital punishment is essential. The inclusion of the phrase "although some people disagree" shows that she will also explain some of the reasons others disagree with capital punishment.

NOW YOU TRY

For each thesis statement, identify the problem from the list and revise the statement to be more effective.

Common Thesis Statement Problems
- Lack of focus
- Lack of supporting points
- Confusing supporting points
- Too much information
- Inappropriate language

1. I believe assisted suicide causes two main problems: difficulty in regulating it and difficulty for patients in making a rational choice.

   Problem _____

   Revised thesis _____

2. The Internet leads to improved communication.

   Problem _____

   Revised thesis _____

3. Several cultural factors lead to the prevalence of child labor in Latin America: family values, the company managers back in the United States, inflation, poor transportation systems, a lack of emphasis on education, and the Catholic Church.

   Problem _____

   Revised thesis _____

4. This paper is about cloning.

   Problem _____

   Revised thesis _____

5. Homeschooling results in closer family ties, flexible time schedules for parent and child, and a desire for more educational choices.

   Problem _____

   Revised thesis _____

ACTIVITIES TO PRACTICE WRITING THESIS STATEMENTS

ACTIVITY **1** Identifying Parts of a Thesis

Work with several classmates to identify the parts of each thesis statement.
- Circle the topic
- Underline the focus once
- Underline the supporting points twice

1. Although our memory of John F. Kennedy has been frozen, he is remembered for many reasons: his political achievements, the way his public behavior reflected American values, and the mystery of his assassination.

2. Several important factors make Bruce Lee extraordinary: his family background, his dramatic life, his skill as a martial artist, and his philosophy of life.

3. Society should develop an awareness of factors that motivate children to act violently, such as family problems and the influence of media, and also consider ways to prevent juvenile violence, including better support for parents and improved monitoring of media.

4. Simplicity, emptiness, directness, and naturalness are four traditional characteristics of Japanese art inspired by Buddhism.

5. There are several reasons why people smoke even though they know it is a habit that can bring death: social pressure, psychological need, and physical addiction.

ACTIVITY **2** Improving Thesis Statements

With your group, consider each thesis statement and decide how to improve it, following the criteria for an effective thesis:
- Does it state your topic and focus, and answer your research question?
- Does it give an overview of your supporting points, which are logically connected to your focus?
- Does it give enough information without too much detail?
- Does it use correct grammar and precise vocabulary?

1. I think genetically modified food is terrible.

   Problems _____

   Revision _____

2. Public transportation has some advantages and disadvantages.

   Problems _____

   Revision _____

3. The topic of this paper is women's rights.

   Problems _____

   Revision _____

4. Confusion and trouble will probably come from the recent changes in laws about medical privacy in the United States.

Problems _____

Revision _____

5. Space travel for ordinary people is exciting and will probably happen soon.

Problems _____

Revision _____

ACTIVITY **3** Writing Thesis Statements

Work in pairs or groups to write a thesis statement that reflects each research question and rough outline. Compare your thesis statements with others in your class.

Rough Outline 1

Research Question:	Why do young people commit crimes?
Focus of Research Question:	Causes
Answers to Research Question:	1. Influence of the media 2. Availability of weapons 3. Peer pressure 4. Lack of family contact

Thesis Statement: _____

Rough Outline 2

Research Question:	What problems do international students face when they study in the United States?
Focus of Research Question:	Classification
Answers to Research Question:	1. Language difficulties 2. Money problems 3. Adjusting to a new culture

Thesis Statement: _____

BUILDING YOUR PAPER

Write a Thesis Statement

Using the research question and rough outline you developed in Chapter 2, write a thesis statement for the research paper you are building. Consider the characteristics of a good thesis statement.

1. It states your topic and focus, which answer your research question.

2. It gives an overview of your supporting points, which are logically connected to your focus.

3. It gives enough information without too much detail.

4. It uses correct grammar and precise vocabulary.

Getting Feedback

Thesis Seminar

The purpose of this activity is to help each writer produce an effective thesis statement. Comments should be focused on ways to make each thesis clear and easy to understand, NOT on judging it as "good" or "bad" writing or judging the writer as a "good" or "bad" writer.

1. In a group of six or more, sit in a circle. Write the Four Characteristics of an Effective Thesis Statement listed above on the board or post them on a large sheet of paper where everyone can see them.

2. One student writes her thesis statement on the board or gives a copy of it to each group member.

3. The person sitting to this student's right comments on Characteristic 1. The next person to the right comments on Characteristic 2, and so on.

4. The student takes notes on any suggested changes from group members. Later, she makes the changes she decides are suitable.

5. Repeat steps 2–4 for each student in the group.

At the end of this exercise, each group member will have critiqued a different thesis characteristic and learned more about what makes an effective thesis statement.

EXPANDING YOUR ROUGH OUTLINE WITH EVIDENCE

Now that you have a thesis statement and a rough outline listing the supporting points for your research paper, it's time to return to the notes you took from your sources in Part Two. So far, your sources have served two important functions. First, in Chapter 1, you explored your theme by reading the sources for general information. Then, in Chapter 2, you took notes while doing a focused reading of your sources that helped you answer your research question. In addition, using the ideas from your sources as a guide, you created a thesis statement and rough outline that will become the framework for your paper.

In this next stage of the writing process, the information in your sources will have a new role. You will select specific information from your notes to use as evidence—to help you explain each of the main supporting points in your thesis statement.

When we use information from articles to explain the main points in our paper, we call that information "evidence." Your reading notes from Chapter 2 include all the information you found to answer your research question. However, it's likely that only some of that information will work as evidence in your paper. You need to decide which information to use as evidence. Your paper will be more convincing if you use the following guidelines when choosing evidence.

 ## Guidelines for Choosing Effective Evidence

1. **Choose information that you understand easily and can explain clearly.**

2. **Choose ideas that are directly related to the point you are making.**

3. **Choose a variety of types of evidence.**

EASY TO UNDERSTAND

Think about whether you understand each idea well enough to explain it in your own words. If you don't understand the information, you won't be able to write about it clearly, and it will be better to omit it.

For example, based on one writer's research question and rough outline, she wrote this thesis statement:

> People become addicted to alcohol because of emotional distress, social pressure, and physical causes.

However, as she began to select evidence to support the idea of "physical causes," she realized that many physical causes of alcoholism were based on complex chemical processes that she did not completely understand. She decided not to use the evidence about chemical issues but to limit her discussion of physical causes to genetic predisposition. She revised her thesis statement:

People become addicted to alcohol because of emotional distress, social pressure, and genetic predisposition.

RELATED TO YOUR POINT

Sometimes it's tempting to include interesting details that are related to your topic in a general way but don't help to explain your specific supporting points.

For example, if your focus is a comparison of the cost, nutritional value, and availability of fast food and health food, you need evidence that illustrates the differences in these two kinds of food. Information about the history of tofu, a common health food, will not be useful in this paper.

NOW YOU TRY

Working with a partner or a small group, decide which pieces of evidence would effectively explain the underlined supporting point in the following thesis statement. Circle *Yes* or *No* and explain the problem, if there is one.

Thesis Statement: Using the Internet gives young people increased literacy but also leads to <u>health problems</u> and <u>isolation</u> from other people.

Evidence: 1. Asked their preferences for spending free time, 19 percent of the student body at the high school chose playing sports; 24 percent, watching TV; 22 percent, listening to music; and 34 percent, surfing the Internet.

   Is the evidence effective? Yes No

   If not, what is the problem? _____

2. In Waltham's study, business people between the ages of 35 and 50 reported spending 10 to 12 hours a day online, thus severely impacting the time they spent with colleagues and family.

   Is the evidence effective? Yes No

   If not, what is the problem? _____

3. Feeling isolated, many teenagers turn to drugs or gang membership to solve their problems, according to interviews conducted by Smith and Paget at the Outsiders Café.

   Is the evidence effective? Yes No

   If not, what is the problem? _____

4. "The problem of feeling estranged from society is much more severe among young people who spend more than four hours a day online," states Martha DePriau, psychologist at Vanderbilt University.

   Is the evidence effective? Yes No

   If not, what is the problem? _____

5. Sixty percent of Internet users between the ages of 12 and 25 reported that they spend more time online than with family or friends.

   Is this evidence effective?   Yes   No

   If not, what is the problem? _____

A VARIETY OF EVIDENCE

Writers can support their ideas with several kinds of information. The following are three common types of evidence that you may find as you look through your focused reading notes. In each example paragraph, the paraphrased evidence is underlined.

Einstein Evidence

Einstein evidence shows that other scholars or thinkers on the topic have come to the same conclusion as you have.

When using this kind of evidence, provide as much information as you can about the expert. For example, you might include where you found the information, the research the expert has done, or the university or institution where he or she works.

> **EXAMPLE**
>
> It has been argued that the reason why some terminally ill patients wish to commit suicide is that they are depressed. Patients suffering from terminal illness might tend to feel negative and hopeless. Edward Marlough, an associate professor of clinical psychology at Columbia Presbyterian Medical Center in New York, argues that <u>in many cases, a dying patient is simply occupied by negative reactions to their critical condition</u> (*"When Patients Want to Die,"* 1999).

Example Evidence

Example evidence consists of specific examples that illustrate the point you are making.

> **EXAMPLE**
>
> The direct and independent connections through the Internet create new relationships among people, relationships that can change the way we think and act. To illustrate this point of view, Brian Belsie, in his article "The Electronic Village" (n.d.) showed how <u>a large number of people living in widely separated areas could form a community simply through electronic communication; in this case, the parents of children who suffered from a certain kind of psychological problem</u> formed an online support group.

Fact Evidence

Fact evidence includes statistics and other objective information. As you read your sources in Part Two, you may find specific facts that you can use to demonstrate the point you are making.

First of all, many people become vegetarians to maintain good health. Vegetarianism can prevent people from getting diseases. Castleman (1995) writes that <u>many studies prove that meat, especially beef, pork, and lamb, likely increase the percentages of heart disease and cancer.</u> In his article, he points out that <u>the rate of vegetarians who die from these diseases is definitely lower than the rate of meat eaters. For example, 28 percent fewer vegetarians than omnivores die from heart disease, and 39 percent fewer die from cancer.</u> The National Cancer Research Institute found that <u>meat-eating women get breast cancer almost four times more often than women who do not eat meat or eat only a little.</u> (*"Why Be a Vegetarian?" 1999*).

Undocumented Evidence

Another kind of evidence, called undocumented evidence, comes not from written sources, but from your experience and things that you know or that are commonly understood to be true.

Suppose you are writing about the causes of alcohol abuse. An example of a personal experience that could be used as evidence would be a story about a friend who began drinking to escape from the stress of her job.

An example of evidence that is commonly known to be true would be that many teenagers want to fit in with their peer group and will feel pressure to behave like the teenagers around them. This information could be used as evidence in a discussion on social pressure as a cause of alcohol abuse. The point that teenagers feel pressure from their peers would not have to be documented; however, linking this pressure to alcohol abuse would.

In academic writing, most evidence is from documented sources, but anecdotal or undocumented evidence can be an effective addition to your paper.

NOW YOU TRY

Working in pairs or in small groups, read the following thesis statement.

Thesis Statement: Being forced into a sedentary lifestyle by the demands of their jobs is making young professionals more health conscious, <u>increasing the popularity of risky sports,</u> and leading to the development of more health foods. . . .

Here are some excerpts from several articles on taking risks. Decide whether each excerpt would support the underlined supporting point in the thesis statement above as Einstein evidence, example evidence, or fact evidence.

1. "The number of people who dive out of planes, for instance, has risen about 5 percent a year since 1990."

    —Bowers, Joe, *"Going Over the Top," 1995*

Type of evidence _____

2. "'Five–four–three–two–one–see ya!' And Chance McGuire, 25, is airborne off a 650-foot concrete dam in northern California. In one second he falls 16 feet, in two seconds 63 feet, and after three seconds and 137 feet, he is flying at 65 mph. . . . McGuire is a practitioner of what he calls the king of all extreme sports, BASE—an acronym for building, antenna, span (bridges) and earth (cliffs) jumping."

—*Greenfield, Karl, "Life on the Edge," 1998*

Type of evidence _____

3. "Michael Apter, a Georgetown University visiting scholar and the author of *The Dangerous Edge: The Psychology of Excitement* explains, 'The safer you make life, the more people feel the need for excitement.'"

—*Bowers, Joe, "Going Over the Top," 1995*

Type of evidence _____

ACTIVITIES TO PRACTICE CHOOSING EVIDENCE

ACTIVITY **1** Finding Documented and Undocumented Evidence

To get an idea of the percentage of documented and undocumented evidence that is appropriate in a well-written paper, analyze one of the student papers in the Appendix A on page 211. Highlight all the documented evidence in one color. Documented evidence is any information that begins or ends with the name of an author or title of a source. Highlight the undocumented, or anecdotal and common knowledge, evidence in another color.

ACTIVITY **2** Finding the Same Idea in Different Articles

1. Work in a small group. Choose one term or idea that as been discussed in several of the articles you have read. Write the idea on a piece of paper.

2. Look through each article to find instances of that idea. Underline each place it is mentioned.

3. Compare the articles. Which article mentions the idea most often? Are there some articles that do not mention it at all? Discuss in your group.

ACTIVITY **3** Choosing Effective Evidence

With several classmates, look at each piece of evidence and decide whether it would be effective to support the underlined supporting point in the thesis statement. Effective evidence should be:

- Information you understand and can explain clearly
- Ideas directly related to the point you're making

For each piece of evidence, circle *Yes* or *No* and explain the problem, if there is one.

Thesis Statement: Ships and planes often vanish in the Bermuda Triangle because of <u>environmental reasons,</u> supernatural causes, or unexplained phenomena.

Evidence: 1. Christopher Columbus observed a huge ball that looked like a meteor falling into the sea as he first sailed near the Triangle on his way to the West Indies in 1492.

Is this evidence effective?　　Yes　　No
If not, what is the problem? _____

2. One hundred miles north of Puerto Rico is the deepest part of the Atlantic Ocean, estimated to be 30,100 feet deep; it is here that most of the accidents between Miami and the Bahama Islands have happened.

Is this evidence effective?　　Yes　　No
If not, what is the problem? _____

3. According to Angelina Campo in "*Mysteries from the Realms of Outer Space*," highly developed beings from outer space have created their own society under the Atlantic Ocean in the area of the Bermuda Triangle, and it is they who abduct the travelers.

Is this evidence effective?　　Yes　　No
If not, what is the problem? _____

4. Roy Hutchins, a retired Coast Guard Captain, said, "Weather within the Triangle where warm tropical breezes meet cold air masses from the Arctic is notoriously unpredictable."

Is this evidence effective?　　Yes　　No
If not, what is the problem? _____

5. The Bermuda Triangle is one of the few places on earth where the compass points to the true north instead of the magnetic north. Because of this, sailors must adjust their direction carefully and the inexperienced may fail to do this, thus losing their way.

Is this evidence effective?　　Yes　　No
If not, what is the problem? _____

ACTIVITY ❹ Working with Expert Groups

To complete this activity, select a supporting point from a thesis statement on a topic that your class is working on.

1. Divide into small groups. Each group is responsible for one source (these are the expert groups).

2. In your group, identify pieces of information from your source that you think would be useful evidence for the idea you support. Discuss why the information would be convincing to a reader.

3. After you identify the useful evidence, form new groups (the sharing groups). Put one member from each expert group in each sharing group.

4. In your sharing group, take turns discussing the evidence each expert group selected.

5. As a group, decide whether the evidence selected is appropriate for the point.
   - Is the evidence easy to understand and explain?
   - Is the evidence appropriate for the point?
   - Does more than one source contain the same idea?
   - Does your group have any questions about specific pieces of evidence?

BUILDING YOUR PAPER

Choose Evidence

Create a list of evidence for each supporting point in the rough outline you wrote.

- As you search for potential evidence in your sources, remember to choose information that you understand and can explain and that is directly related to the points you want to make.

- Try to choose a variety of types of information.

- Try to find two to three pieces of evidence for each supporting point.

CREATING A DETAILED OUTLINE

You can now put together a detailed plan for writing your paper that includes both the supporting points you want to discuss and the evidence you will use to help explain each point. If you plan to use undocumented evidence, you need to include that in your outline, too.

NOTE: The organization of argumentation papers needs special consideration. For information on organization and a sample argumentation paper, see the *Sourcework* website at **http://esl.hmco.com/students.**

You want a plan that is detailed enough to provide a guide as you write. Think of it as a lifeline to hold onto if you get lost. With an outline to return to, you can put your paper aside and not lose track of what you are going to say next.

Criteria for a Useful Outline

1. **It begins with the thesis statement.**

2. **It includes a phrase to explain each supporting point.**

3. **It includes a notation of where you will use each piece of supporting evidence.**

As you begin to write, you may discover that you will discard some of the information or that you need to look for more evidence to support certain points.

As you work, you may change the outline, rearranging the order or adding or deleting sections. Since the outline is a tool for your own use, write it in any way that works for you. The following are three methods that other writers have found useful.

 # Three Outlining Methods

TRADITIONAL OUTLINE

In this outline, the notations, such as "Markoff, p. 1" and "NPR, p. 14" refer to the sources the writer plans to use. The note "personal example" in parentheses reminds the writer she will use a personal anecdote, a kind of undocumented evidence. The note "summarize whole article" means that the writer will use a brief summary of this whole article as evidence here, rather than just paraphrasing a sentence or two. Notes like these help make your outline more effective by reminding you in detail how you plan to use your notes.

I. *Thesis Statement:* Compared with other inventions, the Internet has changed our styles of communication and led to more freedom for individuals.

II. Comparison with other inventions
    A. TV
        1. My friends and I often discuss TV (personal example)
    B. Phone
        1. My family used to use the phone to keep in touch (personal example)

III. Styles of communication
    A. Less time than with old methods of communicating
        1. Less time with people
            a. Markoff, p. 1 (evidence from source)
            b. My family uses phone less (personal example)
        2. Less time with TV
            a. Markoff, p. 2 (evidence from source)

      B. New ways of communicating

         1. Chat rooms

            a. NPR, p. 14 (evidence from source)

            b. My experience in chat rooms (personal example)

         2. Helps with some jobs

            a. NPR, p. 6 (evidence from source)

            b. *Economist*, p. 2 (evidence from source)

   IV. More freedom for individuals

      A. Ordinary people have opportunities

         1. Romero (summarize whole article)

      B. More democracy

         1. *Economist*, p. 1 (evidence from source)

CLUSTER OUTLINE

A cluster outline includes all the same information that a traditional outline does, but is written as connected circles rather than in the linear form of the traditional outline.

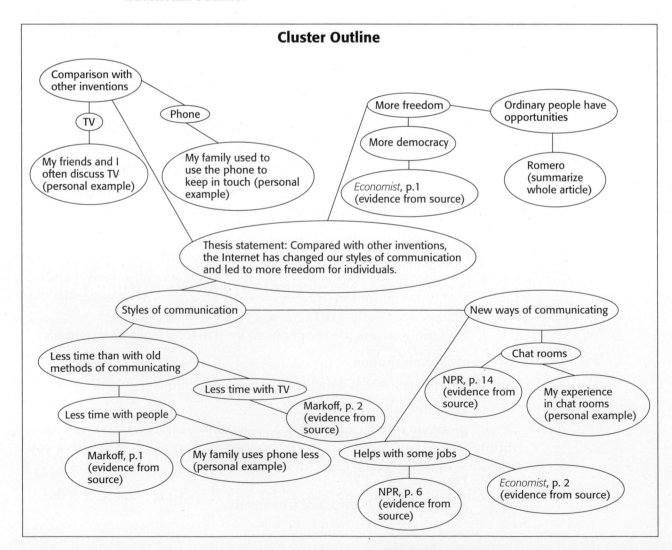

GRID OUTLINE

Like the other outlining methods, a grid outline includes the thesis, supporting points, sub-points, and evidence. Information is organized as a chart, which offers a visual perspective of your ideas, just as a cluster does, while keeping some of the more structured elements of a traditional outline.

Grid Outline		
Thesis: Maintaining a strong family identity and promoting cross-generational communication are two reasons why heritage language programs should be encouraged.		
Supporting Points	Sub-points	Evidence
1. Encourage young people to learn about their family's culture and history.	**A.** Culture	Wilson, p. 56; Tam, p. 12
	B. Family	Grandpa story; Tam, p.13
2. Better communication between generations	**A.** Communication in family	Peterson, p. 8; Hiang, p. 35
	B. Stronger family connection	Wilson, p. 51; Family trip

ACTIVITIES TO PRACTICE OUTLINING

To practice outlining, do one or both of the following activities. Blank outlining grids are available on the *Sourcework* website at **http://elt.heinle.com/sourcework.**

ACTIVITY **1** Outlining a Paper

Working with a partner, read one of the student research papers in the Appendix on page 209, or on the *Sourcework* website. Use one of the outlining methods described and prepare an outline of the paper.

ACTIVITY **2** Filling in a Detailed Outline

To complete this activity, select a representative thesis statement created by one of your classmates or by the whole class.

1. Focusing on one supporting point at a time from the thesis statement, look through your sources or notes to identify two to three pieces of evidence you could use to support each main idea in the thesis.

2. Write the evidence you have selected for each supporting point so that the whole class can see it.

3. Share your list of evidence with the class.

4. Discuss problems you had or questions that came up in your group.

5. With this information, you can create an outline following one of the methods discussed in this section.

BUILDING YOUR PAPER

Write a Detailed Outline

Select an outline format and create a more detailed plan for your paper. In this outline, include the following:

- Your thesis statement
- A phrase that explains each supporting point
- A plan for where you will use each piece of evidence

Getting Feedback

Divide into small groups. Provide a copy of your research paper outline for each person in your group.

1. Take turns reading each person's outline.

2. Discuss each outline using the critique questions below, and jot down comments on your copy of your classmate's outline.

3. When you finish, give all the copies back to the person who wrote the outline.

Critique Questions:

1. In the thesis statement, circle the topic, underline the focus once, and underline the supporting points twice. Does each major section of the outline logically connect to the thesis statement? If not, what changes could be made?

2. Do two or three details support each topic sentence? Is each detail supported with specific evidence from the sources?

3. Is any part of the thesis statement omitted from the outline?

4. Does the outline include any major new ideas that should be added to the thesis?

5. Other comments? Questions left unanswered? Confusing parts?

CHAPTER 4

BUILDING A PAPER:
Create

It's time to write the first draft of your research paper. You have done the essential work of exploring ideas and planning the overall structure of what you want to say. Now you will make a first try at writing the whole paper. Writing is hard work, and producing your first draft is an accomplishment to be proud of. As you write your draft and put all your thoughts together in the same place, you may find connections between your ideas that you did not see before when you were working with separate parts of your paper.

A big part of putting this paper together is combining ideas from your reading notes with what you yourself want to say. Using your detailed outline from Chapter 3 as a guide, you can work section by section to explain each point and support it with the evidence you've chosen from your readings. The more smoothly you can make the connection between the information you are using from other writers and your own ideas, the more effective your paper will be.

Rereading your own first draft, listening to your classmates' feedback, and fine-tuning your writing will help you produce a second draft that presents what you want to say even more clearly.

In this chapter you will practice the following:

- **Writing the body of your paper**

- **Integrating evidence into your paragraphs**

By the end of this chapter you will have written a rough first draft and a more polished second draft that integrates the evidence from your sources into the presentation of your own ideas.

WRITING THE BODY OF YOUR PAPER

Writing can feel chaotic as you fit all your ideas into a form that clearly states what you want to say. But, with the work you have already done to write your thesis statement, collect your evidence, and create an outline, you have a guide for your next task. You are ready to write the first draft of your paper.

Three Steps for Writing the Body of Your Paper

1. **Write a topic sentence for each supporting point in your thesis.**

2. **Review the ideas you plan to discuss about each supporting point.**

3. **Write a first draft.**

WRITING TOPIC SENTENCES

Each main section of your paper will expand on one of the supporting points from your thesis statement. While the sections may vary in length, their basic structure will be similar. Each new section will begin with a topic sentence that refers to a separate supporting point in your thesis. Linking the main idea of each section to the thesis statement helps the reader remember the larger goal of the paper, and directs her to the specific focus of each part. A good topic sentence has three qualities.

- It logically connects to the topic of the thesis.
- It logically connects to the focus of the thesis.
- It repeats a supporting point, but expresses it in a different way.

To see in detail how topic sentences connect to your thesis, look at the thesis statement and topic sentences from a student paper on communication problems between younger and older people.

> **Thesis Statement:**   Emphasis on individualism, loss of focus on extended families, and overscheduled lifestyles are three reasons for the generation gap between younger and older people.

This thesis tells us that the topic of the paper is the gap between younger and older people, and the focus is the causes of this gap. We also know that the first part of this paper will discuss how individualism can create a difference between generations. To establish this connection between her thesis and the first section of the paper, the writer uses a topic sentence.

> **Topic Sentence 1:** The value of independence is one reason why younger and older people become isolated from each other.

- Notice that the topic sentence repeats the focus idea, "reason," and is connected to a supporting point in the thesis, but does not repeat the same words. That is, "the value of independence" in the topic sentence is another way to say "emphasis on individualism." This topic sentence also includes a logical connection to the topic. In other words, "younger and older people become isolated from each other" is another way to express "generation gap."

There are many ways to write a good topic sentence that expresses the ideas in the thesis statement without being repetitive. For this paper, equally good topic sentences for the first body paragraph would be:

Trying not to appear too dependent can cause older people to limit their interaction with their children.

Valuing their independent lifestyles causes adult children and their parents to lose contact with each other.

Looking back at the thesis statement again, we can see that a topic sentence for the second section of the paper, about the loss of focus on extended families, might be:

> **Topic Sentence 2:** The change in family structure from extended families to nuclear families has resulted in less connection between generations.

For the third section of the paper, about overscheduled lifestyles, the topic sentence could be:

> **Topic Sentence 3:** A third cause of the generation gap is the lack of time that family members have to spend with each other.

There are many other, equally good, ways of writing topic sentences 2 and 3, as long as the writer is careful to include a logical connection to all the parts of her thesis statement.

Thinking about language in this way and using it to help your reader see how your ideas are related is often called using "guiding language." For more information about guiding language, see page 110 in Chapter 5.

NOW YOU TRY

For each thesis statement, decide whether the topic sentences are appropriate according to the qualities of a good topic sentence.

- Does it have a logical connection to the topic of the thesis?
- Does it connect to the focus of the thesis?
- Does it repeat the supporting point in a different way?

1. *Thesis Statement:* The negative effects of the Internet can be defined as a deterioration in courtesy while communicating and an isolation from other people.

   Topic Sentences: **A.** The decrease in politeness is common knowledge to those who work in network communication.

   Is this topic sentence appropriate? If not, what is the problem?

   _____

   B. People who use the Internet are lacking one of the most important things human beings need to have: connection to other people.

   Is this topic sentence appropriate? If not, what is the problem?

   _____

2. *Thesis Statement:* Exposure to violence, an inadequate rating system, and too little parental supervision are three reasons why children shouldn't play with video games.

   Topic Sentences: **A.** Children in the United States love to play video games.

   Is this topic sentence appropriate? If not, what is the problem?

   _____

   B. Unclear standards for evaluating video games is another reason why children should avoid video games.

   Is this topic sentence appropriate? If not, what is the problem?

   _____

   C. Too little parental supervision is a third reason children shouldn't play video games.

   Is this topic sentence appropriate? If not, what is the problem?

   _____

ACTIVITIES TO PRACTICE WRITING TOPIC SENTENCES

ACTIVITY **1** Identifying Topic Sentences

1. Select one of the model essays in Appendix A on page 210.

2. Find the thesis statement in the introduction of the essay. Highlight the focus of the thesis in one color. Highlight the overview of supporting points using a different color for each point.

3. In the body of the essay, highlight the topic sentence for each supporting point using the same color you used in the thesis statement.

4. Analyze these topic sentences by answering the following questions:
   - Are the topic sentences for supporting points organized in the same order that they appear in the thesis statement?

- Do the topic sentences repeat the focus idea from the thesis statement?
- Does each topic sentence repeat a supporting point idea? If yes, does the writer use a new way of saying this idea?

ACTIVITY **2** Writing Topic Sentences

For each thesis statement, write a topic sentence to introduce each of the main sections of the paper. Use a separate sheet of paper.

1. Alcohol addiction can lead to mental, physical, and social problems.

2. Social expectations, moral beliefs, and consideration of alcohol as a drug are three differences between American and Japanese attitudes toward alcohol.

3. Drinking behavior can be divided into three categories: social drinking, problem drinking, and alcoholism.

4. Quitting a bad habit requires four steps: acknowledging the problem, brainstorming solutions, devising a plan to quit, and, most difficult of all, monitoring yourself as you follow the plan.

5. Although some people worry that lowering the drinking age will result in alcohol abuse and increased traffic accidents, the legal drinking age should be 18 because it is consistent with other adult rights and responsibilities.

REVIEWING IDEAS FOR YOUR PAPER

Take a few minutes to look over everything you have gathered to help you write this paper: the articles you read, your responses or summaries of the articles, the notes you took on your readings and class discussions, your outline, and your thesis statement and topic sentences.

Then, decide which supporting point to work on first. It can be the first point in your outline or a later one; you can write your paper in any order and arrange the sections into your final order later. Think about the most important things you want to say about this point. It is important to include at least one piece of documented evidence in each paragraph of your finished paper, so jot down some notes to remind yourself what evidence you will use in this section.

As you write, consider several different ways to develop your ideas and make sense of them for your reader. For instance, you can provide examples, definitions, explanations, reasons, summaries, comparisons and contrasts of ideas, alternative perspectives, or personal experiences. Using a variety of strategies to explain your thoughts and ideas will make your paper more interesting and convincing.

When you feel comfortable with your planning, move ahead to your next step: the writing itself.

WRITING A FIRST DRAFT

Writing a first draft may be the most difficult stage of writing because you must begin with an empty page. However, keep in mind that, although your page is blank, your mind is actually full of ideas about this paper because you have been working on it and thinking about it for a long time.

Writing your ideas down is almost certain to be messy. Most of us cannot write a perfect first draft with everything clearly explained the first time. Moreover, you may be surprised at the new things you learn about your topic just from setting the words down on the page. This may lead you to make changes in your plan for the essay as you write. For example, you may decide to rearrange the order of supporting points, to leave gaps where your ideas are not yet clear, or to make other revisions. All of these changes are a normal part of the writing process.

No One "Best" Way

There is no one "best" way to write a draft. You can faithfully follow the outline you have made or start in the middle and go back to the beginning later. You may decide to write the easiest parts first to encourage yourself or to write the hardest part first to get it over with. You may write one long paragraph about each supporting point. Later, for your second draft, you can divide that paragraph into shorter ones and write a topic sentence for each.

You may use a computer or write by hand. You can write it all in one sitting or write a few sentences at a time, and then get up and wander around. Write everything that comes to mind; you can always cross it out later. If you can't think of what to say in one section, leave space and go back to it later.

The point is to keep at it until you complete a first draft. Then, you have something to work with and never have to return to an empty page.

Getting Out of Writer's Block

Writer's block is the feeling you have when your mind goes blank and you have no ideas. You may feel that you'll never be able to write again, that you don't have anything to say about your topic, or that you would rather do anything than write. This feeling strikes all writers from time to time. Some people say it is actually a healthy sign that our brain is working on our ideas and has simply gotten stuck in one place.

Here are some ideas that may help you to get out of writer's block.

1. **Start with what you have already accomplished and then continue into new ideas from there.**
   - Read over what you have already written–your notes, outlines, and so on–and, without thinking in depth about what you've just read, immediately start your draft with whatever comes to mind.
   - Copy over sections of what you have already written. New ideas may come to you while you do this, and if they do, write them down even if they are only one word at a time.

- Whenever you stop, leave yourself a note about what you will write next, so you won't have to wonder what to say when you get back to work.

2. **Talk to yourself or someone else about your paper. Once you have described your ideas informally, writing the paper will just be an expansion of the same ideas in more formal language.**

   - Write a paragraph telling what you think your paper will be about when you finish it.

   - Pretend you are writing a letter to a good friend about your topic instead of writing an academic paper.

   - Call up a friend and talk about your paper. Tell him or her what you plan to write.

3. **Start with something easy. Seeing certain sections finished will encourage you so that it won't be hard to go on to more challenging parts.**

   - If you are stuck on one section of your paper, set that aside and work on another part for a while. You can return to the more difficult section later.

   - Do something that doesn't take a lot of thought, such as working on your reference list or proofreading what you have already written.

4. **Take regular breaks the whole time you're working on the paper.**

   - Take a walk around the block. Promise yourself that you will take a 10-minute walk every hour.

Another way to help yourself with your writing is to get assistance from a friend or professional tutor or editor. However, it's important to keep in mind that working through the writing process yourself will give you the skills and confidence you need to write academic papers on your own. If you get too much help with your paper, get too much advice from a friend or tutor, or if you copy (plagiarize) a paper, you miss the valuable practice in the writing process and you won't be able to apply what you have learned in the class to your own writing later.

First Draft, Working Draft

Like your working thesis statement and your working outline, your first draft will be a working draft; it will change as you continue to work on it. But, as with the thesis and outline, having the draft in front of you will make the process of expanding your ideas and refining your paper much easier. You will have done the hardest part and can return to work on smaller pieces, until the writing is just the way you want it.

BUILDING YOUR PAPER

Write a First Draft

Write a rough first draft of your paper. Your goal is to get your ideas down, so they will be much easier to work with. Later you may rearrange the order, add missing parts, fine-tune your wording and grammar, and so on. Because your goal is simply to produce a rough draft, set yourself a time limit two hours is probably a good length of time to allow.

If, after an hour and a half, you find that you are a long way from finishing, speed up your writing. You might skip the introduction and conclusion, skip some details, or simply note where you will use each piece of evidence. At this stage, don't worry about correct spelling or grammar.

Getting Feedback

Bring your rough draft to class and sit in a circle with a small group or the whole class. Take turns telling the group one thing you really like about your paper and one thing that you are not yet satisfied with.

INTEGRATING EVIDENCE INTO YOUR PARAGRAPHS

Now that you have a first draft, you can work on each part of it until you are satisfied that your writing conveys what you want to say. A good place to begin your revision is by looking at each body paragraph to make sure that your evidence helps to make your ideas clear and easy to understand.

You have already written a topic sentence for each section of your paper. If a section has more than one paragraph, you can now make sure each one has a topic sentence. Each paragraph consists mostly of your own ideas combined with information you have taken from sources. To effectively use that source information, you need to incorporate it gracefully into your work.

EXAMPLE OF A PARAGRAPH WITH EVIDENCE

Topic sentence:	The value of independence is one reason why young and old people become isolated from each other.
Explanation of topic sentence with supporting evidence:	Being independent is an important quality of life for most Americans. Since childhood, people have been taught to be independent. The notion continues through their lives until they become old. Margaret Mead (1971), an American anthropologist, writes in her article, "Grandparents Have Copped Out," that old people don't want to be a burden to their children so they try to live their lives independently. That is, old people do not want to interfere with their children's lives. Young people also believe their lives will be better without their parents as constant companions.
Concluding sentence:	Consequently, communication between the generations is limited and isolation gradually occurs.

Three Steps for Integrating Your Evidence

To integrate each piece of evidence from your sources into your own well-written paragraph, follow these steps.

1. **Paraphrase or quote each piece of evidence.**

2. **Introduce the evidence.**

3. **Connect the evidence to the topic sentence.**

QUOTING AND PARAPHRASING EVIDENCE

The first step in using each piece of evidence is to decide whether to quote it directly or to paraphrase it. Paraphrasing is more common in academic writing. As discussed in Chapter 1 on page 6, a paraphrase uses your own words to accurately restate what the author said. Less frequently, evidence is presented in a direct quotation, using the exact words of the original source with quotation marks around the author's words.

The examples below show how a quotation and a paraphrase of the same piece of evidence differ.

EXAMPLES

Original excerpt from source to be used as evidence:	To behave aggressively is no longer considered unfeminine and unattractive. Girl characters are expected to be assertive and achievement-oriented.
	—Hopkins, Susan, "Bam! Crash! Kapow! Girls are Heroes Now"

Quotation of this excerpt:	According to Hopkins (n.d., p. 13), "To behave aggressively is no longer considered unfeminine and unattractive. Girl characters are expected to be assertive and achievement-oriented."
Paraphrase of this excerpt:	According to Hopkins (n.d.), females in movies and books today are often hard-driving and ambitious; unlike in the past, it is now socially acceptable for women to act boldly and forcefully.

Using Quotations

We use direct quotations in only a few circumstances:

- When the original is written in poetic language or provides a unique image as in this description of the differences between a woman and her Chinese grandmother:

  "The difference between (my grandmother's and my) feet reminds me of the incredible history we hold between us like living bookends. We stand like sentries at either side of a vast gulf."

  —*Wu, Janet, "Homework Bound"*

- When the original was spoken or written by a famous person and is generally recognizable as a famous saying. For example, we would never try to paraphrase the beginning of President Abraham Lincoln's Gettysburg Address:

  "Four score and seven years ago our fathers brought forth upon this continent, a new nation, conceived in Liberty, and dedicated to the proposition that all men are created equal."

Using Paraphrases

Much more often, writers paraphrase evidence from sources. In some cultures, it's considered acceptable or even good taste to copy from the writings of experts or classical authors. However, in Western academic culture, writing someone else's ideas or words as if they were your own without acknowledging the original author is called *plagiarism,* and is considered very dishonorable behavior. In the academic environment at colleges and universities, copying someone else's work can result in a failing grade and possible expulsion from the institution. In public life too, plagiarism is a serious offense; people have lost jobs or have had to pay thousands of dollars in damages when they were convicted of plagiarism.

Remember to Document

In addition to paraphrasing almost all the pieces of evidence you plan to use, you will also need to document, or acknowledge, the original author. This means that you write the name of the author and/or the name of the article when you mention it in your paper. This is not difficult to do, but it is very important. It lets the reader know that you are presenting information from another person. Referring to the original author helps to establish your honesty and reliability as a writer, and it is expected in academic writing in US universities. Documenting evidence is discussed in detail in Chapter 5 beginning on page 123.

Using the methods described in Chapter 1 on page 7, you can paraphrase the information you plan to use as supporting evidence in your essay. Recall that a good paraphrase meets these criteria:

- It means the same as the original.

    –No new ideas are added.

    –No important ideas are deleted.

- It differs enough from the original to be considered your own writing.

- It refers to the original.

For more practice with paraphrasing, turn to the optional Paraphrasing Challenges on page 90.

INTRODUCING THE EVIDENCE

Once you have decided whether to paraphrase or quote each piece of evidence, you need to frame it, or introduce it, telling where it comes from.

- Include the author's last name every time you use evidence from your sources.

- The source title is optional. Include the title the first time you introduce a source, if you think it is important for the reader to know.

- A description of how to formally document and cite your sources is given in Chapter 5 beginning on page 123.

Here are some formats for introducing your source.

1. Format choices when you know the name of the author.

EXAMPLES

Author:	Jim Clark
Article:	College Success
Choice 1:	[In the article, "College Success"] Clark (2010) writes that students should study two hours for every hour in class.

<u>Prepositional Phrase</u> w/title (optional)	<u>Subject</u> Author & date	<u>Verb</u> simple present	<u>Noun Clause</u> (*that* + full sentence) • paraphrase or quotation • present tense
In the article, "College Success," **OR** In "College Success,"	Clark (2010)	writes	that students should study two hours for every hour in class.

Choice 2:   According to Clark (2010) [in "College Success"], students should study two hours for every hour in class.

Prepositional Phrase w/author & date	Prepositional Phrase w/ title (optional)	Full Sentence • paraphrase or quotation
According to Clark (2010),	in "College Success,"	students should study two hours for every hour in class.

Choice 3:   Clark (2010) writes [in his article "College Success,"] that students should study two hours for every hour in class.

Subject Author & date	Verb simple present	Prepositional Phrase w/ article title (optional)	Noun Clause (*that* + full sentence) • present tense
Clark (2010)	writes	in his article "College Success,"	that students should study two hours for every hour in class.

2. Format when you don't know the name of the author

When you don't know the name of the author, use the article title. In this situation, the article title is the subject of the sentence.

EXAMPLES

The article "College Survival Tips" (2007) recommends that students prepare a daily schedule.

Subject Article title & date	Verb simple present	Noun Clause (*that* + full sentence) • paraphrase or quote
The article "College Survival Tips" (2007) **OR** "College Survival Tips" (2007)	recommends	that students prepare a daily schedule.

Sometimes it is useful to include information about the author if he or she is an expert on the topic. Do this only the first time you use a source.

EXAMPLES

Clark (2010), director of the College Success program at Winston University, writes that students should study two hours for every hour in class.

<u>Subject</u> Author & date	<u>Noun Phrase</u>	<u>Verb</u> simple present	<u>Noun Clause</u> (*that* + full sentence) • present tense
Clark (2010),	director of the College Success program at Winston University,	writes	that students should study two hours for every hour in class.

Common Verbs for Introducing Evidence

The verb you choose when introducing evidence can give the reader a clue about your opinion of the information.

If you have a neutral stance towards the evidence, use these verbs:

	writes	
	states	
Clark (2010)	remarks	that students should study two hours for every hour in class.
	explains	
	notes	

You can signal your disagreement or doubt about a piece of information by using one of these verbs:

	argues	
Clark (2010)	claims	that students should study two hours for every hour in class.
	suggests	

In this situation, after you have presented the idea, the reader will likely expect you to provide a contrasting opinion.

Clark (2010) argues that students should study two hours for every hour in class. On the other hand, other experts in the field state that too much studying causes student burnout and stress.

To present information from a study, use one of these verbs:

	found	
Clark's (2010) research on successful college students	showed	that students who study two or more hours for every hour in class are more likely to earn a GPA of 3.0 or higher.
	demonstrated	

 For more information on how to present your opinion or controversial information in your writing, visit the *Sourcework* website at **http://esl.hmco.com/students.**

CONNECTING THE EVIDENCE TO THE TOPIC SENTENCE

Finally, you complete the integration process by connecting each paraphrase or quotation with the flow of your own writing. Explain why you are using each piece of evidence and what links it to the topic sentence of the paragraph. This is similar to what you would do in a conversation. If the person you are talking to asked, "Why are you telling me this fact?" you would explain where you found the fact and why you think it is important. You can provide the connecting explanation before the evidence, after the evidence, or in both places.

A more extended look at the example paragraph from the paper on communication between younger and older people mentioned on page 79 reveals how the writer smoothly integrated the evidence into her writing.

EXAMPLE OF A PARAGRAPH WITH INTEGRATED EVIDENCE

Topic sentence:	The value of independence is one reason why young and old people become isolated from each other.
Connecting explanation:	Being independent is an important quality of life for most Americans. Since childhood, people have been taught to be independent and the notion continues through their old age.
Evidence:	Margaret Mead (1971), an anthropologist, writes in her article, "Grandparents Have Copped Out," that old people don't want to be a burden to their children so they try to live their lives independently.
Connecting explanation:	In other words, old people do not want to interfere with their children's lives. Young people also believe their lives will be better without their parents as constant companions and advisors.
Concluding sentence:	Consequently, communication between the generations is limited and isolation gradually occurs.

In this paragraph:

- The connecting explanation that comes before the evidence explains how the idea of independence is connected to old age.

- The evidence is given as a paraphrase and includes the name of the author, the article title, and some information about the author. In paragraphs that follow this one, the writer will include only the last name of the author, Mead, when this source is introduced.

- The connecting explanation that comes after the evidence provides further information that relates the value of independence to the relationship between the young and the old.

NOW YOU TRY

The following is a well-constructed paragraph in which the evidence has been smoothly integrated into the writing.

The first characteristic of risk is that the outcome of the activity is uncertain. When the person begins the activity, he is not sure whether or not he will be successful. In her article "Taking the Bungee Plunge," Gina Bellafonte (1992, p. 80) writes about this uncertainty. "We build sustainable confidence not by taking life-threatening risks, but by gradually working at things we never thought we could achieve." In other words, a risky activity does not have to be dangerous, but it must involve trying to accomplish something we are not sure we are capable of doing. The key here is that we try and succeed in doing something that is not easy for us to do. This also points to a second characteristic of risk; a risky activity must be challenging.

1. Put brackets around the topic sentence.

2. Underline once any sentences or phrases that provide connecting information before the evidence.

3. Circle the title of the article and the name of the author.

4. Put parentheses around the quote that is used as evidence and double parentheses around the paraphrase of that quote.

5. Underline twice the connecting explanation after the evidence.

6. Underline with a wavy line the conclusion and/or transition to the next paragraph.

Including Background Information

In many cases, as you integrate a piece of evidence from a source into your writing, you will notice that the source idea you want to paraphrase refers to an earlier section of the passage. In this situation, it is necessary to briefly explain the background information leading up to the part you are using as evidence in your paraphrase. In other words, a paraphrase must include enough of the original passage so that it makes sense; this is part of doing a good job of integrating evidence into your paragraph.

The following original sentence is from paragraph 3 of "The Deadly Noodle" in Part Two, page 181.

Original: But the trend has turned out to be more insidious and more widespread than previously thought.

—Hastings, Michael, 2003

Weak Paraphrase: The fad is even more common and difficult to get rid of than expected (Hastings, 2003).

- It isn't enough to simply paraphrase this short passage; you must begin by explaining what "the trend" is. Looking at the context in the original article on page 181, we can see that the paragraph discusses how more and more people all over the world are becoming overweight by eating American fast food. A good paraphrase will explain this.

Stronger Paraphrase: The tendency for people everywhere to gain weight by eating American fast food is more prevalent and more difficult to stop than expected (Hastings, 2003).

NOW YOU TRY

Write a stronger paraphrase of the section of the following passage that is in **bold**. As you study the weak paraphrase, consider how to include enough background information so that the paraphrase makes sense.

Original: This year's report focuses on the growing global "consumer class"—defined as individuals whose "purchasing power parity" in local currency is more than $7,000 a year (roughly the poverty level in Western Europe). As economies expand—accelerated by globalization that has opened up markets, greater efficiency in manufacturing, and advancing technologies—that consumer class has grown rapidly. **It's the main reason there are more than 1 billion cell phones in the world today.**

—Knickerbocker, Brad, If Poor Get Richer,
Does World See Progress? 2004

Weak Paraphrase (of statement in bold): That's why people currently own more than 1 billion cell phones worldwide.

Stronger Paraphrase (including some background information):

_____

_____

_____

Avoiding Dumped Evidence

Dumping a piece of evidence from a source into your writing means inserting the quotation or paraphrase without a proper introduction or explanation. When this occurs, the reader is left to figure out the purpose of the quote or paraphrase. In the example, the writer has simply dumped the quote into the paragraph with no supporting information.

> **Weak Integration:**   An uncertain outcome is one characteristic of risk. In her article "Taking the Bungee Plunge," Bellafonte (1992) writes that "we build sustainable confidence not by taking life-threatening risks, but by gradually working at things we never thought we could achieve." Another characteristic of risk is that the activity must be challenging.

- Notice in this example how the writer simply includes a quotation with no explanation of its relationship to the topic sentence either before or after it.

NOW YOU TRY

Consider the information on how to integrate evidence and then identify two or more problems with dumped evidence in this paragraph.

Younger and older people are segregated in American culture according to one article. In other words, the young and the old do not communicate or interact enough with each other. This problem is caused by a lack of contact between them. The article says that old people don't want to be a burden to the young.

Problem 1 _____

Problem 2 _____

Problem 3 _____

ACTIVITIES TO PRACTICE INTEGRATING EVIDENCE

ACTIVITY ❶ Analyzing the Organization of an Essay

1. Working with a partner or in a small group, look at the student paper "Risky Business" in Appendix A on page 210.

2. Underline the thesis statement.

3. Circle each supporting point in the thesis and identify the section of the paper that discusses that point.

4. Discuss how the writer introduces and connects each piece of evidence in that section.

ACTIVITY **2** Identifying Evidence in Paragraphs

1. With a small group, read the two paragraphs below. Underline each piece of outside evidence.

2. Discuss the following questions about each paragraph:
   • What is this paragraph about?
   • How many pieces of outside evidence are used?
   • Does each piece of evidence support the topic sentence?
   • Is each piece of evidence well integrated?
   • Does the paragraph flow logically and smooth**ly**?

3. Discuss your answers with the class.

Paragraph 1: The selling of human eggs raises a legal problem. In fact, US law does not allow people to buy and sell human organs, except for sperm and eggs ("Millions Check In," 1999). Dr. Jeffery Kahn, Director of the Center for Bioethics at the University of Minnesota, confirms that it is an offense against federal law to deal in human parts, aside from human blood and tissue. On the other hand, he also argues that there are many important ways in which eggs should be considered more like tissue than like organs (Kahn, 1999). Meanwhile, in attempts to circumvent the law, several entrepreneurs are offering human eggs from beautiful women for sale on the Internet ("Eggs for Sale," 1999). And so far, such online commerce seems to be beyond the reach of the law. Objecting to these egg auctions in cyberspace, Ron Wyden, the Democratic senator from Oregon who wrote the 1992 federal law regulating fertility clinics, has called the operation "crass commercialism" (Lemonick, 1999).

Paragraph 2: As people around the world become more affluent, their diets get worse. According to Ted Wilcox (1999), a writer for the "New York Times," Japanese immigrating from the high-carbohydrate Pacific to high-fat America have a greater risk of heart disease the more westernized their diets become. Carolyn Henderson, a high school student in Tennessee, says that Mexican restaurants are becoming more popular everywhere. What is a safe level of cholesterol? Scientists in a laboratory in Texas wrote an article saying that as a country's food gets richer, infectious disease and malnutrition are replaced by heart disease, certain cancers, and obesity (Russo, 2000). People are eating more meat and dairy products in countries such as Cuba, Mauritius, and Hungary. Not surprisingly, the disease rates in these countries are changing along with the change in diet (Martinez, 2001). The American Heart Association National Cholesterol Education Program (1999) says that fat should be no more than 30% of our diet.

ACTIVITY **3** Grading Paragraphs

1. With your group, read each of the three paragraphs. As you read, consider the following:
   - Does it have a clear topic sentence?
   - Does it have at least one piece of outside evidence?
   - Is the outside evidence carefully integrated?
   - Does it have a brief conclusion and/or transition to the next paragraph?

2. Rate each paragraph according to this scale:

   A = Excellent. Meets all criteria for a paragraph with well-integrated evidence.

   C = OK, but needs work. Has some, but not all, characteristics of a good paragraph using outside evidence.

   F = Unacceptable. Doesn't have any characteristics of a good paragraph using outside evidence.

3. After completing your analysis of the paragraphs, discuss your ratings with the class and compare them with the teacher's rating.

Paragraph 1:   Gender roles come from social factors such as culture and family as well as from biological factors such as age and physical characteristics. Because men have more testosterone, they have more physical energy and are more aggressive. This makes them like sports, which makes them more competitive. Therefore, men are more interested in dominating others than in helping them. In social life, man is less nurturing because when he gets a promotion in his job, he has less time to spend with his family (Farrell, 1986). Also, Houston (1973) mentions that she knows about Asian gender roles because her family taught her. Houston writes, "It would have embarrassed me to see my brothers doing the dishes."

Grade _____

Paragraph 2:   One group of people who oppose xenotransplantation* are animal rights advocates. These people state that the new science causes misuse and exploitation of animals' lives (Cassidy, 1994). To develop a new medical practice requires lots of precise and complicated testing. During the process, if scientists make some small errors, then they need other healthy animals to start the experiment over. Consequently, the "old" animals are deserted and need to be killed. Animal rights activists wonder how many animals need to die due to the mistakes in experiments. They suggest that there must be

---

* *Xenotransplantation* is the transfer of an organ from one species to another, for example, transferring a pig's heart to a human.

an alternative way that could replace animals for testing (Cassidy, 1994). Sacrificing animals without considering the great pain and torture which the animals suffer as well as their right to live, is, according to these activists, selfish and immoral.

Grade _____

Paragraph 3:   First of all, many people become vegetarians to maintain good health. Vegetarianism can prevent people from getting diseases. Castelman (1995) writes that many studies prove that meat, especially beef, pork, and lamb likely increase the percentages of heart disease and cancers. In his article, it is proved that the number of vegetarian deaths is definitely lower than meat eaters. For example, 28 percent fewer vegetarians die from heart disease than omnivores do, and 39 percent fewer die from cancer. The National Cancer Research Institute also found that meat-eating women get breast cancer almost four times more than women who do not eat meat or eat little meat ("Why Be Vegetarian?" 1999). Hypertension, gallstones, constipation, and diabetes are also problems (Cerrato, 1991). Dworkin (1999) cites a Loma Linda University study that says vegetarians can live seven years longer than people who eat meat. Another positive health point of vegetarianism, according to Dworkin, is that vegetarians are generally slim and have stronger bones. Knowing these health benefits, many people are becoming vegetarians.

Grade _____

OPTIONAL

Paraphrasing Challenges

Paraphrasing can present some special challenges. Using paraphrasing well requires you to truly understand the original and to present this information as clearly and accurately as possible. Below are five challenges you may encounter as you paraphrase your evidence.

1. PARAPHRASING WORD-BY-WORD

It's tempting to simply substitute synonyms or change grammatical structures without considering the overall context of the sentence you are working with. Here are two examples of the problems that can result.

Problems with Synonym Substitution

Original: A hero has a story of adventure to tell and a community who will listen.

—Tollefson, Ted, "Is a Hero Really Nothing But a Sandwich?" 1993

Weak
Paraphrase: A hero has a tale of experience to share and a community who will hear (Tollefson, 1993).

- Because this paraphrase relies only on synonym substitution, it is not really a paraphrase; it's too similar to the original. Also, the substituted vocabulary doesn't have exactly the same meaning as the original. For example, "experience" is broader in meaning than "adventure," and "hear" is more passive than "listen."

Stronger
Paraphrase: Heroes have both a unique experience to share and a community that is eager to listen to it (Tollefson, 1993).

NOW YOU TRY

Write a stronger paraphrase of this original sentence after you study the weak paraphrase.

Original: The process by which sunglasses have gained worldwide popularity is a fascinating one that began, surprisingly, in the justice system of medieval China.

—"How Sunglasses Spanned the World," n.d.

Weak Paraphrase: The procedure by which sunglasses have earned global fame is a very interesting one that started, amazingly, in the fairness system of middle China ("How Sunglasses Spanned the World", n.d.).

Stronger Paraphrase:

_____

_____

Problems with Incorrect Grammar

> Original: Without Gandhi, India might still be a part of the British Empire.
> —*Sudo, Phil, "Larger Than Life," 1990*
>
> Weak Paraphrase: Without Gandhi, India could stay a part of the British Empire until now (Sudo, 1990).

- This paraphrase is grammatically incorrect. The new adverb phrase, "until now," although similar in meaning to "still," requires a different verb tense.

> Stronger Paraphrase: Great Britain might still be governing India if Gandhi hadn't been there (Sudo, 1990).

NOW YOU TRY

Write a stronger paraphrase of this original sentence after you study the weak paraphrase.

Original: Opponents of standardized testing believe tests are a limited way of assessing students.
        —*MacDonald, Moira, "Does Province-Wide Testing Distort Reality?" 2001*

Weak Paraphrase: MacDonald (2001) thinks that people who want to use standardized testing to know the students' ability or knowledge is very limited.

Stronger Paraphrase:

_____

_____

2. DEALING WITH POETIC OR IDIOMATIC LANGUAGE

When you're paraphrasing sentences from sources that are poetic or that use idiomatic language, it's best to focus on the overall meaning of the sentence and use the tell-a-friend method (Chapter 1, page 7).

You can run into problems if you try to use the Grammar Toolbox method (see the *Sourcework* website at **http://elt.heinle.com/sourcework**) with these kinds of sentences.

Original: *snakes* Like serpents, we keep shedding the skins of our heroes as we move toward new phases in our lives.

—*Tollefson, Ted, "Is a Hero Really Nothing But a Sandwich?" 1993*

Weak Paraphrase: We never stop changing our heroes when we face different stages of our lives, as if we were snakes (Tollefson, 1993).

- The phrase, "like serpents" in the original sentence is poetic or a "figure of speech." It means that people are flexible or changeable, which is also a characteristic of snakes. In this paraphrase, the reference to a snake has no meaning because the image of "shedding our skin" has not been included.

Stronger Paraphrase: Because we face different challenges at each stage of our lives, the people we consider heroes also change (Tollefson, 1993).

NOW YOU TRY

Write a stronger paraphrase of this original sentence after you study the weak paraphrase.

Original: *metaphor* Medical science, focused on curing the ills of the body, has often treated the mind like an annoying younger brother: a presence to be ignored whenever possible.

—*Goode, Erica, "Your Mind May Ease What's Ailing You," 1999*

Weak Paraphrase: Goode (1999) writes that in medicine, the mind is like a little brother and doctors are interested only in the body.

Stronger Paraphrase:

_____

_____

3. MANAGING PASSAGES WITH STATISTICS

The information in a source passage that contains several statistics can be dense and thus tricky to paraphrase. Sometimes, drawing a picture or making a chart of the information in the original will help you to understand it and provide a way to present it clearly.

Original: The problem [*of youth addiction to cell phones*] seems to be growing. A Japanese study revealed that children with cell phones often don't make friends with their less tech-savvy peers. A Hungarian study found that three-fourths of children had mobile phones, and an Italian study showed that one quarter of adolescents owned multiple phones and many claimed to be somewhat addicted to them. A British study also recently found that 36 percent of college students surveyed said they could not get by without cell phones. But this may be more a sign that students view cell phones as a modern necessity like a car, said David Sheffield, a psychologist who conducted the study at Staffordshire University in England.

—*Birdwell, April Frawley, "Addicted to Phones?" January 18, 2007*

Traditional
Paraphrase: More and more young people may be becoming addicted to cell phones. Four studies have verified this trend. A study in Japan showed that children who have cell phones don't play with children without phones. Research results indicated that 75 percent of youngsters in Hungary already have cell phones, and that 25 percent of teenagers in Italy have them and say they may be addicted to them. Also, about one-third of college students questioned in a British study said that their cell phones were a necessity. But, according to David Sheffield, the psychologist who did the British study at Staffordshire University, all of this information could simply show that today's younger generation thinks of cell phones as older generations have thought of cars—as an essential tool (Birdwell, 2007).

Paraphrase presented as a chart:

Youthful addiction to cell phones	
Japan	Kids with cell phones refuse to be friends with kids without phones
Hungary	75 percent of kids have cell phones
Italy	25 percent of teenagers have cell phones; many claim addiction
Britain	36 percent of college students cannot manage without cell phones

NOW YOU TRY

Create a chart that presents the information in this thesis sentence.

Original: In the most sprawling cities in the United States, 49 of every 100,000 residents die each year in traffic crashes. The least sprawling cities have fewer than 20 people per 100,000 die in fatal crashes each year.

—*Ewing, Reid, "Measuring Sprawl and Its Impact" 1997*

4. HANDLING PASSAGES WITH OPINION OR BIAS

When the author of the original passage expresses an opinion or bias, your paraphrase must include the point of view along with the facts he or she states.

Original: I think it's a very simple deduction that the music is Negro music to begin with; and for these guys (critics) to write about the music as though it's an American music, that everybody plays equally, and that we all love one another and we're all brothers—to me, really, that's a lot of horseshit.

—*Lott, Tommy Lee, "The 1960s Avant-Garde Movement in Jazz," 2001*

Weak Paraphrase: Lott (2001) thinks that it's easy to see that this is really black American music and the critics say all Americans play this music the same way and love each other like family.

- This paraphrase does not include the author's strong disagreement with the critics, which he voices in the phrase "that's a lot of horseshit." This opinion must be included in the paraphrase.

Stronger Paraphrase: Lott (2001) says that it's clear that this music is uniquely black American music, not music appreciated by all in the United States, and he strongly disagrees with critics who say that all Americans love the same music like a big happy family.

NOW YOU TRY

Write a stronger paraphrase of this original sentence after you study the weak paraphrase.

Original: "It is inappropriate and simplistic to treat cohabitation as the major cause of divorce," says Larry Bumpass, a sociologist at the University of Wisconsin.

—*Labi, Nadya, "A Bad Start? Living Together May be the Road to Divorce," 1999*

Weak Paraphrase: Larry Bumpass (cited in Labi, 1999) says that cohabitation might be a major cause of divorce.

Stronger Paraphrase:

_____

_____

5. DEALING WITH LONG PASSAGES

When you want to use the evidence in a long passage from a source, you can paraphrase by summarizing it, mentioning only the key ideas (underlined here) and summarizing others (italicized here).

Original: Alleging that whaling is inherently cruel, as the British do, often comes with the further claim that whales are somehow "special": *they are extraordinarily intelligent, perhaps, or spiritual, noble or peaceful, or they have some mixture of these qualities that makes killing them more reprehensible than, say, killing cows or pigs.* Science has little to say about this sort of speculation. Whales look peaceful enough, though bull whales of some species bear the scars of fierce fighting with other males.

—*"A Bloody War," 2004*

Strong
Paraphrase: Many, such as the British, say that whaling is brutal because whales are unique and more human-like than other, domestic animals. However, there is no scientific proof of this, and in fact, male whales often fight among themselves, as shown by their scars ("A Bloody War," 2004).

NOW YOU TRY

Practice paraphrasing the following longer passage.
- Identify the key ideas to paraphrase by underlining them once.
- Select the ideas to summarize and underline them twice.
- Write a short paraphrase of the passage.

Original: Scientific research on reproductive cloning in other mammals shows that there is a markedly higher than normal incidence of fetal disorders and loss throughout pregnancy, and of malformation and death among newborns. There is no reason to suppose that the outcome would be different in humans. There would thus be a serious threat to the health of the cloned individual, not just at birth, but potentially at all stages of life—without obvious compensating benefit to the individual bearing this threat.

—*White, J. "Science, Cloning and Morality," 2003*

Paraphrase:

_____

_____

_____

_____

ACTIVITIES TO PRACTICE PARAPHRASING

ACTIVITY **1** Paraphrasing Challenging Passages

Work with a partner or in a small group.

1. Choose one of the following excerpts from articles in Part Two of this textbook.

2. Identify the challenge in the excerpt you're working with. In some cases, you may need to look at the original article in order to understand the context for the excerpt.

3. On a separate piece of paper, write a paraphrase of your excerpt and share it with your class. You may want to write it on the board or on an overhead transparency.

4. As a class, critique the paraphrase of each pair of students or small group according to the criteria for a good paraphrase:

   • It has the same meaning as the original.

      –All main ideas are included.

      –No new ideas are added.

   • It is different enough from the original to be considered your own writing.

      No more than four or five words in a row are from the original source.

      –Grammar and vocabulary are changed as much as possible.

   • It refers directly to the original source.

      –Includes name of author and/or name of source

Excerpt 1 (page 187): **Air quality.** Between 1970 and 1997, U.S. population increased 31 percent, vehicle miles traveled increased 127 percent, and gross domestic product increased 114 percent – yet total air pollution actually decreased by about 31 percent.

Charles, John A., The Environmental Benefits of Globalization,
Globalenvision.org, July 14, 2004

Challenge with excerpt 1:

_____

_____

Excerpt 2 (page 203): It is difficult to direct a snowball as it careens down the slope; thus, it is now – when there are only a handful of functional humanoids around the world – that we must decide the direction in which to push.

—*Bruemmer, David, Humanoid Robotics: Ethical Considerations,*
www.inl.gov/adaptiverobics/humanoidrobitics/ethicalconsiderations.shtml, May 30, 2006

Challenge with excerpt 2:

_____

_____

Excerpt 3 (page 158):   Type T's are not just the mountain-climbing daredevils of the world however. They are often our best inventors, entrepreneurs, and explorers. They are CEOs, surgeons, and civil rights leaders. Take high altitude mountaineer Dr. Kenneth Kamler, for example, a New York microsurgeon and listed in the New York Guide to Best Doctors as well as in Who's Who in America. We wouldn't be the progressive, vibrant society we are today if no one was willing to take risks. Farley argues that history's most crucial events are shaped by Type T individuals exhibiting Type T behaviour, from Boris Yeltsin to Martin Luther King, Jr. The act of emigration, he says, is an intrinsically risky endeavor that selects individuals who are high in sensation seeking. Consequently, countries built upon immigrant population—America, Canada, Australia—probably have an above-average level of risk takers. He warns that much of the current effort to minimize risk and risk taking itself runs the risk of eliminating "a large part of what made this country great in the first place."

—Smith, Julia, Living on the Edge: Extreme Sports and Their Role in Society,
Summitpost.org, August 9, 2006

Challenge with excerpt 3:

_____

_____

Excerpt 4 (page 182):   "Where in the past they produced their own fruits and vegetables, now they're swamped with canned soda and mutton fat imported from New Zealand," says Yach of WHO. "Call it the Coca-Colafication of the Pacific Islands."

—Hastings, Michael; Theil, Stefan; Thomas, Dana. The Deadly Noodle,
Newsweek, January 20, 2003

Challenge with excerpt 4:

_____

_____

Excerpt 5 (page 189):   What tools do people need to become architects of their own lives?

—Ma, Yo-Yo, Paths of Globalization: From The Berbers to Bach,
New Perspectives Quarterly, Spring 2008

Challenge with excerpt 5:

_____

_____

ACTIVITY **2** Trading Paraphrases

Work with a partner or in a small group.

1. Select two to three passages from an article you are reading in Part Two for the research paper you're building.

2. Using the "tell-a-friend" method on page 7 or the "chunking" method on page 8 or a combination of the two, paraphrase the passages you have selected.

3. Evaluate your paraphrases using the criteria for a good paraphrase from Activity 1 on page 97.

4. Trade your paraphrases with another pair or group.

5. Read the other students' paraphrases and see if you can identify the original passages in the article.

ACTIVITY **3** Sharing Paraphrases

1. Choose a paraphrase that you have worked on, either for a current or past writing assignment, but found particularly difficult to write. Bring both your paraphrase and the original passage to class.

2. Write both the original passage and your paraphrase on the board or on an overhead transparency.

3. With a small group or with the class, discuss what the problem is with the paraphrase. Consider the five challenges on pages 90–96 in your discussion.

BUILDING YOUR PAPER

Write a Second Draft

Write a second draft of your paper, paying special attention to how well your evidence is integrated into each paragraph.

Getting Feedback

1. Choose one body paragraph from your second draft. Make a copy of the paragraph for each member of your small group.

2. Take turns reading the paragraphs aloud while the others read along silently and make notes.

3. After you read your paragraph, listen to your classmates' comments and make notes about possible changes to your paragraph. Collect the copies from your classmates so you can use their notes in your revision.

4. After you listen to each of your classmates' paragraphs, give the writer feedback answering these questions:

   • Does the paragraph meet the criteria for a well-constructed paragraph?

   • Is the outside evidence introduced and explained following the steps for integrating evidence on page 79?

CHAPTER 5

BUILDING A PAPER:
Refine

Now that you've written one or more drafts of your paper, your goal is to make sure you've presented your ideas so that they are clear to the reader. Your job is to create a reader-friendly paper that smoothly guides the reader from one idea to the next. To do this, you will need to read through your sentences one by one with your reader in mind, considering how well each sentence presents your ideas and how clearly these ideas link to each other. To help you identify strengths and weaknesses in your paper, it is useful to communicate directly with your reader. Your readers for this paper are your teacher and classmates. By talking with or writing to your reader, you can think about how another person might understand your paper.

To refine your paper, you will add some finishing touches to your introduction and conclusion and to the language you use to link ideas clearly. You will also formally document your evidence. Based on your readers' comments and your own editing, you can polish your paper so it is cohesive and rich in detail.

In this chapter you will practice the following:

- Revising your introduction and conclusion

- Revising your use of language for cohesion

- Documenting your evidence

By the end of this chapter, you will have written an effective introduction and conclusion, used lexical and grammatical techniques to make your writing cohesive, and documented your evidence. After considering feedback from your classmates, you will write the final version of your research paper.

WRITING INTRODUCTIONS AND CONCLUSIONS

Because introductions and conclusions form the reader's first and last impression of your paper, they deserve special attention. Often, in writing the body of the paper, the introduction and conclusion are hurriedly written and not very effective. Now is the time to revise these two sections with the reader in mind. Revising your introduction and conclusion at the same time can ensure that the beginning and ending of your paper link together smoothly.

Elements of an Effective Introduction

As your first contact with your reader, the introduction is an opportunity to engage your reader's interest and identify the purpose of your essay. In an effective introduction, you accomplish three things:

1. **Engage your reader and introduce your topic.**

2. **Establish your purpose.**

3. **State your thesis.**

EXAMPLE OF AN EFFECTIVE INTRODUCTION

Celebrating the revolution, French citizens sent King Louis XVI to the guillotine. Every Halloween day in ancient Rome, the most evil criminals were executed at the city square. In the 1800s, in an effort to deter crime in the United States, hundreds of bank robbers, killers, and horse thieves were hanged in front of the public. Capital punishment has been a useful and powerful tool to protect justice and deter crime. However, in the last half of the 20th century, the death penalty has faced increasing opposition. Many people, especially members of churches, are against capital punishment. Most advanced countries have eliminated the death penalty ("Down With the Death Penalty," 1998). While it is true that the death penalty has some negative points, it is still a powerful and useful tool. Therefore, so as to deter crime, to give fairness to victims and their families, and to punish inhumane criminals, our society should keep the death penalty.

- **Introduction to the topic**: In the opening sentences, the writer engages the reader's curiosity by giving examples of public executions from three historical periods. From the first three sentences, we assume that the topic will be the death penalty, but wonder what the writer will say about it because the examples he gives are from such different situations.

- **Purpose**: Next, the writer explains why the topic is important. He states, "Capital punishment has been a useful and powerful tool to protect justice and deter crime." Then, he goes on to describe some of the controversy over execution as a punishment and offers his opinion about it. Thus, in the middle part of the introduction, the writer tells us his purpose for writing: to show that capital punishment "is still a powerful and useful tool."

- **Thesis:** The last sentence of the paragraph is the thesis statement, which commonly, though not always, appears at the conclusion of the introduction.

ENGAGING YOUR READER AND INTRODUCING YOUR TOPIC

The beginning of the introduction is sometimes called the "hook" because it grabs your reader's attention and directs it toward what you have to say.

As you work on your hook, ask yourself what would first catch a reader's attention or what might immediately draw a reader in. If necessary, you should also give just enough background information so that a reader new to your topic will have a basic understanding of it.

Techniques for Writing a Hook

The following techniques are some of the ways to create an effective hook. Your introduction can include more than one.

- Use a quotation or a surprising fact or statistic from your sources that relates to the focus of your topic.

   For example, the introduction to a paper on male violence could provide statistics on the percentage of violent crimes committed by males.

- Describe a problem, dilemma, or controversy associated with your topic.

   For instance, the introduction to a paper on assisted suicide could discuss the dilemma of balancing the rights of individuals with the medical obligation of doctors.

- Tell a story.

   See the introduction in the Now You Try on page 103.

- Relate a personal reason for your interest in the topic.

   For example, a paper about the changing status of women in business might begin with a story about the early career of a successful businesswoman.

- Define a word that is central to your topic.

   An argument paper on genetically modified food could begin with a brief definition of the term "genetically modified."

- Make a historical comparison or contrast.

   See Example of an Effective Introduction on page 101.

NOW YOU TRY

Read the introduction that follows. With a partner or a small group, discuss which of the six techniques for writing a hook the writer uses.

Introduction: I was eating breakfast in a restaurant in Portland when Mike came in and sat at a table beside mine. He wore new jeans and a jacket, but what caught my attention more was that he had short hair and looked clean. Was he the same man I had seen a couple of times before coming into the restaurant looking like a homeless person and asking for empty cans and bottles in order to get some money? Yes, he was Mike. After finishing his breakfast, Mike asked for the check and paid as a normal customer. I was wondering how he had changed, so I asked the waiter about him. The waiter told me that Mike is a veteran and that he had just received his pension from the government after years of waiting. Due to bureaucratic problems, he had not gotten his pension for many years and had become homeless. Like Mike, there are a lot of homeless people that you see on the streets. According to the National Survey of Homeless Assistance Providers and Clients (NSHAPC), 23 percent of the total homeless population are veterans (Homelessness, 1999). The causes of homelessness are numerous and complex. The lack of both affordable housing and public assistance as well as the breakdown of the families are some of the principal causes of homelessness in the United States.

What hook technique(s) did this student use? _____

ESTABLISHING YOUR PURPOSE

After you have engaged your reader and introduced your topic, your next job is to explain which aspect of the topic you will write about. Obviously, in one paper, you cannot say everything there is to say about a subject, so it is here that you identify what particularly interests or concerns you about your topic. You may raise a new issue about it that has not been considered before, provide a comprehensive definition, give a detailed history, argue for or against it, and so on. This is where you tell the reader the purpose for writing your essay.

STATING YOUR THESIS

Finally, you state your thesis. Your thesis statement is the single sentence that clearly tells what your paper will be about. So far, in your first draft, you have had a working thesis. Now you can polish it so that it specifically explains how your paper will address the issue you raised in your introduction.

NOW YOU TRY

Working with a partner or in a small group, answer these question about the introduction that follows:

1. How does the writer spark reader interest?

2. What is the topic of the paper?

3. What is the writer's purpose for writing this paper? What aspect of the topic will she address?

4. What is the thesis statement?

Introduction: Two years ago, my brother was killed in a bicycle accident. He was very important to me, and losing him was a terrible experience. Since his death, I have thought a lot about the value of life. I have come to realize that life does not have any price. We can never be compensated for the loss of someone we love. People who support the death penalty feel that through the death of another person, they can pay for the life of a person who has been murdered. They believe that the death penalty will offer justice to the victim's family. However, the death penalty is not a good way to resolve problems of crime because the judicial system can make irreparable mistakes and the moral cost is too high.

Elements of an Effective Conclusion

Just as the introduction is your first opportunity to connect with your reader, so the conclusion is an opportunity to guide your reader to the close of your research paper. A strongly written conclusion leaves your reader not only with a clear understanding of the central point in your paper but also with a final comment that provides an interesting closing thought. An effective conclusion has two parts:

1. **A final analysis of the main points of your paper.** This is not a restatement of your thesis, but a new way of expressing your central ideas.

2. **An ending comment that inspires your reader to continue thinking about your topic.**

This introduction and conclusion are from a research paper about the effects of globalization.

EXAMPLE OF AN EFFECTIVE CONCLUSION

Introduction: What do we do when we have a problem? Leave it alone? Or try to solve it? Most people say that globalization creates more and more problems, such as increasing the gap between the rich and the poor. However, this difference between people who have a lot and those who have only a little is not the result of an intention to increase the income gap in the world; instead, it is a result of how well the First World nations have been managing their economies. In truth, the developed countries have been supporting developing countries, especially by providing jobs and other opportunities so that starving people can survive with dignity. There is an expression that says, if you give a man a fish, you feed him for a day; if you teach a man how to fish, you feed him for a lifetime. This saying illustrates how globalization is a positive force because it supports the lives of the poor with jobs, education, and access to improved technology.

Conclusion: ***[Summary of main points]*** Globalization is essential for people in Third World countries to rise from their present state of poverty. Because of globalization, more people than ever before have employment in meaningful jobs and literacy at all levels is spreading throughout the world. Technology such as the Internet, cell phones, and chances to travel connects people in all countries and helps decrease the income gap between "haves" and "have-nots." ***[Ending comment]*** I refer the reader back to the expression about teaching a man to fish; globalization provides the necessary tools for the poor to "eat for a lifetime."

- In this conclusion, the writer has provided a final analysis of the main points in her essay. Notice that the analysis includes the thesis ideas, but expresses these ideas in a new way. The final sentence of the conclusion links back to a proverb mentioned in the introduction. This strategy provides a strong connection between the beginning and ending of the essay.

Techniques for Writing an Ending Comment

- Echo the approach used in the introduction, using different wording.

  See the conclusion example above on globalization.

- Use a quotation.

  For example, in a conclusion for a paper supporting capital punishment, you could include a quote from a victim's family on why they believe in the death penalty.

- End with a powerful fact or other detail related to the topic of the paper.

  In a paper arguing for stronger recycling programs, you could conclude with a statistic that shows the amount of garbage produced each year.

- Recommend a course of action, if called for in the material you present.

  To conclude a paper discussing reasons for male violence, you could offer a few suggestions for overcoming these causes.

NOW YOU TRY

Read the following introduction and find the thesis statement. Circle the focus of the thesis and underline the supporting points. Then read, discuss, and evaluate each of the possible conclusions. Decide which conclusion would be the most effective match for this introduction.

Introduction: In the state of Oregon it is legal for a doctor to help a terminally ill patient to commit suicide. A doctor can prescribe a pill or injection to complete the process of assisting the patient to die peacefully and with less pain. Some people say they would rather accept the terminally ill patient's wish to die because they feel that it is a kind of torture to see them suffering from intolerable pain. Others say they can't agree with assisting patients who want to die because there are some obvious problems which lead these patients to this decision. Problems in regulating assisted suicide and difficulties for patients making the choice to end their lives are two reasons why assisted suicide should not be legalized.

Conclusion 1:   In conclusion, problems in regulating assisted suicide and difficulties for patients making the choice to end their lives are two important reasons why assisted suicide should not be legalized. In Oregon, a very small number of people have used the assisted suicide program ("Insight on the News," 1999). However, rather than thinking that this means that legalized assisted suicide is a good idea, it should motivate the medical community to overcome the remaining problems that cause that small number of people to feel that dying is better than living.

Discussion: How does the writer restate the thesis idea in a new way?
What technique does the writer use for writing an ending comment?
Is this a good conclusion for a paper that begins with the introduction above?

Conclusion 2:   Assisted suicide causes many problems. The process is easy to abuse. The boundaries of when assisted suicide is appropriate means that it is difficult to control. For example, it is not always easy to determine if and when a patient will die. Moreover, emotional factors and underlying problems, such as intolerable pain, influence many patients to decide that they want to die. A Korean proverb says, "When a person falls in the water, he will grab even straws to pull himself out." I'm sure many terminally ill patients feel the same way. When faced with such pain, death seems to be the best way to escape. Society needs to find ways to improve the end of life for people so that the choice to live is more hopeful than the decision to die.

Discussion: How does the writer restate the thesis idea in a new way?
What technique does the writer use for writing an ending comment?
Is this a good conclusion for a paper that begins with the introduction above?

Conclusion 3:   Even though many people agree with physician-assisted suicide, few people choose it in their own lives. In Oregon, only a few people have followed through on their request for assisted suicide. Many doctors think it is hard to determine when patients will die. In addition, the difficulty in distinguishing between a patient's rational thought and emotional depression as well as the fact that the medical community has not been successful at finding ways to ease people's pain, raise more problems.

Discussion: How does the writer restate the thesis idea in a new way?
What technique does the writer use for writing an ending comment?
Is this a good conclusion for a paper that begins with the introduction above?

ACTIVITIES TO PRACTICE EVALUATING INTRODUCTIONS AND CONCLUSIONS

ACTIVITY ❶ Evaluating Introductions

With your group, read and discuss the following three introductions for their effectiveness. Then, make notes in the chart to evaluate and compare them.

Introduction 1: She wakes up in Japan and eats toast and sausage made in Germany for breakfast with her father, who checks the movement of the yen rate in the daily paper. She works at a Chinese pharmaceutical company and usually eats fast food like MacDonald's for lunch before she goes to English conversation school. She is a typical young person in the world today. Nowadays, our life itself is globalized. But the problem of globalization is still controversial. Although some people worry that it aggravates the problem of obesity all over the world, globalization is good because we can benefit from it in three ways: economics, health, and culture.

Introduction 2: Have you ever taken standardized tests? Many people around the world have participated in standardized tests as a way to enter a new higher level school or to prove that they have learned in school. Some people think standardized tests help improve education; however, some people disagree with standardized tests. Although standardized testing is a controversy around the world, national and local governments will continue to use standardized tests to measure schools and students. Standardized tests improve the quality of education in two ways: motivating students and providing an effective measurement of how schools are doing.

Introduction 3: It is wonderful for people all over the world to communicate with each other through the Internet, or to enjoy foods from the opposite side of the globe. On the other hand, finding a case of mad cow disease in the United States makes beef disappear from the Japanese marketplace. These are both sides of the coin. In the article, "Globalization: Good or Bad?" Keith Porter (2004) writes "Globalization is much like fire. Fire itself is neither good nor bad. Used properly, it can cook food, sterilize equipment, form iron, and heat our homes. Used carelessly, fire can destroy lives, towns, and forests in an instant." While many people debate this issue, globalization has also influenced women's expectations of marriage recently.

	Introduction 1	Introduction 2	Introduction 3
1. Which technique(s) did the writer use for writing a "hook"?			
2. Where does the writer present the issue or aspect of the topic that will be addressed in the paper?			
3. What is the focus of the thesis? What is the overview of supporting points?			
4. Overall rating of the introduction? 4 3 2 1 excellent good fair weak			

ACTIVITY **2** Evaluating Conclusions

With a partner or small group, read the introductions and conclusions of each sample student essay in Appendix A. In each essay, find the thesis statement. Circle the focus of the thesis and underline the supporting points. Make notes in the chart to analyze each conclusion.

	Conclusion "Risky Business"	Conclusion "Expectations of Marriage"	Conclusion "Vegetarianism"
1. How does the writer restate the thesis idea in a new way?			
2. What, if any, ending comment technique(s) does the writer use?			
3. Overall rating of the conclusion? 4 3 2 1 excellent good fair weak			

BUILDING YOUR PAPER

Revise Your Introduction and Conclusion

Revise the introduction and conclusion of your research paper draft. As you revise, consider the following:

Introduction revision

- How does your introduction attract the reader's attention?
- Where do you establish your purpose and explain the aspect of the topic you will discuss?
- What is your thesis statement?

Conclusion revision

- Does your conclusion offer a final analysis of the central points in your paper?
- Does your conclusion have an ending comment that leaves the reader with an idea to think about?

Getting Feedback

Make copies of your introduction and conclusion. Bring enough copies for several classmates to read. Work in groups of three or four.

1. Decide how much time to spend on each person's paper.
2. Have the first person read his introduction and conclusion aloud while the others read along silently.
3. After the reading, discuss the introduction and conclusion:
   - Identify the hook in the introduction.
   - Identify the thesis statement.
   - On the basis of the introduction, what do you think the paper will be about? What questions will the paper answer?
   - How does the writer connect the conclusion to the introduction? What technique does the writer use for an ending comment?
   - Tell the writer about any parts of the introduction and conclusion that are unclear to you.
4. When the first person's time is up, repeat the process with the next person until everyone in the group has had a turn.

BUILDING COHESION IN YOUR PAPER

As you revise your writing, your goal is to create a cohesive, reader-friendly paper that is easy to understand. When writing is cohesive, ideas are clearly linked so that the reader can follow them. Now is the time to ensure that your writing is cohesive by looking closely at the language you have used.

 # Five Techniques for Building Cohesion

1. **Use guiding language.**

2. **Create lexical chains.**

3. **Use pronouns clearly.**

4. **Keep verb tense consistent.**

5. **Link old and new information.**

USE GUIDING LANGUAGE

When you created your outline and wrote your first draft, you had to decide which ideas to include and how to organize each section so that the ideas would flow logically from one point to the next. This organization may now be clear to you, but not necessarily to your reader.

To lead your reader from one idea to the next, you can use guiding language—words, phrases, and sentences—that clarify the connections. Paragraphs are a good starting point for a review of your guiding language. Each paragraph begins with a topic sentence, followed by sentences that add ideas to develop the paragraph's focus. As you review these sentences, consider how they develop the central idea of the paragraph and whether this is easy for the reader to follow.

In the following paragraph from an essay on standardized testing, the writer uses sentences to explain a reason, to give evidence, to provide examples, and to present an alternative perspective. She uses guiding language to help make some of these functions clearer. In addition, her use of documentation lets the reader know when she has provided outside evidence.

The functions of the sentences are noted in the margin, and the guiding language the writer used is in bold.

EXAMPLE

Guiding Words and Phrases

Topic sentence →	It has been argued that standardized testing motivates students to work harder. **When** students face the pressure of achieving a certain test score, they are forced to work hard. They know that they will not be able to progress towards their goal without
Explains a reason →	that test score. In "A Self Fulfilling Prophecy," Rotbert (2001) notes that teachers and students feel an obligation to improve their standardized test scores. They feel that the test score is the primary measure that others will use to judge their ability and **so**
Provides an alternative perspective →	they place a great deal of effort on achieving the highest score possible. **However**, under the pressure of test scores, they may work harder, but they don't work deeply. In
Explains outside evidence →	"Standardized Testing: A Defense," Ashworth (1990, p. 71) admits that "when it comes to figuring out the system, most students learn to be con artists." **In other words**, they avoid learning their school subjects and focus only on test-taking strategies
Provides an example →	that they think will help them beat the test. **For example**, they study patterns of test questions and methods for quickly finding answers. Their goal is to get high scores
Provides an additional idea with an example →	on tests, and they don't care where their answers come from. They **also** don't focus on subjects that are not covered by tests **such as** art and current events (Kohn, 2000).
Summarizes point →	**Thus**, standardized testing may motivate students to study intensely, but the quality of education doesn't improve because students' efforts reflect only a shallow approach to learning.

The following is a chart of signal words and phrases commonly used in academic writing.

Kind of phrase	Example 1	Example 2
Phrases to signal an example	***For example,*** Students avoid learning their school subjects and focus only on test-taking strategies that they think will help them beat the test. *For example,* they study patterns of test questions and methods for quickly finding answers.	**General point** + *such as* + **noun** Students avoid learning their school subjects and focus only on test-taking strategies that they think will help them beat the test *such as* studying patterns of test questions and methods for quickly finding answers.
Phrases to signal an alternative perspective	***However,*** **+ alternative perspective** Students feel that the test score is the primary measure that others will use to judge their ability, and they place a great deal of effort on achieving the highest score possible. *However,* under the pressure of test scores, they may work harder, but they don't work deeply.	***Although*** **[first perspective], + alternative perspective** *Although* students may feel that the test score is how others will judge their ability and they will work hard to achieve the highest score possible, under this pressure they may work harder, but they don't work deeply.

Kind of phrase	Example 1	Example 2
Phrases to signal possible objections to an idea	***Some might argue that +* objection** The students' goal is to get high scores on tests, and they don't care where their answers come from. *Some might argue that* this approach to learning leads to shallow thinking.	***Opponents of this point might state that +* objection** The students' goal is to get high scores on tests, and they don't care where their answers come from. *Opponents of this approach to learning might state that* it leads to shallow thinking.
Phrases to signal a discussion about the cause of something	**X happens. *Therefore,* Y happens** Students feel pressure to achieve a high score on standardized tests; *therefore,* the tests motivate them to study harder.	***When* X, Y happens** *When* students feel pressure to achieve a high score on standardized tests, they are motivated to study harder.
Phrases to signal an elaboration or interpretation of outside evidence	***In other words,* + sentence** In "Standardized Testing: A Defense," Ashworth (1990, p. 71) admits that "when it comes to figuring out the system, most students learn to be con artists." *In other words,* they avoid learning their school subjects and focus only on test-taking strategies that they think will help them beat the test.	***[Author]'s point is that, what [author] means is that*** In "Standardized Testing: A Defense," Ashworth (1990, p. 71) admits that "when it comes to figuring out the system, most students learn to be con artists." *Ashworth's point is that* students avoid learning their school subjects and focus only on test-taking strategies that they think will help them beat the test.
Phrases to signal an elaboration of a point you are making with a slight shift in focus	**Subject + *also* + verb** Their goal is to get as high a score as possible on the test and they don't care where their answers come from. Students with this perspective *also* don't take time to study subjects that are not in the test.	***In addition,*** Their goal is to get as high a score as possible on the test and they don't care where their answers come from. *In addition,* students with this perspective don't take time to study subjects that are not in the test.
Phrases to signal a summary of your point	***Thus,* + summary** *Thus,* standardized testing may motivate students to study intensely, but the quality of education doesn't improve because students' efforts reflect only a shallow approach to learning.	***The point/issue/problem is that* + summary** *The issue is that* standardized testing may motivate students to study intensely, but the quality of education doesn't improve because students' efforts reflect only a shallow approach to learning.

While transition signals are useful, your writing will be smoother if you do not overuse this guiding language technique. A well-developed paragraph with plenty of explanatory details and a few well-chosen transition signals will do the best job of helping your readers understand your meaning. In fact, an overuse of transition signals, coupled with a lack of explanatory details, can actually make writing feel choppy and less cohesive.

In addition to single words and short phrases, full sentences can also be used to show your reader how ideas are related. These guiding sentences can be used to signal transitions within paragraphs, and they are also helpful in leading your reader from one paragraph to the next.

In the following paragraph excerpt, the sentence in bold leads the reader to the next idea that will be discussed in the paragraph.

EXAMPLE

Guiding Sentence within Paragraph

One reason young people commit suicide is because of pressures from their daily lives. According to Merritt (2000), growing up is more stressful today than it's ever been before. Merritt writes, "the cumulative weight of life's stresses makes growing up a difficult experience for many young people, one that can seem overwhelming to some" (p. 89). **Family conflict and school pressure are two examples of issues young people often find difficult to deal with…**

- In this paragraph, the writer mentions two examples—family conflict and school pressure—that he will discuss to illustrate his point about the stresses in a young person's life that might lead to suicide. By including this guiding sentence that summarizes what he will explain next, the writer prepares the reader for the information he will include in the rest of his paragraph.

In this example from an essay on heroes, the last sentence of the paragraph points toward the focus of the next paragraph.

EXAMPLE

Guiding Sentences between Paragraphs

End of paragraph:	Basically, heroes live for ideals and their principles function as a catalyst that motivates society. However, <u>sometimes a hero's ideas conflict with some members of society.</u>
Topic sentence of next paragraph:	<u>Because heroes must often face some opposition to their ideals and their effort to change society,</u> they must also be brave, a second characteristic of heroes.

- Here the writer introduces the idea about heroes and conflict at the end of one paragraph. In the next paragraph, he begins the topic sentence with a direct connection to this idea of conflict before leading his reader to his paragraph's focus that heroes must be brave.

NOW YOU TRY

Read and discuss the following introductory paragraph of a paper on cross-cultural conflicts and adjustment.

- Circle the guiding words and phrases.
- Underline the guiding sentences.
- Discuss whether you think the student uses guiding language effectively in this paragraph.

Introduction: "What a wonderful country. The people are so friendly. I love it here." These are the expressions that a newcomer student says after two weeks in the host country. In contrast, "They do everything backward. I can't make friends" and "I miss my home country" are also expressions from a newcomer student, but after four months in the host country. This is what students normally say during their experience studying abroad. When a person decides to study abroad, he expects that the experience will be enjoyable and beneficial; however, he may not see beyond this optimistic expectation. There are many challenging issues a student can face while studying abroad. For example, there are financial, transportation, and housing challenges. Also, there is the language issue which some people consider the most difficult. Furthermore, cultural values and norms in the new country may also cause some difficulties for students. In fact, culture shock and reverse culture shock are two unexpected challenges that students might face during their experience studying abroad.

CREATE LEXICAL CHAINS

Repeating key words or related words can help to emphasize important ideas and show how ideas are organized. These repetitions are called lexical chains. As you write your paper, it is useful to brainstorm a list of words and phrases you can use as alternative ways to discuss your central ideas.

In this excerpt, from a paper about studying abroad, notice how the writer uses two lexical chains.

EXAMPLE

Lexical Chains

The first <u>benefit</u> of **studying abroad** is personal growth. The **International Education of Students** (IES) surveyed all **IES students** who **studied overseas** from 1950–1999 and found that these **students** said that they developed many positive personal characteristics through their **international experience**. When **students live in another country**, they are willing to try many new things in an effort to adapt to the **host country**…

> The next <u>advantage</u> for **international students** is improving their knowledge and understanding of both their own and their **host country's culture**.

- The underlined words form one short lexical chain to explain the idea of "something good." These repeated ideas help the reader follow the organization of the paper.
- The bold phrases form another, longer lexical chain of referring to the idea of "studying abroad." This lexical chain draws the reader's attention to the writer's topic throughout the passage.

NOW YOU TRY

Notice how lexical chains are used in the articles in Part Two. You may choose to focus only on the article from the theme you are writing about, or you may want to look at the use of lexical chains in all three articles.

In the section *Risking Change,* turn to "Eve's Daughters," on page 161, lines 1–12. In these introductory paragraphs, Polster is introducing her reader to the topic of her paper, the characteristics of heroes.

- Underline the words *hero* and *heroism* each time they are used. What do you notice about their use throughout the introduction?
- Circle the words and phrases in the lexical chain that refer to the idea of characteristics. What are some of the different words that the author uses to express the idea of characteristics?

In the section *Globalization,* turn to "Spiritual Perspectives on Globalization" on page 176, lines 1–18. In this section, Rifkin is describing globalization's effect on various aspects of human life.

- Underline the word *globalization* throughout this passage. Notice how Rifkin uses this lexical chain to present each effect that he will discuss.

In the section *Technology,* turn to "Mind Over Mass Media" on page 199, lines 1–20. In these beginning paragraphs, Pinker is introducing his topic of the relationship between technology and the brain.

- Underline any words or phrases that are related to technology.
- Circle any words or phrases that are related to thinking or the mind.
- Notice how these two lexical chains are present throughout the passage. If you look closely, you'll notice that often words from these two lexical chains appear in the same sentence.

USE PRONOUNS CLEARLY

Pronouns are a simple but useful tool for linking ideas together; they signal the reader that an idea is directly connected to a previously mentioned idea. When readers see a pronoun, they immediately return to the original noun, if only for a moment, and consider how the two are related.

Compare the two examples of the use of the pronoun *they*.

Pronoun Reference

Example 1:   The length of each stage of culture shock may vary from one person to another. **They** usually occur in the same order, however.

- The pronoun "they" refers to the phrase "stage of culture shock."

Example 2:   Students who study abroad state that their world view has changed because of their interactions with people in their host culture. **They** also have a broader world view through this interaction.

- In this example, it is not clear who "they" is. Is it "students who study abroad" or "people in the host culture"? When a pronoun and the word that it refers to, the referent, are not clearly linked, cohesion breaks down and the reader can become frustrated. This most commonly happens when it is not easy to identify which idea the pronoun is referring to.

This/that and *these/those* are demonstratives used to refer to ideas that have already been presented. Academic writers commonly use demonstratives as pronouns (when by themselves) or as adjectives (when paired with a "catch-all noun," or general noun, such as "this *characteristic*" or "these *problems.*") Demonstratives, either alone or with a catch-all noun, refer to an entire passage that has already been discussed and connect it to a new idea.

EXAMPLE

Demonstrative Pronouns

The third stage of cultural adjustment is the resolution stage. The student succeeds in understanding the new culture more deeply. His language expands and he is able to express himself. He is able to open the door to the new culture. According to Oberg (1960), during this stage the student develops his own approach to the new culture that will help him when he faces a new difficulty. **This** allows him to feel more relaxed and at ease in his day-to-day life.

- In this passage, the demonstrative pronoun "this" refers to the student's new approach to dealing with cultural differences.

Catch-all nouns are very useful when you want to summarize an idea rather than describe it with specific details. The need for catch-all nouns arises most often in two situations:

   –just before you are about to explain an idea, as in the topic sentence of a paragraph,

   –after you have already described the idea and want to refer back to the broader idea, but not the specifics.

In this passage, the phrase in bold summarizes three previous ideas.

EXAMPLE

Demonstrative adjective + catch-all noun

> My purpose for coming to the United States was not to enter the university. I was interested in volunteering as a nurse in a developed country, so I wanted to improve my English skills. I also wanted to learn about the U.S. medical system. **These reasons** were related to my professional goals rather than furthering my education.

- The demonstrative pronoun "these" signals that the ideas have already been described, and the catch-all noun "reasons" refers to the broader idea of why the writer came to the United States. The phrase summarizes three ideas: "volunteering as a nurse," "improve my English skills," and "learn about the U.S. medical system."

Here is a list of some catch-all nouns commonly used in academic writing.

approach	difficulty	problem
aspect	factor	reason
characteristic	feature	result
circumstance	issue	tendency

NOW YOU TRY

Read and discuss the following paragraphs from Part Two. You may choose to focus only on the article from the theme you are writing about, or you may want to look at all three articles. For each paragraph do the following:

- Circle each pronoun (*he, she, it, they*) and draw an arrow back to its referent, the word or phrase that it refers to.
- Underline the use of a demonstrative pronoun paired with a catch-all noun. Identify the ideas your underlined phrase refers to.

In *Risking Change,* turn to "The Role of the Corporation in Supporting Local Development" on page 168, lines 35–44.

In *Globalization*, turn to "World Publics Welcome Global Trade—but Not Immigration" on page 178, lines 44–56.

In *Technology*, turn to "Addicted to Phones?" on page 195, lines 19–34.

KEEP VERB TENSE CONSISTENT

It may surprise you to learn that the most common verb tense used in academic writing is simple present, followed by simple past as the second most common. Good academic writers usually rely on the simple present tense and change to other tenses only when there is a very specific reason to do so.

Keeping your verb tenses within one time frame—present, past, or future—without switching unnecessarily from one tense to another helps to build cohesion within your writing. When you do need to switch from one time frame to another, clearly signaling this change will help your reader.

Guidelines for Verb Tense Choice

1. Use the simple present and simple past unless there is a clear reason to choose another verb tense.

   - Simple present is used to present general information, facts, opinions, and research findings. It is also used in citations and paraphrases.

   - Simple past is used to refer to specific events that began and ended in the past.

2. Provide a signal word or time phrase when switching time frames.

   - Use time phrases that help the reader understand the context of the past event, such as "at that time," "in the past," or "in 2001."

   - Use a time phrase also when switching back to present tense if this will help your reader.

By keeping her verbs consistently within one time frame and providing a clear signal when she moves into a new time frame, the writer of this paragraph has helped build cohesion.

Verb Tense Choice

Culture shock **is** a response people **have** when they **leave** their own culture and **stay** for a long time in a different culture. Homesickness, sadness, insomnia, and feeling vulnerable **are** common symptoms of culture shock. Because of these symptoms, people usually **have** a negative feeling about culture shock, but Dr. Carmen Guanipa (1988) **explains** that culture shock **is** a good chance to look at one's life objectives, and also it **is** a chance to learn and **develop** new perspectives. Students **can learn** about themselves and **improve** their personal character from culture shock. Therefore, though culture shock **has** a negative image, students **shouldn't worry** too much because it **can be** a great opportunity for personal growth. When I **came** to the United States last year, I **experienced** culture shock. I **was** sometimes depressed and sometimes excited.

- The writer uses the simple present tense to explain facts about culture shock. She also uses the simple present tense in her citation verb. When she moves from a general discussion of culture shock to her personal example, she shifts to the past tense because she is discussing a specific situation that occurred in the past. She carefully signals this shift with the phrase "when I came to the United States last year."

NOW YOU TRY

Read and discuss the following paragraphs from Part Two. You may choose to focus only on the article from the theme you are writing about, or you may want to look at all three articles.

In *Risking Change*, turn to "Is a Hero Really Nothing but a Sandwich?" on page 160, lines 1–12.

- Underline each verb and identify the tense.
- Why does Tollefson use past tense in the first paragraph?
- When does he switch from past to present tense? Why do you think he switches his tense here?
- Why does Tollefson use simple present tense in the second and third paragraphs?

In *Globalization*, turn to "Globalization and Local Culture" on page 179, lines 31–40.

- Underline each verb and identify the tense.
- In lines 31–40 which verb tense is most commonly used? Why?
- Notice in lines 41–45, the verb tense shifts. Has the writer provided a signal for this tense shift? Why do you think the author shifts tense?

In *Technology*, turn to "Technology, Progress, and Freedom" on page 194. Read the entire article.

- Underline each verb and identify the tense.
- Which verb tense is primarily used? Why do you think the author chose this verb tense?
- In the second paragraph, the verb tense shifts. Why?

LINK OLD AND NEW INFORMATION

In the structure of your paragraph, the sentences work together to explain the idea you have introduced in your topic sentence. The central point in your topic sentence is expanded in the second sentence. This idea is then carried into the third sentence, further building your paragraph's topic. One by one, the sentences work together to support and explain the point you want to make.

A final strategy for building cohesion is to connect old and new ideas with a sentence pattern often used in academic writing: placing old information in the first part of the sentence, followed by new information in the later part of the sentence.

At times, it's possible to develop this pattern of old and new information for an extended passage. Here's how it works:

EXAMPLE

Linking Old and New Information

Old Information	New Information
1. Culture shock and reverse culture shock	have several stages in common.
2. These shared stages	include a honeymoon stage, a disintegration stage, and an adaptation stage.
3. During the honeymoon period,	students feel elated by the freshness of the culture.
4. This excitement occurs	whether a student is entering a new culture or returning to their home culture after a long absence.
5. When students return home,	their reaction to the familiar sights of their own culture can surprise them.

- Notice how the new information of one sentence is moved to the beginning of the next sentence. It is now the "old" information, and new information is added to the sentence.

Passive voice is a useful tool for structuring this pattern of linking old and new information. In this paragraph on culture shock, the writer creates the pattern of connecting old and new information. Notice how she uses the passive voice in the third sentence (in bold) so that she can put the idea of a problem (from sentence 2) into the old information position of sentence 3.

EXAMPLE

Linking Old and New Information Using Passive Voice

Old Information	New Information
1. One uncomfortable issue that students might come across from their study abroad experience	is culture shock.
2. Recognizing the stages of culture shock will not make it disappear,	but like any problem, noticing it is the first step toward coping with it.
3. Once the problem is understood,	the student will feel less frustrated.
4. Learning how to overcome a difficult experience	is part of what a person can learn when he or she lives in a new culture.
5. Experiencing a new culture	is the best teacher for personal growth.

NOW YOU TRY

Analyze how the writer links old and new information in this passage about family communication.

- Beginning with the first sentence, find the new information and write it under the new information column. Find the phrase in the next sentence that presents this idea as old information. Write it in the old information column.

Adolescents indirectly learn strategies from their parents about how to settle conflicts by watching their parents communicate at home. I grew up in a modern Asian family, and I'm very lucky to have my parents, who are very open-minded, but my mother is also very traditional. She never brings up any argument with my father in a rough way; she always uses the calming strategy to deal with problems that happen in my family. Her communication style has taught me not to be aggressive when having conflict with my friends. When I have a fight with my friends, I never yell at them.

Old Information   **New Information**

Sentence 1: _____   parents communicate at home

Sentence 2: I grew up in a modern Asian family ✎ _____

Sentence 3: _____ ✎ _____

Sentence 4: _____ ✎ _____

Sentence 5: _____ ✎ _____

ACTIVITIES TO PRACTICE BUILDING COHESION

ACTIVITY **1** Analyzing Cohesion in a Paper

Select and read one of the research papers in Appendix A, page 209. Alone or with a partner, analyze the writer's use of cohesion techniques.

1. Look for one or more examples of each technique: guiding language, lexical chains, clear pronoun use, consistent verb tense, and links of old and new information.

2. Share your findings with classmates who have analyzed the same paper.

3. Do you feel the writer uses the cohesion techniques effectively? Why or why not?

ACTIVITY **2** Advising a Writer

Print a copy of the essay "Barriers for International Students" from the *Sourcework* website. This is the first draft of a student paper. Imagine that you must advise this student on ways he can improve his paper. You don't want to discourage him, so choose what you feel are the five most important problems with his paper. Consider what you have learned about building cohesion and creating a reader-friendly paper. Be prepared to share your advice with the rest of the class.

ACTIVITY **3** Discussing Cohesion in Your Paper

Select one or two paragraphs from your paper to discuss with your classmates. Bring two to three copies of these paragraphs to class. Take turns discussing each group member's paper.

1. Read the passage aloud to the group.

2. Take two or three minutes to quietly analyze the writer's use of guiding language, pronouns and catch-all nouns, lexical chains, consistent verb tense, and links of old and new information.

3. Discuss one example of an effective use of cohesion techniques that the writer uses.

4. Discuss ways that the writer might further build or improve his or her cohesion within the passage.

BUILDING YOUR PAPER

Revise Your Paper for Cohesion

Take some time now to analyze and revise your research paper draft for the use of cohesive language.

- Check your use of guiding words, phrases, and sentences. Delete signal phrases where they are not necessary. Insert guiding language where the reader might need additional help to follow your ideas.

- Consider your use of lexical chains. Do you have a good balance between repeating key words and using alternative ways of expressing those key ideas?

- Check to make sure your pronouns clearly refer to a preceding idea. Make sure each use of catch-all nouns is clear.

- Review your verb tenses in each paragraph. If you use tenses other than simple present and simple past, be sure you have a clear reason for doing so. Also, check for unclear shifts in tense.

- Look for opportunities to link old and new information in sentences. Make sure that each sentence builds clearly on the information in the preceding sentence.

DOCUMENTING YOUR EVIDENCE

You must properly document all the evidence from sources that you use in your research paper. Whether you use direct quotes or paraphrases, it is essential to identify the original source so that your reader knows where the information came from. The process of acknowledging your sources is called **documentation.** When you document a source, you tell the reader exactly where you found the information.

 # Three Reasons to Document Sources

1. **To let the reader know that you have carefully researched your ideas.**

2. **To tell the reader where to find the original source if she wants to learn more about your topic.**

3. **To avoid plagiarism, a serious offense in academic writing in the United States.**

Each field of study uses a particular system of documentation. The system presented in *Sourcework* is APA, which stands for American Psychological Association. This information has been taken from the *Publication Manual of the American Psychological Association, Sixth Edition.* APA documentation is commonly used in business, engineering, and the social sciences. Other documentation formats include MLA (Modern Language Association) used in the humanities, CBE (Council of Biology Editors) used in the life sciences, and Chicago (follows the *Chicago Manual of Style)* for humanities and social sciences.

For links to documentation systems not presented in *Sourcework* go to the website at **http://elt.heinle.com/sourcework.**

RULES FOR DOCUMENTING SOURCES

As with most documentation systems, APA documentation occurs in two places in your research paper:

1. Within the text of your paper (in-text citations)

2. At the end of your paper in a reference list

Here are examples of how the documentation for the same source looks in these two places.

EXAMPLE

APA Documentation

Within a paper
(in-text citation):   Elaine Harper (2001) writes that later born children are more
                          likely to pursue nontraditional careers.

At the end of a paper
(reference list entry):   Harper, E. (2001). *Birth order and adult personality.* New York: Collins, Inc.

- The citations in your paper and on the reference page at the end of your paper work together as a formal documentation system. As you document your sources, keep in mind that your goal is to help the reader identify the source of your information. To ensure this, be consistent in the format you use.

In-Text Citations

When you include a paraphrase or quotation in your writing, you will need to acknowledge the source. In other words, you will need to *cite your source.* In the APA system, a citation includes the following three pieces of information.

- The name of the author
- The year of the source
- The page number (required only for quotations)

Citations occur in one of two places: within the sentence or at the end of the sentence.

CITING YOUR SOURCE WITHIN THE SENTENCE

	Last name of the author	Date	Reporting verb
Author and date are separate.	Last name only	• Include the year only • Place in parentheses • No extra punctuation. If no date is given write n.d.	• Choose an appropriate verb to introduce your evidence (see list of verbs in Chapter 4 on page 83). • Use the simple present tense.
Example	Bellafonte	(1992)	argues

EXAMPLE

Bellafonte (1992) argues that genetic factors have played a role in
last name   **year**   **reporting verb**
people's need to take risks.

CITING YOUR SOURCE AT THE END OF A SENTENCE

	Name of the author	Date	Title
Author and date are placed together	• Last name only • Place in parentheses.	• Year only. If no date is given write n.d. • Place after author's name. • Put a period after the parenthesis mark.	Not included
Example	(Bellafonte,	1992).	

EXAMPLE

Extreme sports provide only a short-term superficial sense of satisfaction (Bellafonte, 1992).

NOW YOU TRY

Practice writing in text citations using the information below.

Author: Ann Fishburn

Date: May 3, 2000

Paraphrase: Freedom to explore, a caring community, and exciting art projects are three important characteristics of an art program.

Citation within the sentence:

_____

_____ freedom to explore, a caring community and exciting art projects are three important characteristics of an art program.

Citation at the end of the sentence:

Freedom to explore, a caring community, and exciting art projects are three

important characteristics of an art program _____

SPECIAL CITATION SITUATIONS

Here are several common situations that occur when you write from sources that require special citation formats.

Quotations

Occasionally, you will use a direct quotation from your source. All quotations require a page number.

- Put quotation marks around quoted material.
- Put the page number after quoted material in parentheses.
- Put a period outside parenthesis.

Citation within
the sentence: Souza (1997) writes that "these spiraling human demands for resources are beginning to outgrow the earth's natural resources" (p. 31).

Citation at the end
of the sentence: "The key to building a sustainable society rests with changing cultural attitudes among young people" (Hawkins, 2006, p. 188).

NOW YOU TRY

Write a citation for this direct quotation.

Source Author: Jane Donner

Source Date: March 15, 2000

Quotation: "Volunteering in our community helps both the community and ourselves." Page 112

Citation   _____

Idea Taken from More Than One Source

Sometimes you will want to include an idea that is mentioned by more than one of your sources. In this case, you'll need to include all the sources in your citation.

- Use the end-of-sentence format.
- List the authors alphabetically.
- Separate sources with a semicolon.

We cannot rely on technology to solve our problems (Feisk, 1995; Punon, 1995).

NOW YOU TRY

Write a citation for this paraphrase of an idea taken from two different sources.

Author: Daniel Birge *Date:* 2001

Author: Kate Spoon *Date:* 2000

Paraphrase: Critical thinking must be a central part of university studies.

Citation _____

Unknown Author

If the author's name is not given, you will need to use the title of the source instead.

- Use quotation marks around the source title.
- Include the year.
- Use the full title in the first citation. In later citations, use only the first two to four words of the title.

Citation within the sentence:	"Choosing Your Friends Wisely: How to Develop Lasting Friendships" (2004) describes three common mistakes that occur in new relationships.
End-of-sentence citation:	There are three common mistakes that occur in new relationships ("Choosing Your Friends Wisely: How to Develop Lasting Friendships," 2004).
Subsequent citation:	"Choosing Your Friends" (2004) presents results from a survey on long term friendships suggesting that learning how to argue respectfully is a key to making friendships last.

NOW YOU TRY

Write a citation for this paraphrase of an idea taken from a source without an author listed.

Source Title: "Study Skills for University Success"

Source Date: June 2002

Paraphrase: Success in college depends on effective study habits.

   Citation   _____

Groups as Authors

Some sources are written by a government agency, corporation, organization, or association without an author name given. For these sources use the title of the organization.

- Use the full title of the organization in the first citation.
- If the title is long, shorten the title in subsequent citations.
- Include the year.

> The Society for Conservation Biology (2007) presents five main threats to biodiversity.

NOW YOU TRY

Use the information below to write either a citation within the sentence or an end-of-sentence citation.

Group Title: National Organization for Women

Date: January 13, 2009

Paraphrase: Women still receive lower salaries on average for work than men.

   Citation   _____

   _____

Source with More Than One Author

If a source is written by two authors or by three or more authors, you will need to use slightly different citation formats.

Source with two authors:	• List the authors in the order they appear in the source.
	• Use an ampersand (&) when using the end-of-sentence format.
Cited within the sentence:	Blackburn and Little (2005) note that exposure to secondhand smoke can increase the risk of lung cancer by over 30 percent.
Cited at the end of the sentence:	Exposure to secondhand smoke can increase the risk of lung cancer by over 30 percent (Blackburn & Little, 2005).

Source with three or more authors:	• When citing the source the first time, list the name of all the authors in the order they appear in the source.
	• In subsequent citings, use the end of sentence format. List the first author only followed by the phrase "et al."
Cited within the sentence:	Kapline, South and Findel (2003) write that dark chocolate contains four times more antioxidants than green tea.
Cited at the end of the sentence:	Dark chocolate contains four times more antioxidants than green tea (Kapline et al., 2003).

NOW YOU TRY

1. Write a citation for this source written by two authors.

Authors: Jenny Pope and Marge Green

Date: 2003

Paraphrase: Most students change their major at least once during their undergraduate studies.

Citation   _____

2. Write an end-of-sentence citation for this source written by three authors.

Authors: Gene Jones, Richard Letham and Wendall Brout

Date: 2004

Paraphrase: The primary difference between a digital camera and a traditional film camera is how they capture the image.

Citation _____

Indirect Source

Often sources include paraphrases and quotes from experts on the topic. You may want to use this information that is included in the source but comes from someone other than the author.

- Include background information about the person whose idea you are using.
- Use an end of sentence format.
- Write "cited in" and then the last name of the author(s) of your source.
- No extra punctuation is needed.

According to Joan Sinker, a San Francisco psychologist, increasing wealth does not result in greater happiness (cited in Hamblen, 2001).

- In this case, Hamblen wrote the article and, in her article, she included a quote from the psychologist Joan Sinker. The student writer wanted to use Sinker's idea so this is how she documented her information.

NOW YOU TRY

Write a citation for this paraphrase of a quote by Patricia Manning, a spokesperson for the American Cancer Society, in an article by Matt Simms.

Source Author: Matt Simms

Source Date: January 21, 2003

Evidence Author: Patricia Manning

Paraphrase: According to Patricia Manning, a spokesperson for the American Cancer Society, the health effects of second-hand smoke are still being studied.

Citation _____

Writing the Reference Page

As discussed on pages 123–130, documenting your sources includes both citing sources within your paper and on a reference page. The list of your references (your sources) is the second of the two-part documentation process. Include the references at the end of your essay on a separate piece of paper. The format of information in the reference list corresponds to the citations within your paper. For example, the author's last name occurs in both the citations within your paper and in the reference list.

EXAMPLE

In-text citation: Harper (2001) writes that later-born children are more likely to pursue nontraditional careers.

Reference list entry: Harper, E. (2001). *Birth order and adult personality*. New York: Collins, Inc.

EXAMPLE REFERENCE LIST

References

book
Althen, G. (2003). *American Ways: A Guide for Foreigners in the*
author   date   book title

United States, Yarmouth, Maine: Intercultural Press, Inc.
city/state of publication   publishing company

website
Oberg, L. (n.d.). Culture shock and the problem of
author   no date   article title

adjustment to new cultural environments. Retrieved from
http://www.worldwide.edu/travel_planner/culture_shock
Web address

movie
Reitzell, B. (Producer), & Coppola, S. (Director). (2003).
authors   date

Lost in Translation [motion picture]. United States: Focus Features.
movie title   producing company

periodical
Sitique, R. (2002, March 15). Reverse culture shock: Returning home.
author   date   article title

Transitions Abroad Magazine 37, 5.
periodical title

no author
Stages of reverse culture shock. (2006, July 14). Retrieved from
article title   date

http://www.wings.buffalo.edu/studyabroad/rculture.html
Web address

periodical retrieved online
Sumka, S. (2006). The impact of study abroad: Educational travel
author   date   article title

as a model for responsible tourism. Retrieved from
http://www.transitionsabroad.com
Web address

periodical retrieved   Thantick, P. & Thomson, C. (2007, Winter). Culture shock and
from database   **authors**   **date**   **article title**

social support. *Social Psychiatry, 40,* 777-781.
periodical title

GENERAL FORMATTING GUIDELINES
FOR APA REFERENCE LISTS

1. Double-space all entries.

2. Have the first line of each entry at the left margin; indent subsequent lines five spaces.

3. Use the author's full last name and only the initial of his or her first name.

4. If there is more than one author, separate the names by a comma and put an ampersand (&) before the last author's name.

5. If the author's name is unknown, write the title of the article first.

6. Organize the entries alphabetically by the author's name, if known, or the title of the article.

7. At the end of each item in an entry, type a period, unless the entry ends with a Web address.

NOW YOU TRY

Identify the five general formatting mistakes in the reference list below. Use the **Guidelines for APA Reference Lists** above to help you.

References: Nancy Merrit. (1997). *Teen suicide: Light in the shadows.* Sacramento: Full House Press.

Brook, S. (1998, February). Some things you should know about preventing teen suicide. *Psychology Today,* 51, 20–25.

Author Unknown. (1997). Youth suicide. Retrieved March 6, 1999 from http://www.juring.my/befrienders/youth

Mulrine, A (1999, December) Preventing teen suicide: It starts with straight talk. U.S. News and World Report 68, 55–57.

Problem 1 _____

Problem 2 _____

Problem 3 _____

Problem 4 _____

Problem 5 _____

REFERENCE LIST FORMATS FOR SPECIFIC TYPES OF SOURCES

Each type of source has specific rules for how it should appear on a reference page. Here are guidelines for five common types of sources that students use.

 Go to the Purdue University Online Writing Lab at **http://owl.english.purdue.edu/** for more information about formats for sources.

Periodicals

Periodicals include magazines, newspapers, and journals that are published regularly (for example, daily, once a month, or once a season or quarter). Information you will need:

- Author
- Date of the periodical
- Title of article
- Title of periodical
- Volume number of periodical if given (also include issue number if available)
- Page numbers of the evidence you use
- Web address if retrieved online

Reference entries for periodical:

(periodical retrieved online):

Evangelista, B. (2009, November 15). Internet harms real relationships.
author   **date**   **article title**

San Francisco Chronicle. Retrieved from
periodical title

http://www.seattlepi.com/health/412332_internetaddiction1116.html
                    Web address

Corpet, F. (2002, September 3). Global warming revisited.
author   **date**   **article title**

Science Today, 52, 24.
  periodical **volume** **page**
  title   **#**   **number**

Specific Guidelines for Periodicals

- Capitalize only the first word of the article title, the first word of the subtitle, and any proper nouns.
- Do not underline the title or enclose it in quotation marks.
- Capitalize all important words of the periodical or newspaper title.
- Italicize the periodical title and volume number.
- Include the page numbers after the volume number.
- Write "Retrieved from" and the Web address for online periodicals.

NOW YOU TRY

Write a reference list entry for this periodical:

Author:	Martha Summer
Title of Article:	Five Steps to Success in College
Title of Magazine:	American Survey
Date and Volume:	September 21, 2000, Volume number 36
Page Numbers:	14–15

Reference list entry _____

Article Retrieved from an Electronic Database

Libraries often provide several databases that can be used to search for sources of information. EBSCO, InfoTrac, PsychINFO, and WilsonWeb are examples of a few. Sources found via a database follow the same format as a periodical. Do not include information about the database.

Information Retrieved from a Website

For information retrieved from a website with no available print source, it is important to include the following information:

- The author, if available.
- The title of the article or title of the website if article title is not given.
- The web address used to retrieve the information.
- If no date is given for the website, write "n.d."

Information retrieved from a website:

Collins, K. (n.d.). A mission to educate. Retrieved

author   **date**   **title of source**

from http://www.americanlandinstitute.org

Web address

NOW YOU TRY

Write a reference list entry for this information retrieved from a website:

Website Title: Career Browser: What do you want to be?

Date: None given

Web Address: http://www.collegeboard.com

Reference list entry _____

Books

In addition to the author, date, and title, reference list entries for books also require the city of publication and the name of the publishing company.

Reference for a book:

Caplan, A. (1998). *Due consideration: Controversy in the age of medical miracles.*

author   date   book title

New York: John Wiley & Sons.

  city of publication/publishing company

Specific guidelines for books

- Italicize the title of the book
- Capitalize the first word of the title, the first word in a subtitle, and proper nouns only.
- List the first city of publication only.

NOW YOU TRY

Write a reference list entry for this book.

Author: Richard Rodriguez

Date: 1982

Title: Hunger of memory: The education of Richard Rodriguez

City of Publication: New York

Publishing Company: Bantam Books

Reference list entry _____

REFERENCE PAGE CONVENTIONS AND PUNCTUATION

What Gets Capitalized?
- The first word in book titles and article titles
- The first word in a subtitle that comes after a colon
- All important words and words four letters or longer in the title of a magazine

What Gets Italicized?
- Titles of books
- Titles of periodicals
- Volume numbers for periodicals

NOTE: Do not italicize titles of articles and chapters of books.

Where Do Periods Go?
After each piece of information:
- –author
- –date
- –name of article
- –page number in information about a periodical
- –initial of an author's first name

NOTE: Do not place a period at the end of retrieval information for an electronic source (e.g., a Web address).

Where Do Commas Go?
- In between the last name and the initial of the author's first name
- After each author's name when listing two or more authors
- After the title of a periodical
- After a volume number
- After the year in a date that includes a month
- Before a Web address

ACTIVITIES TO PRACTICE DOCUMENTING SOURCES

ACTIVITY ❶ Correcting Documentation Mistakes

Practice with in-text citations. With a partner, find the six mistakes in the following citations. One of the citations is correct and one has two errors.

1. Brown suggests that we have the ability to develop a sustainable society (1996).

2. Human population will grow in relation to technology's ability to support it (1995, Weiskel).

3. Urban centers are often associated with ecological destruction. (Weiskel, 1995)

4. Cohen (1995) believes that organized religion is not always the cause of increased population growth.

5. "There is no single numerical answer to the question of how many people the earth can support (Cohen, 1995)

6. People tend to see heroes as role models (Lark, 1992 and Sudo, 1997).

ACTIVITY ❷ Peer-Editing for Documentation

1. For homework, insert an in text citation for each piece of outside evidence in one or more paragraphs of your research paper draft.

2. Bring a copy of your draft to class.

3. Trade papers with a partner.

4. Read your partner's paper, checking the format for each citation.
   - Circle any citations that are not correctly formatted.
   - Circle any pieces of outside evidence that have not been cited.

5. Discuss your suggestions with your partner.

BUILDING YOUR PAPER

Document Your Evidence

Check your research paper draft for each piece of paraphrased and quoted evidence from the sources you have used in your paper.

- Complete an in-text citation for each piece of evidence within your paper.

- Create a reference page that lists all the sources you used in your paper.

Write the Final Paper

At last you are ready to write the final draft of your paper. Use the work you have done in refining your introduction and conclusion, and what you have learned about creating a cohesive paper to complete this last stage of the writing process. When you are finished, you will have a piece of writing that you can be proud of.

Refer to the *Sourcework* website for suggestions on how to get feedback from your classmates as you work on this final draft of your paper.

Reflecting on What You Have Learned

Now that you've completed the hard work of writing a research paper, it's time to reflect on what you've learned about yourself as a writer. Take a moment to consider what you feel are some of the insights you've gained through this process and what you have discovered about yourself as a writer.

Share some of the things you have learned with your classmates and teacher.

CHAPTER 6

BUILDING A PAPER:
Independent Research

After you've written a guided research paper, you may have the chance to undertake a research and writing project on your own. In that case, you have some interesting work ahead of you.

The first step is to determine a topic that appeals to you and will fit the time and resources you have. Research and writing are more fun if the subject interests you enough to spend time on it. A good topic has enough information so that you can write a paper about it, but not so much that you can't cover it all in the time you have.

Once you settle on a topic, you will search for sources related to your idea. As you sift through the information, you must decide what to use. Set aside whatever is too opinionated, complicated, unreliable, unrelated, or unsuitable in any way.

Finally, with a clear focus for your paper and with the sources you want, you are ready to write your research paper, following the same writing process you practiced in Chapters 1 through 5. You may review those chapters to remind yourself of the steps for writing an effective paper.

In this chapter you will practice the following:

- Choosing a topic and writing a research proposal

- Finding and evaluating sources

By the end of this chapter, you will have chosen a suitable topic and written a research proposal. You'll have learned how to locate and evaluate sources and written a list of references. You'll be ready to begin writing your independent research paper.

CHOOSING A TOPIC, WRITING A RESEARCH PROPOSAL

For some writing assignments, your teacher will select the topic and research question. In other cases, you will choose your topic, do the research to find appropriate sources, and write a paper incorporating the evidence you gather from your reading. Although the writing process is much the same as that for more structured assignments, you must first take the preliminary steps of clarifying your topic and research question, and finding sources that will help you answer your question.

You may be given a general topic, as in this assignment:

> Research Paper Topic: Select a topic in psychology that you find interesting and use the research paper to learn as much as possible about the subject.

In this case, it's up to you to decide what to write about, how to focus your ideas, and what questions to address.

 # Three Steps for Choosing a Research Topic

1. **Find ideas for topics.**

2. **Narrow your topic.**

3. **Write a research proposal.**

FINDING IDEAS FOR TOPICS

As you think about your topic, there are several things you should keep in mind.

- Look for a subject that you want to learn more about. It's not easy to write a good research paper if you're not interested in learning about the topic.

- Make sure your topic is covered in a number of sources. You will need a variety of sources to give your paper depth.

- Think about whether it can be written in the time you have available. Realistically assess how long it will take you to find your information, organize your paper, and write it.

- Choose a subject that is appropriate for your level of knowledge. A subject that is too technical or that requires specialized knowledge you don't have will take a lot of extra time.

Here are some places where you may find good ideas for topics.

Your Experience and Interests

- Is there an issue that has affected your family, your community, or your country that you'd like to learn more about?
- Do you have a special interest that you'd like to explore?

Classes

- Look over your class syllabus and readings. Do you see any topics you would like to explore in more depth?
- Think about issues you have studied in previous classes. What more could you learn about these?

The Web

- Explore some of your topic ideas online by typing in key words and phrases. You may discover related subjects and ideas that are new and interesting to you.

Newspapers and Magazines

- Go to the library and skim national newspapers and magazines (e.g., *Time, Newsweek, The Smithsonian, Discover, The Economist*) to learn about interesting subjects or current topics in the news.

NARROWING A TOPIC

When you find a subject you want to explore further, think about the time you have available. The subject of a research paper should be specific; it should be limited to the amount of information you can reasonably expect to include in the time you have.

Here are some topics that other students have considered. In each case, the writer began with a general topic, then moved to a more focused idea, and finally narrowed the idea to a suitable topic for a research paper.

General Topic	Focused Topic	Narrowed Topic
1. Dogs	Dogs and humans	Use of dogs in psychotherapy
2. Architecture	Japanese architecture	Influence of Buddhism on Japanese architecture
3. Sports	Snowboarding	Reasons for popularity of snowboarding
4. Family	Korean families	Cultural conflicts in raising Korean children in the United States
5. Genetic engineering	Help for infertility	Selling human eggs on the Internet

As you think about your topic and how you might narrow it, you may choose to use Wikipedia, an online collaborative encyclopedia that can provide you with an overview of your topic, be a source of useful search terms, and offer some interesting directions you could take with your topic. While most instructors will not accept Wikipedia as a reliable source for your final research paper, at this exploratory stage, Wikipedia can be an excellent tool.

Some Common Problems with Topics

Some topics don't work well for research papers because:

1. There isn't enough information available.

   - You may need to shift the focus of your topic or use different key words to search for information.

2. Information is available, but the sources contain too much jargon or are too technical for your level of knowledge.

   - Some aspects of "genetic engineering," topic 5 on the previous page, require a great deal of background knowledge of chemistry and biology. However, the writer in this case was able to find an area of genetic engineering, "selling human eggs on the Internet," that was interesting to her but did not involve a detailed knowledge of science.

3. The topic is too broad; that is, the topic does not have a specific enough focus.

   - All the focused topics listed would probably fall into this category; whereas, the narrowed topics are all subjects of suitable scope for research papers.

ACTIVITIES TO PRACTICE DEVELOPING TOPICS

ACTIVITY **1** Brainstorming Topics

1. For five minutes, brainstorm a list of things you know something about or might even be an authority on. List everything.

2. Now, for five more minutes, brainstorm a list of things about a topic you'd like to learn more about. Be as specific as possible. Don't worry if something appears on both lists.

3. Now look at both lists. Circle one item from either list that you want to research more closely. For five minutes, brainstorm a list of questions about this topic that you would like to learn the answers to.

4. Share your topic and questions with a partner or group of classmates. They may have more questions to suggest.

ACTIVITY **2** Answering Questions

1. On one side of the room, your teacher will post these three questions about global issues:

   - What events in the twentieth century had the greatest impact on the way we live?

- What are the five most pressing global issues of today?
- What changes have you noticed in your own country in the last five years?

On the other side of the room, your teacher will post these three questions about a personal view of history:

- What historical figure do you admire and why?
- What scientific discovery would you like to know more about?
- What historical event in your own country or elsewhere would you like to know more about?

2. Sitting in a circle, each person in the room, including the teacher, briefly answers one question from each side of the room.

3. After each person speaks, discuss whether the response would make a good topic for a paper, considering questions such as:

- Would you be interested enough in the topic to spend many hours, from a few to several weeks, investigating and writing about it?
- Would you be able to find enough information about it?
- Is the topic something you and your readers can understand, or is it too technical to explain easily?
- Is the topic broad enough so that it can be explored in some depth?

ACTIVITY ❸ Writing Questions on the Walls

1. Write a topic you're considering for a research paper at the top of a large sheet of newsprint and post the sheet on the classroom wall. Each class member will do the same, covering the walls with sheets, each with a topic at the top and plenty of blank space below.

2. Walk around the room and jot down questions you have about each topic on the sheets. Everyone else, including the teacher, will be doing the same.

3. After everyone has had a chance to write questions on each posted topic, sit together and spend a couple of minutes clarifying the questions.

4. At the end of class, take your sheet home and use the questions from others to help you focus on your topic.

Example of a posted topic with some questions generated by classmates and teacher:

Topic: Food

Questions: How do food taboos develop in different cultures?
How do food taboos develop in different cultures?
What role does food play in social rituals?
Why do people become vegetarians?
What are the causes of eating disorders?
Who discovered chocolate?

ACTIVITY **4** Exploring Topics Online

1. At home, select three topics that interest you. For each topic do the following:

    - Search the Internet for 20–30 minutes to explore the ideas and issues related to the topic.

    - List the websites that you found for the topic.

    - Write a paragraph that explains why you are interested in the topic, and what ideas you found during your search.

2. In class, share your topic ideas with your classmates. Discuss what makes the topic appealing to you, and whether you see any potential problems with the research subject.

Writing a Research Proposal

When you're writing on a topic of your own choice, creating a research proposal is one of the best ways to clarify what you will write about. A good research proposal

- is about 75 to 100 words long.

- is written in informal language.

- includes the topic you will research.

- gives an explanation of why the topic interests you.

- mentions several questions you hope to answer about the topic.

The research proposal may help you think about how you will approach your topic; it's a place to define your focus as well as to express doubts or mention problems you anticipate.

Here are some research proposals.

SAMPLE RESEARCH PROPOSALS

Proposal 1:   On the bus that I take, there is a dog that is a guide for a blind woman. I love dogs and I thought it would be interesting to learn about the different ways that dogs can help people. I want to know what kinds of services are the most common for dogs to do. I'd like to learn about whether there are certain types of dogs that are better as service dogs, and how the dogs are chosen and trained. I think my topic might be too broad, so I may have to focus on only some kinds of service, or I may have to cut out how the dogs are trained. I'll see which part of the subject is most interesting to me, and I will focus on that.

Proposal 2:   My original idea was to write about a comparison of Swiss and U.S. schools, but since it is impossible to get references on Swiss schools in such a short time, I will concentrate on U.S. schools, with a few references to Swiss schools. In particular, I will discuss whether rules for classroom behavior encourage a humanistic school climate and/or self-discipline.

Proposal 3:   I watched a video about the great Pacific Ocean garbage patch, and I want to learn more about it. It is a huge area of the Pacific Ocean that is covered in plastic garbage. I want to know why the plastic garbage collects there, and what problems it causes. I'm really worried about pollution, and so I decided to focus on this specific example of a pollution problem. What I really want to focus on for my research are the solutions of the Pacific Ocean garbage patch. What can we do to get rid of it? I think my research will have three parts. First, I want to describe the problem. What is the Pacific Ocean garbage patch? Second, I want to discuss how to remove it. Third, I want to find out—at least one or two ways—how we can prevent another one.

BUILDING YOUR INDEPENDENT PAPER

Choose a Topic and Write a Research Proposal

Choose a topic and write a research proposal about it that includes an explanation of your interest in the topic and possible questions you would like to answer in your paper.

FINDING AND EVALUATING SOURCES

Now that you've chosen your topic and developed some research questions, you have a clearer idea of what you are writing about. You're ready to look for suitable sources to help you answer your questions.

 Three Steps for Finding Sources

1. **Search for information.**

2. **Evaluate sources.**

3. **Write a working reference list.**

SEARCHING FOR INFORMATION

Searching for your sources can lead you in many new and interesting directions. Because you have a deadline for completing your assignment, you will have to balance the fun of exploring new ideas with the need to find a useful collection of sources for your assignment.

As you search, you may even change or revise your topic. You may find sources that interest you more than your original topic and decide to pursue a new subject. Or, a topic may sound great at the beginning, but a lack of suitable sources may force you in a different direction.

The words and phrases you use to find information on your topic are an important key to your success as a researcher. Before you begin your search, think about what you already know about your topic. Then, create a list of words and phrases that are related. This will be your search term list. As you continue to search, consider your topic from many angles and look for other key vocabulary that you can use as search terms.

Finally, make note of any material that could help answer your research question. Save articles and website links on your computer or write the address of useful sites in a research notebook. Later, you can delete articles that are not useful.

You will probably want to include information from several different kinds of sources to give your paper more depth. Here are some common places to find information for a research paper.

The Internet

The Internet is one place where information is easy to access and read. But be careful—many sites contain unreliable information and hidden biases. When you use the Internet to find information on your topic, you will probably find numerous sites, but many will not fit your needs. Here are some tips for conducting an efficient search online:

1. Get to know the various search engines. Although different search engines may uncover some of the same sites, you will find that each also offers some unique sources. Google, MSN, and Yahoo are three search engines, but there are many others.

2. The "hit list" of many search engines is organized according to the sites most frequently requested rather than the date published. This means you may find a good source buried deep within your list of potential sources.

3. When you type in your search term:
   - List the most important key word first (e.g., *stress and health effects*).
   - Use lowercase letters (e.g., *falconry* rather than *Falconry*).
   - Enter phrases in quotation marks (e.g., "assisted suicide").
   - Use *AND* when looking for combined subjects (e.g., marijuana AND "medical use").
   - Use *AND NOT* when excluding a subject (e.g., marijuana AND NOT legislation).

Electronic Databases

Another good place to look for sources is in electronic databases, usually available through libraries. These provide full or partial texts of articles in periodicals, newspapers, encyclopedias, and other reference works.

EBSCO Host, InfoTrac, and ProQuest are three examples of electronic databases that are commonly available in libraries. They focus on articles in periodicals and newspapers and provide reliable sources for academic work.

Books

Books are a good source for general background information on a topic, as well as for reliable, in-depth information, but you may not have time to read a whole book. The introduction of a book often provides a useful overview of the subject. Using the table of contents and index can help you find specific information.

Newspapers

Newspapers are a good place to look for short articles, but be aware that the information may be focused too specifically on their place of publication.

Interviews

If you find the right person to talk to, an interview can provide information directly related to your research. Sometimes, it's difficult to find an appropriate person to interview, and it may take time to set up an interview. But if you can arrange it, an interview is an excellent primary source of information.

EVALUATING SOURCES

As you assemble a list of sources, you may find that your problem is not finding enough information, but deciding which information to use. You can save time and effort by briefly evaluating the sources before you read each article in detail.

Guidelines for Evaluating Sources

Is the source about the topic?

Looking at the title and related notes can often give you a sense of the main idea of the article. Notice whether it is likely to be too general or too specific for your topic. Some articles may be very scientific and technical; others may concentrate on only one aspect of the topic while you plan to write about it in a more general way.

For example, if you plan to write about the effects of smoking on college students, but you find an article about the chemical composition of tobacco smoke, that article is probably too technical for your purposes.

Is it enough information or too much?

To judge this, look at the number of pages. A one-page article may give you a little bit of information and may be worth looking at if its title sounds good.

On the other hand, it probably won't give you much substance, so you'll need other sources to supplement it. Conversely, a 10-page article will keep you busy reading for a long time and may be more information than you really need.

What kind of information does it offer?

Some articles provide statistics and the results of scientific studies about the issue. Other anecdotal articles tell personal experiences related to the topic. Look for the kind of information that you plan to focus on in your paper.

Is it up-to-date?

Look at the publication date. If your topic is a current problem, you probably don't want to use articles that are more than six to eight years old. But, if you're writing about historical trends that led to a current problem, you will want sources that go back a number of years.

How is the information biased?

Every article is written with an audience in mind, but some are written with the intent to present only one point of view or to persuade the reader to the writer's opinion. It is fine to use such an article as a source as long as you are aware of the opinion, or bias. Look at who the writer is and what organization she or he represents. Read carefully. Look for words with positive or negative connotations or statements that make unrealistic claims.

Some Special Considerations in Evaluating Websites

Websites are perhaps the easiest sources of information to access and yet may be among the most biased. Anyone can create a website about any topic. This means that a website with information about your topic may be written by an expert or simply be the ideas of someone who wants to share them. For most university assignments, you are expected to support your ideas with evidence from people or organizations that have carefully researched the topic and are generally accepted as reliable. Before you use a website as a source for an academic paper, consider these factors.

Guidelines for Evaluating Websites

Look at the web address to see where it comes from.

- Government sites (.gov) are often reliable sources of facts and statistics.
- Educational sites (.edu) are usually dependable places to find reliable information.
- Nonprofit organizations (.org) may be objective or may be promoting a social cause and, therefore, may be biased in favor of or against a certain point of view.
- Commercial providers (.com) charge for use of the site and thus have control over content. These are not considered objective sources.

Determine who wrote the page.

- Is it a personal website? If so, the opinions may be solely those of the writer, and you need to find out more about the writer in order to evaluate the site.

- Is there a place on the website to find out more about the author? Are the author's credentials provided? If the author has done research or published in her field, then she has expertise in the subject and you can safely assume the information is reliable.

- If the site is written by an organization, is the purpose of the organization provided? If the organization is selling a service or product, the information it provides is not objective. Sometimes you can learn something about the author or organization by truncating the URL to locate the website (e.g., *www.religioustolerance.org/euthanas.htm* can be truncated to *www.religioustolerance.org* to find information about the Religious Tolerance organization).

Consider whether the information is up-to-date.

- If your topic is one that changes rapidly, you need a site that is updated frequently.

- Check the links on the site to see if they are current.

Notice whether the format is easy to access.

- Is the information easy to find and understand? If the source is confusing to navigate, you may be better off looking elsewhere.

- Is the site free? If you must pay for information, you know that the site is created to make a profit and may not be objective. Some information, such as that in newspaper archives, also requires a fee but is entirely reliable.

ACTIVITIES TO PRACTICE FINDING SOURCES

ACTIVITY ❶ Evaluating Sources from a Database

For this activity, you need access to a computer lab.

1. Go to the website for any large library; it can be academic or public. Follow the links to the databases and choose EBSCO Host, which is a collection of many databases.

2. As a class, select a topic to search for (e.g., causes of stress or gun control) and enter the key phrase into the EBSCO Host database.

3. Working with a partner, print out the first few pages of the list of articles about the topic generated by EBSCO Host.

4. Using the Guidelines for Evaluating Sources on page 147, decide which articles might be useful. Write *Y* on sources you think will be useful, *N* on sources you know won't be useful, and *M* on sources that might be useful.

5. Discuss your evaluations with the class.

ACTIVITY ❷ Evaluating Websites

For this activity, you need access to a computer lab.

1. As a class, select any search engine. Use "birth order" as a search term.

2. With a partner, evaluate the reliability of the first five websites that your search engine generates. Use the Guidelines for Evaluating Websites on page 148.

3. As a class, discuss which sources you believe are reliable and which are not. Give reasons for your opinions.

ACTIVITY **3** Conferencing with Your Teacher

For this activity, you need access to a computer lab.

1. Schedule a time to meet with your teacher for 20 to 30 minutes. Bring your research proposal with you.

2. Discuss possible search terms and type one of these terms into EBSCO.

3. With your teacher, evaluate the usefulness of the sources. Remember to keep a list of new search terms as you skim titles and articles.

4. Print or mark any potentially useful sources.

5. If your search is not generating the information you want, consider how you might modify your topic based on the information you are getting.

6. You will not find all your sources during this conference, but you will begin to get an idea of whether your topic will be manageable.

WRITING A WORKING REFERENCES LIST

This list of 10 to 15 sources is your "working references list." It will include some sources that look promising now but that you'll end up not using, and you may add other sources later. However, at this point the working references list will provide a good start for finding information for your paper.

A working reference list should include the topic and research question at the top. For each source, the references list should include the title, author, date, and short description of the content of the source.

EXAMPLE

Working References List

Topic: Birth Order

Research Question: How does birth order affect personality?

Sources:

Title	Author & Date	Source & Description
University of Maine Cooperative Extension Bulletin #4359	Judith Graham • unknown	website http://www.umext.maine.edu • This article gives an overview of the typical personalities of oldest, middle, and youngest children. It's very general.
The Power of Birth Order	Jeffrey Kluger • Oct. 17, 2007	*Time* Magazine website http://www.time.com/time/health • Some statistics and discussion on what science has to say about whether or not birth order affects personality.
Born to Rebel: Birth Order, Family Dynamics, and Creative Lives	Frank Sulloway • 1996	Book: New York: Pantheon Books • Sulloway researched eldest born and youngest born people from history.
Brothers and Sisters: The Order of Birth in the Family	Karl Konig • 1963/2004	Book: Edinburgh: Floris Books • Longer discussion on personality characteristics and birth order in families.
Empirical Studies Indicating Significant Birth-Order-Related Personality Differences	Preview By: Daniel Eckstein • Winter 2000	EBSCO article: *Journal of Individual Psychology*, Winter 2000, Vol. 56 Issue 4, p. 481, 14p • An overview of 150 studies on birth order and personality.
How Birth Order Affects Your Personality	Joshua K. Hartshorne • Jan. 2010	Scientific American online http://www.scientificamerican.com/article.cfm?id=ruled-by-birth-order • Arguments against birth order as a key factor in personality.
Birth Order Effects on Personality and Achievement Within Families	Janet Smith • Nov. 1999	*Psychological Science*, Vol. 10 Issue 6, p. 482, 7p • Discusses family relationships. Has some good statistics.
The Identification of Birth Order Personality Attributes	Lawrence Nyman • Jan. 1995	EBSCO: *Journal of Psychology*, Vol. 129 Issue 1, p. 51, 9p • Scientific study of African-American and Latino college students and birth order.

BUILDING YOUR INDEPENDENT PAPER

Create a Working References List

Write a working references list of the sources you have found. Begin with your topic and research question. Your list should include 10 to 15 sources and have the following information for each:

- Title, author, and date
- Where you found the source
- A short description of the source

Remember not to rely only on the Internet for your sources. Consider books, periodicals, and electronic databases as well. Take time to evaluate each source before including it in your working references list.

WRITING YOUR NEXT RESEARCH PAPER

Now that you've chosen a topic, written a research proposal, learned how to collect and evaluate your sources, and written a working references list, it is time to retrace the steps in the writing process. Use Chapters 1–5 in this book to guide you through the process of writing a research paper.

PART TWO
Sources for Research

INTRODUCTION TO PART TWO

The articles in this part of *Sourcework* provide the sources you will use to help you think about your topic and find evidence for your guided research paper. As you write, you will often flip back and forth between the articles you are reading and the writing activities you are doing in the chapters in Part One.

Each of the three Themes presented here has the same structure:

Table of Contents
- List of the articles in the Theme

Getting Started Activities
- Discussion of what you already know about the topic and learning about the source authors

Introduction to the Theme
- Brief description of the Theme

One or two framing articles
- Sources for your writing
- Set out key issues connected with the topic

Three articles about one aspect of the Theme
- Sources for your writing
- Provide several points of view on this aspect

Three articles about a second aspect of the Theme
- Sources for your writing
- Provide several points of view on this aspect

Questions for Writing
- Writing assignments about each Theme
- More writing assignments that require additional research

For additional resource lists on the Themes in Part Two and on the following additional Themes, go to the *Sourcework* website at **http://elt.heinle.com/sourcework.**

1. Birth Order and Personality
2. Standardized Testing
3. Expectations of Marriage
4. Taking Risks
5. Homeschooling

RISKING CHANGE:
Working for a Better World

GETTING STARTED 1

You must become the change you want to see.

—Mahatma Gandhi

You must do the thing you think you cannot do.

—Eleanor Roosevelt

Only a small group of dedicated citizens can change the world; indeed, it's the only thing that ever has.

—Margaret Mead

How wonderful it is that nobody need wait a single moment before starting to improve the world.

—Anne Frank

They imprisoned me for almost 30 years. If I now come into the bright light of freedom filled with hate and determined to get even, then I will be their prisoner for the rest of my life.

—Nelson Mandela

The quotations above are comments made by individuals who have written about and worked toward changes in society. To begin thinking about the topic of social change—taking risks and making change—do the following activity with a small group.

1. Choose one of the quotations that interests you and find several other classmates who would like to discuss the same quotation.

2. In your group, discuss what you know about the speaker and what you think about the quotation. You can include your thoughts about what the quotation means, why the person said it, why you agree or disagree with it, give examples from your experience that have shown it to be true or not true, or share any other ideas that come to mind.

3. As a group, present a summary of your discussion about the quote.

GETTING STARTED 2

For homework, do an Internet search on the author(s) of each article in this Theme. In class, share what you found.

 ## Introduction to the Theme

Most of us hope to make a better world. We want to make changes, both to help ourselves be better people and to help others, but we also recognize that making change, whether personal or societal, demands the courage to take risks and face uncertainty. The first article frames the theme by looking at the role of risk taking in life.

On a societal level, there have always been a few people who have led the way into change, taking the first risks and setting the standards for others. Some people call them heroes. Every society throughout history has had such heroes and heroines, people who stand out as inspirations for others to follow. They may be recognized leaders—politicians, warriors, scientists, or artists—or they may be less conspicuous, so-called "ordinary" individuals thrust into leadership by circumstance. Some would say that they define us; the heroes we choose reveal our own values. The next three articles examine the types of people who step forward to make change in their world.

While we all want a better world, we may differ on just what "better" means and on how to achieve the ideal world we seek. Many attempts to create a better world involve violent conflict, in which one group forces change on another in the form of war or conquest. Yet history also includes a record of nonviolent changes that are less damaging, more humane, and even more lasting than war. Some of these changes happen on a small scale and are initiated by one committed individual working on a project of personal concern. Others apply methods of nonviolent resistance and conflict resolution to a social or political issue. The last three articles present several ways of making nonviolent social change.

Framing Article:
Why Do People Take Risks?

*Living on the Edge: Extreme Sports and Their Role in Society**

Julia Smith

August 9, 2006

http://www.summitpost.org/

With regard to extreme sports, the perception of the general public is that people who choose to take risks are irresponsible 'adrenaline junkies' who are ultimately a burden to society. When a person takes unnecessary risks, and becomes injured or in need of rescue, the expenses for coming to their aid are often borne by taxpayers. It should
5   not be surprising then, that these same taxpayers question why they should have to pay for these seemingly foolish actions. A backcountry rescue after skiers trigger an avalanche, for example, will cost thousands of dollars. Skateboarders cause damage to both private and public property, and injure themselves. While these issues have been discussed at great length in the media, rarely does discussion focus on the negative
10   impact of limiting access to these types of risky sports. What would be the effect on society if we made it more difficult for people to engage in these types of activities? In fact, by curbing a person's passions and limiting access to their chosen sports–even those the public may consider risky–these athletes may well find outlets for their energy that is much more burdensome to society.

*This article is from a British publication and contains some British spellings.

15   While it is true that extreme sports do not appeal to the masses, there are still a significant number of people to whom these activities are an important and fulfilling part of their lives. It is our differences that make a society interesting, so while it may not be for everyone, high-risk activities contribute to the diversity of our culture. We all crave adventure to some degree or another. As author, outdoorsman, and Idaho State

20   University faculty member, Ron Watters explains in his essay "The Wrong Side of the Thin Edge", everyone needs a little adventure. But some people need more than the normal forms of life's excitement and take it one step further, participating in high-risk activities—sports played on the edge, where the consequences are far greater, and where as the great American mountaineer and outdoor philosopher Willi Unsoeld

25   once said, 'It has to be real enough to kill you' (258). Psychologist Frank Farley has studied thrill seeking risk-takers for decades, and has developed the term "Type T" (for thrill seeking). Farley describes Type T personality types as "risk-takers and adventurers who seek excitement and stimulation wherever they can find or create it" (qtd. in Roberts).

30   Type T's are not just the mountain climbing daredevils of the world however. They are often our best inventors, entrepreneurs, and explorers. They are CEOs, surgeons, and civil rights leaders. Take high altitude mountaineer Dr. Kenneth Kamler for example, a New York microsurgeon and listed in the New York Guide to Best Doctors as well as in Who's Who in America. We wouldn't be the progressive, vibrant society we are today

35   if no one was willing to take risks. Farley argues that history's most crucial events are shaped by Type T individuals exhibiting Type T behaviour, from Boris Yeltsin to Martin Luther King, Jr. The act of emigration, he says, is an intrinsically risky endeavor that selects individuals who are high in sensation seeking. Consequently, countries built upon immigrant population—America, Canada, Australia—probably have an above-average

40   level of risk-takers. He warns that much of the current effort to minimize risk and risk-taking itself runs the risk of eliminating "a large part of what made this country great in the first place" (qtd. in Roberts).

But for all their positive attributes, Type T personalities also have a dark side. They often bore easily, and without other options their craving for stimulation can lead

45   them to abuse drugs and alcohol, gamble, or engage in other destructive behaviours. Marvin Zuckerman, a psychologist at the University of Delaware and a pioneer in the study of risk's biological roots notes that without healthy psychological outlets, "the main forms of sensation seeking include sex, drugs, heavy drinking, gambling, and reckless driving" (qtd. in Roberts). People who engage in extreme sports do take

50   risks, but there are far more dangerous 'highs' they could be seeking. Rock climbing, mountain biking, and snowboarding offer a high that can only be achieved through self-discipline, hard work, and a healthy lifestyle. People who are serious about extreme sports are highly trained athletes who take care of their bodies and tend to be very safety conscious.

55   There is evidence to show that the Type T personality is something people are born with. It isn't a lifestyle choice. In fact, risk taking has been linked to levels of dopamine, a chemical found in the brain that regulates mood and pleasure. Published research conducted by Dr. Ernest Noble of the University of California links the D2 and D4 dopamine receptor genes to risk-taking behaviour. After his 1998 study, Noble estimated

60   that 20 per cent of people are born with the D2 dopamine receptor while 30 per cent are born with both the D2 and the D4 dopamine receptors (CBC Online Archives).

The predisposition to risk-taking is not a new genetic development. It is likely hardwired into our evolutionary makeup from ancient times, when our survival depended upon the ability to hunt and defend ourselves from attack from predators or other humans. We have been successful in eliminating the vast majority of risk from our daily lives: seatbelts, airbags, and other safety advancements have greatly reduced the dangers associated with driving a car. Most people wear helmets when they bike and rollerblade. Coffee cups even warn us now that the beverage we are about to enjoy is extremely hot. As Watters explains:

The world has become far too safe, and heretofore unknown lands are mapped in far too much detail. As a consequence, we need as many outlets as possible for people to participate in challenging outdoor activities. We need wilderness lands; we need rock climbing areas; we need wild rivers; we need outdoor schools, and given proper environmental safeguards, we need free and unfettered access to outdoor areas. The right to risk is unalienable. It makes our society healthier and more vibrant (259).

It is getting increasingly difficult to take any risks in the course of a day, and yet we still have this innate need for exhilaration. Without relatively safe outlets for this drive, people predisposed to risk-taking behaviors will seek out other activities, with potentially greater personal, social, and economic consequences.

Instead of shunning and discouraging extreme athletes, we should celebrate them for their differences and do what we can to support them as they climb higher, go faster, and push the limits of human endurance and athleticism. As T.S. Elliot once said, "Only those who will risk going too far can possibly find out how far one can go." With public support, extreme athletes can expand our boundaries and contribute to our diverse and evolving society. By curbing their passions and limiting access to activities some consider too dangerous, we may be inviting even greater risk in the form of addictions, crime and health problems the end result of which is a heavy burden for society to bear.

Works Cited

"Hardwired for Thrills—Extreme Sports: Faster, Riskier, More Outrageous." Canadian Broadcasting Corporation Online Archives. 25 Feb. 1998. 12 March 2006. http://archives.cbc.ca/IDC-1-41-1727-11912/sports/extreme_sports/clip5

Roberts, Paul. "Risk." *Psychology Today* Nov/Dec 1994. 12 March 2006. http://www.psychologytoday.com/articles/pto-19941101-000027.html

Watters, Ron. "The Wrong Side of the Thin Edge." To the Extreme: Alternative Sports, Inside and Out. Ed. Robert E. Rinehart and Synthia Sydnor. Albany: State University of New York Press, 2003: 258–259.

Triad. 摘此. 3个item

People Who Make Changes

a kind of Sandwich.

Is a Hero Really Nothing but a Sandwich?

Ted Tollefson

May/June, 1993

Utne Reader

For several years a picture of Warren Spahn of the Milwaukee Braves hung on my closet door, one leg poised in mid-air before he delivered a smoking fastball. Time passed and Spahn's picture gave way to others: Elvis, John F. Kennedy, Carl Jung, Joseph Campbell, Ben Hogan. These heroic images have reflected back to me what I hoped to become:

5   a man with good moves, a sex symbol, an electrifying orator, a plumber of depths, a teller of tales, a graceful golfer. Like serpents, we keep shedding the skins of our heroes as we move toward new phases in our lives.

Like many of my generation, I have a weakness for hero worship. At some point, however, we all begin to question our heroes and our need for them. This leads us to

10   ask: What is a hero?

Despite immense differences in cultures, heroes around the world generally share a number of traits that instruct and inspire people.

A hero does something worth talking about. A hero has a story of adventure to tell and a community who will listen. But a hero goes beyond mere fame or celebrity.

15   *Heroes serve powers or principles larger than themselves.* Like high-voltage transformers, heroes take the energy of higher powers and step it down so that it can be used by ordinary mortals.

The hero lives a life worthy of imitation. Those who imitate a genuine hero experience life with new depth, zest, and meaning. A sure test for would-be heroes is what or whom do

20   they serve? What are they willing to live and die for? If the answer or evidence suggests they serve only their own fame, they may be celebrities but not heroes. Madonna and Michael Jackson are famous, but who would claim that their adoring fans find life more abundant?

Heroes are catalysts for change. They have a vision from the mountaintop. They have the skill and the charm to move the masses. They create new possibilities. Without

25   Gandhi, India might still be part of the British Empire. Without Rosa Parks and Martin Luther King Jr., we might still have segregated buses, restaurants, and parks. It may be possible for large-scale change to occur without charismatic leaders, but the pace of change would be glacial, the vision uncertain, and the committee meetings endless.

Though heroes aspire to universal values, most are bound to the culture from which

30   they came. The heroes of the Homeric Greeks wept loudly for their lost comrades and exhibited their grief publicly. A later generation of Greeks under the tutelage of Plato disdained this display of grief as "unmanly."

Throughout most of the world, it is acknowledged that heroes need a community as much as a community needs them.

35   And most Americans seem to prefer their heroes flawless, innocent, forever wearing a white hat or airbrushed features. Character flaws—unbridled lust, political incorrectness—are held as proof that our heroes aren't really heroes. Several heroes on my own list have provided easy targets for the purveyors of heroic perfectionism.

The ancient Greeks and Hebrews were wiser on this count.

Eve's Daughters

Miriam Polster

2001

Gestalt Journal Press

When we move beyond the classic stereotype of heroes, we can see that many ordinary women and men are actually heroes. Furthermore, heroes are more numerous than we may have thought. Although heroes of the everyday may not receive the great acclaim accorded the classic hero, the value of private heroism
5   may be greater precisely because we see everyday heroes up close; they are so near, so intimately connected. They are family, co-workers, neighbors, and their heroism takes place in commonplace settings and in response to everyday challenges.

Our images of heroes provide an inventory, if you will, of heroic characteristics.
10 And while some of these characteristics may be basic to all heroism, others may be distinctly related to whether the hero is a woman or a man. A useful definition of heroism must include both types.

Five Shared Characteristics of Heroism

Heroism takes many forms. Out of the roster of qualities ascribed to heroes over the
15 ages, I would like to focus on five.

1. All heroes are motivated by a profound respect for human life.

2. Heroes have a strong sense of personal choice and effectiveness.

3. Their perspective on the world is original, going beyond what other people think is possible.

20 4. They are individuals of great physical and mental courage.

5. Heroes are not measured by publicity. Whether a heroic act receives worldwide attention or occurs in an obscure setting with only a single witness, a heroic act is still heroic.

Respect for Human Life

25 The hero profoundly believes in the value and dignity of human life. The one act that most people would agree is heroic is risking one's life to save another. The annual Carnegie Hero Fund Commission endorses this opinion by giving medals and cash awards to women and men who have saved lives. In 1990, eight women won awards for acts ranging from saving people from assault to rescuing people from runaway
30 automobiles or from drowning (Carnegie Hero Foundation, 1990). Mythology is full of hero tales about unfortunate victims apparently doomed if not for the intervention of the hero.

Valuing life can also mean preserving the dignity with which a life is to be lived. Many of the chores that women have quietly but heroically performed over the years
35 have been the simple services that support the dignity and welfare of the people in their care, adults as well as children. Feeding, clothing, and keeping others clean are all humble tasks, but how quickly a life deteriorates when these basic needs go untended. Many women have faced overwhelming odds—and many continue to face them—on

untamed and unpublicized frontiers: in the schools and clinics of our city slums, in
40 wartime hospitals, collecting and distributing food and clothing to the homeless.
All ways of preserving lives.

Faith in Her Effective Exercise of Choice

The hero has a profound faith in herself as an essential influential force. An unhappy
circumstance is not simply to be endured. Personal action is called for, and she chooses
45 to act. She balances her own energy against the opposition and moves to make changes.

One heroic woman who went beyond resignation is Betty Washington. She set
herself and others to work toward their common goal. She singlehandedly recruited
and organized people for a citizen's watch program to rid her Boston neighborhood
of the drug dealing and crime that were threatening to take it over. This made her a
50 publicly marked target, vulnerable to reprisal. But here is how a modern hero talks:
"Either you speak out and take the risk, or you die in the cesspool" ("Heroes, Past and
Present," 1987, p. 63).

The heroic woman believes, and reminds others, that common experience and
accepted opinion can be changed, and she is willing to be the catalyst, even though
55 she may confront opposition and criticism.

Original Perspective

The hero has an original perspective that distinguishes her from others who settle for
agreement and conformity or are too beaten down to ask necessary questions. The
relationship between the hero and the established order of things is fluid; she insists
60 on her freedom to perceive, within the context of things-as-they-are, the way things
could be.

Doubting the inevitable rightness of unquestioned assumptions has gotten women
into trouble ever since Eve. It leads to unwelcome questions, but opens a new view
of old behavior. Looking at voting privileges in an untraditional light, the suffragists
65 began to question the historic restriction of the vote to white male property owners
only. The trite answer, that there was a classic precedent, that this policy had been
good enough for the ancient Athenians—did not satisfy. In our own times, the whisle-
blower exposes the wrongdoing, fraud, or inefficiency in his or her workplace, where
one is not supposed to rock the boat. Rocking the boat, however leaky it may be,
70 requires an original perspective and involves risk of reprisal, slander, ridicule, demotion
and even loss of job.

Courage

It is almost redundant to say that heroism requires courage, both physical and mental;
personal cost takes a backseat to getting the job done. The traditional hero often risks
75 death or injury. In our sensationalistic age, the defiance of death has become one of
the accepted signs of heroism. In disregarding her personal welfare, the hero may
appear to be courting death. This is an oversimplification. In truth, she simply considers
the risk of death or injury to be less important than her purpose.

Women unconcerned with personal sacrifice have often given years of devoted
80 service to a cause or a person. They have persisted at unconventional efforts with little
recognition or encouragement, willingly surrendering their personal comfort in order
to pursue their goals. One example is Marie Curie, who persevered in her research in

the face of the disrespect and open disapproval of women scientists that characterized her time (and that still taint our own). Mother Theresa, whose lifelong devotion to the
85 victims of poverty and disease is known throughout the world, is another compelling example.

The mental courage of the hero permits her to be aware of accepted "truths" and yet not be restricted by them. When the child in the fairy tale says loudly that the emperor isn't wearing any clothes, that child speaks from innocence, not from courage. The
90 heroic woman, however, knows the danger and nevertheless asserts an unwelcome truth. But she speaks from the integrity of the clearsighted. For her, it isn't enough merely to think the unorthodox; she chooses to espouse it publicly.

Since the heroic act may involve going against the habits and customs of the community, opposition is inevitable; supporters of the status quo do not happily
95 welcome disagreement. The hero needs the mental and emotional stamina to sustain energy and intelligence in the face of personal loss, disapproval, or ostracism. Obviously, one of the most powerful sanctions a community can impose is the threat of ostracism or expulsion. This can be formal, as when a society executes, expels, or jails its dissidents, or informal, as in exclusion from social interactions, passing people over
100 for promotions, or ridicule that isolates psychologically.

Public or Unpublic Heroism

Public heroes are what we usually think of when we think of heroes. They have great impact and are noble examples for a number of people. Drama, awe, and admiration accompany them, and recognition is underscored by ceremonies that accord them even more fame.

105 But the grandness of these celebrations can sometimes overshadow a far more pervasive and important factor in the lives of most people: the heroes of the intimate setting. The actions of parents, teachers, relatives, neighbors, and occasionally even strangers provide an immediacy that profoundly colors a person's life.

All heroism is characterized by these five basic traits I have just described: respect
110 for human life, faith in one's ability to make a difference, original perspective, physical and mental courage, and public or unpublic impact. They are not all equally evident in every heroic life or act; sometimes one or another may dominate. These five characteristics do not constitute a hierarchy of heroism; they are not intended to provide a scale on which heroism can be rated. They are guidelines by which we can
115 recognize the heroism that fills our everyday experience. They help us to appreciate heroism in its ordinary guise, unaccompanied by background music or special effects, and to find the heroic elements in our own lives.

Extreme Do-Gooders—What Makes Them Tick?

Jina Moore

September 7, 2009

Christian Science Monitor

www.csmonitor.com

Most people in the world, it's fair to say, want to do a little good. At the very least, we try to follow a kind of secular golden rule: Try to do no harm. But in our communities and around the world, there's a kind of person who takes all this further—to an extreme, even. They're called, most often, "social entrepreneurs," and some of them
5 have become famous, at least in certain circles: Muhammad Yunus, the 2006 Nobel

Peace Prize laureate, is revered in do-good financial circles for pioneering microfinance, a lending system for the very poor. Some rub shoulders with the famous: Jody Williams, whose global campaign against land mines won the 1997 Nobel Peace Prize, found a fan in Britain's late Princess Diana. Others are treated like rock stars themselves: Mention

10 Paul Farmer, the public-health innovator and subject of the bestseller "Mountains Beyond Mountains," and grown graduate students swoon like tweens at a boy band concert.

From protecting our natural environment to improving our children's education to combating global poverty and disease, we've come to rely on extreme do-gooders to

15 tackle the world's toughest problems. And they're happy to do so, even though their dedication will cost them in the long run. Few of them will make as much as they could in the private sector. They may lose a relationship with a loved one to their work, or miss their kids' big moments.

All of which raises the obvious: Why? What makes these people tick, and how do

20 they sustain a lifetime of commitment to a change that might take generations to see? "We call it a moment of obligation," says Lara Galinsky, of the Echoing Green Foundation, whose 471 fellows have raised more than $1 billion for their causes since 1987. "It's usually not a dramatic moment; it's a gathering of moments, but it's very clear. It's when something gathers such force that you can't ignore it."

Lara is not comment

25 It doesn't happen that often. There is only 1 social entrepreneur for every 10 million of the rest of us, according to calculations of Ashoka, an organization that funds social entrepreneurs around the world. Ashoka founder Bill Drayton bases his calculations on nearly 30 years' worth of seeking out the elusive combination of vision and passion that social entrepreneurs put into practice.

30 "The core defining element is that they simply cannot come to rest ... until their dream has become a new pattern across all of society," says Mr. Drayton. "This is very different from everyone else: the scholar or the artist expresses an idea, and they're happy. The manager ... make[s] the company work. The social worker, the professional, help people ... make their lives better. None of that would remotely satisfy the social

35 entrepreneur. Their job is to change the system."

Whether they're fulfilled visionaries or ascetic volunteers doesn't change the ways in which they make a difference, of course. Changing the system has a lot of prerequisites: A good idea, financial and human resources, and a will of steel, to name a few. But most important may be the often elusive chutzpah.

40 "You see the world as changeable because you can change it. The vision of self and vision of world are related," says Drayton. "If you come from a background [where] everyone says 'You can't, you can't, you can't'—you won't. You won't have practiced it. You won't have defined yourself that way."

That self-definition can have roots in several places—school, home, social circle—

45 but it may also be especially American. Alexis de Tocqueville famously analyzed the American tendency for helping one's community, and though social scientists like Robert Putnam have alleged that our communitarian impulses are dying off, the United States still fosters a unique form of social engagement. "The unique thing about a voluntary association," says Marshall Ganz, a lecturer at Harvard University's

50 John F. Kennedy School of Government, "is that you don't have the economic or political power to fire people or put them in jail. You have to elicit a voluntary contribution, so that requires a lot more reference to core values."

For every extreme do-gooder, there are probably—thankfully—uncounted others who want to see social change, sharing their talents and time at a pace most of us can
55 handle. There are, Dr. Etzioni says, "millions of people who make a contribution despite the fact that they have many other duties … [by] going and bringing orphans into our home, doing community service, teaching people to read, being a pal. There are hundreds of ways we do that."

Ways of Making Change

Agents of Change and Nonviolent Action

Hardy Merriman

April 8, 2008

Conservation Biology, Vol. 22, Issue 2

Nonviolent action is a way for ordinary people to fight for their rights, freedom, and justice. It is frequently associated with moral or ethical nonviolence, but I will address it here as a distinct phenomenon, separate from any moral or ethical underpinnings so as to expand on how it works as a pragmatic way to exert leverage in a conflict.

5   Nonviolent action is based on the insight that power in a society is ultimately derived from people's consent and obedience. In contrast, the prevailing—and factually incorrect—view is that power in a society is based on whoever has concentrated wealth and the greatest capacity for violence. But just as the economy is a subsystem of the biosphere—and therefore is ultimately governed by the laws of
10 the biosphere—so too, systems of power that are seemingly based on violence and money are actually subsystems of thousands or millions of people's broader behavior and obedience patterns. If those people shift their loyalties, behavior, and obedience, the balance of power in a society, and in the world, shifts. Simply put, if people do not obey, then rulers or corporations cannot rule.

15 Nonviolent action, therefore, wields power by creating shifts in people's loyalties, behavior patterns, and obedience at a collective level. This can happen dramatically, for example, as it did in the Indian Independence Movement, the U.S. Civil Rights Movement, various labor movements such as the United Farm Workers in the mid to late 1960s, and the downfall of Ferdinand Marcos in 1986, Augusto Pinochet in
20 1988, Apartheid in South Africa in the early 1990s, Slobodan Milosevic in 2000, and the authoritarian system in Ukraine in 2004. Or, shifts can happen more subtly, as when people choose to shop at locally owned businesses, boycott a product, or work to develop alternative institutions and economies. Regardless of its myriad manifestations, all acts of nonviolent actions fall into one of three categories: acts of
25 commission—that is, people doing things they are not expected, supposed, or allowed to do; acts of omission—that is people not doing things they are expected, supposed, or required to do; or a combination of acts of commission and omission (G. Sharp. 2005. *Waging Nonviolent Struggle: 20th Century Practice and 21st Century Potential.* Porter Sargent Publishers, Boston).

30 To promote shifts in people's obedience and behavior patterns, it is important to understand why people obey and behave as they do in the first place. Reasons differ

from society to society, but two of the most common reasons for obedience that I encounter in my work with activists around the world are that people believe there is no alternative way of behaving and they lack confidence that their actions make
35 a difference. Many people have forgotten that they are the true power holders in their society. Of course formal education, corporations, governments, and media all reinforce the narrative that power resides among a few individuals in a government building or corporate headquarters and that money and guns (on which they have a monopoly) are the ultimate source of strength. This narrative suits their purposes
40 well. Successful nonviolent movements throughout history, however, have awakened people to the fact that through their collective actions, people who are organized around a common vision and act strategically are far stronger than armies and money. Any contemporary grassroots movement that wants to gain traction should take note of this fact and make it a central point of its rhetoric to remind people that
45 they are powerful.

Taking this one step further, successful movements not only tell people that they are powerful, they demonstrate people's power by setting clear, achievable objectives and then documenting and publicizing their victories. The victories themselves may be limited, but their impact on mobilizing people can be enormous. For example,
50 the U.S. Civil Rights Movement concentrated its strength on desegregating buses in Montgomery, Alabama, in 1955–1956 and desegregating Nashville lunch counters in 1960. The Indian Independence Movement focused its effort on gaining concessions from the British on the Salt Acts and other laws in 1930–1931. Once achieved, these objectives were small relative to the mammoth task of overturning segregation in the
55 entire U.S. South or gaining independence in India. But their real impact was in their catalyzing effect on the movements themselves. These victories showed people that their actions mattered and that they were capable of making a difference, which led to great increases in support and mobilization and propelled these movements to the national and international center stage.

60 These objectives were not achieved merely because the U.S. Civil Rights Movement or the Indian Independence Movement occupied the moral high ground. They were achieved also because of hard work, creativity, and skillful political analysis. This is true of all successful nonviolent action. Nevertheless, many neglect this fact and instead assume that nonviolent action consists primarily of public protests, expressions of
65 outrage, and moral injunctions or that its success depends on a charismatic leader or some sort of mystical power. It does not. Nor does it require people who are ideologically committed to pacifism or ethical nonviolence. What it does require is an inclusive vision that unites people, sound strategic planning, effective public communications, and the identification of appropriate methods for the situation.
70 There is no one-size-fits-all recipe—nonviolent action is place-specific. Although the principles that govern it, such as power being based on obedience, are constant across all struggles, its application depends on the context and particulars of a given society. Whether it manifests as bold public action, subtle shifts in buying patterns, or both (most movements have a wide variety of tactics designed to be used by people
75 with different levels of involvement), it provides a way for people to use or create political space in their society from which to leverage concessions from an entrenched adversary.

Fortunately, a lot of intellectual work and research has been done about how people can, and historically have, used nonviolent action to achieve great results.

80 This research is now being discovered by activists and members of civil society who recognize the power and potential that nonviolent action holds. Demand for this knowledge is increasing. You won't read about this in most newspapers, and you won't find a lot of politicians talking about it, but if you talk to activists and members of civil society around the world, they will tell you. They are the ones who have

85 already "begun it." They recognize that it is the people in a society who are the agents of change and that structural change is created from the ground up. They are not waiting for a person to lead them because they understand that most government and corporate leaders will not take the lead to do what is right if their populations are disengaged and do not know how to hold them accountable. Therefore, people

90 around the world are increasingly looking toward nonviolent action (which they may use in conjunction with voting, the legal system, or other traditional means) as a pragmatic way to empower their communities to win human rights; freedom; justice; transparency; women's, indigenous people's, and minority rights; and environmental protection. Regardless of the objective for which nonviolent action

95 is used, its prerequisite is the same: a reframing of the concept of power in people's minds. Sharing this knowledge to awaken people to their power is an essential task in shifting humanity's course.

The Role of the Corporation in Supporting Local Development

Muhammad Yunus

2000

Reflections, Vol. 9, Number 2

I was not thinking of creating a bank for poor people when the Grameen idea came to me. The idea had to do with the circumstances in which I found myself. I came back to Bangladesh in 1972, when it became an independent country. It was a devastated country, and I came back from the United States to participate in rebuilding the nation.

5 I started teaching economics at Chittagong University. As the economy slid down sharply, we had a terrible famine in 1974. I was teaching elegant theories of economics while seeing people dying of hunger outside the classroom. I saw that what I was teaching meant nothing to those who were dying, and I thought that as a human being, I should see if I could be of some use.

10 People were taking loans from loan sharks, and were getting exploited. I went around with a student to make a list of people who were borrowing from loan sharks. When my list was complete, we had 42 names, and the total loan was $27. I was shocked by the smallness of the figure. All I had to do was give $27 to these 42 people so they could return the money to the loan sharks and be free. Another question then

15 came to my mind. If I can make so many people so happy with such a small amount of money, why should I not do more? I wanted to do more. The idea to connect the bank located on the campus with the people who live next door came up. I suggested to the bank manager that he should lend money to the poor people. He said, "No way! A bank cannot lend money to poor people." Our debate went on for several weeks, and

20 then he said, "Why don't you go to the senior people? I cannot do such a thing. There is no use arguing with me." So I talked to the senior officials, but everybody told me the same thing. After several months of running around, I offered myself as a guarantor. That is how it all began.

Whenever I needed some rules in my work, I just looked at how conventional banks

25 operate. Once I learned about their procedures, I did the opposite. Conventional banks

are always looking for people who have lots of money and wealth, in order to lend more and make more money. We reversed that principle. To Grameen, the less you have, the more attractive you are. If you have nothing, you have the highest priority. We also dismissed the whole idea of collateral. We dismissed lawyers. We do not have
30 guarantees. Conventional banks focus on men; we focused on women. They look for the rich men; we look for the poor women. Conventional banks are owned by rich men, and we reversed that too. Grameen Bank is owned by poor women. What is amazing is that the system works. People pay back. Why do they pay back? Because it makes sense to them. Because for the first time, they are getting an opportunity that they never had.

35 **Social Business and the Limits of Charity**

There is only one definition of business in the capitalist system: to make money. There is no other interpretation of that concept. Profit maximization is the goal of the business: the more profit you make, the more everybody benefits. I feel uncomfortable with that concept, because the theoreticians behind it interpret human beings too
40 narrowly. They have created this artificial human being who is one-dimensional. All his enjoyment comes from one source, which is making money. But real people are multidimensional human beings. Not only do they enjoy making money, they also enjoy giving away money. They enjoy touching other people's lives and making a difference in the world. Economics does not admit that.

45 My proposition is that in order to justify the totality of the human being, we need to create another kind of business. Social business is the business of doing good to others. It is a non-loss, non-dividend company with a social objective. Social business also refers to any profit-making business owned by poor people. We created social businesses of several kinds. Grameen-Dannon Company is a joint venture company
50 that produces yogurt. Our objective is to reach millions of malnourished, poor children in Bangladesh. We are putting all the micronutrients they need in the yogurt and then selling it at the cheapest possible price.

Beside social business, the only alternative that we have to help others is through charity. We could have conceived of the yogurt venture as a gift to the children, and it
55 could have become a charitable program. However, there are several differences between the charitable program and a social business. One particular difference is that the charity dollar has only one life. You can use it only once; it goes and never comes back. As part of a social business, a non-loss company, the dollar never stops. The social business dollar has endless life. You create an institution, so it can grow and can change direction.

60 Now, if all the children are already fully nourished, you do not need to give them any more of that special yogurt; you can move on to something else. You can continue to produce other products that will address other aspects of health. The company is dedicated to a social goal, so you can continue that social goal without running out of money, and that is a more powerful concept.

65 **The Power of Dialogue and Opportunity**

One point that I have been raising again and again is the power of opportunity. Through Grameen Bank we constantly see, for example, a person who a few years back did not know anything, had never touched money. Now that person is changed completely, an enthusiastic entrepreneur. She is running an expanding business.
70 All human beings are packed with all the entrepreneurial, creative, and innovative capacity they need to succeed. All human beings in the world have the same capacity

and creativity. We have been encouraging our borrowers to send their children to school. Their children are now in colleges. Right now more than 21,000 students are in medical schools, engineering schools, and universities.

75 Occasionally, when I go to the villages, I see a mother who is still working in the Grameen Bank. She started 12 or 15 years ago with a tiny loan to raise chickens, and gradually improved her life and bought a car. She now has several cars, and has sent her daughter to school to become a doctor. The mother could have been a doctor too, but she never got the opportunity. What is poverty really? If you look at these
80 experiences, again and again, you come to the conclusion that poverty is not in the person. It is not created by the person who is poor. Poverty is created by the system. I am sure that the daughter of the doctor will not go back to illiteracy. She will push the envelope further. What is wrong with the system? Why could they not fix the system? If you want to remove poverty, instead of trying to fix those who are poor, we should be
85 trying to fix the system.

This is our planet. We have not come from any other planet. This is our home. If this is our home, we have to make sure that it is a safe place. We must hand over this planet to our next generation safer and healthier than we found it. That will be our responsibility. Today it does not look like we are doing that. It looks as if we
90 are the last generation, enjoying the world as much as we can. And all that comes back to the concept of the businesses that we run. Because the only thing we have is a robot-like maximization of profit. We cannot forget everything else. We have to bring back those other considerations and values. Profit maximization is not the answer.

Outside View: Liberation by the People

Jack DuVall

September 22, 2004

United Press International

Abraham Lincoln suggested that any people have the right to rise up and replace an oppressive government with one that upholds their rights and freedom. Since his time, however, there is not a single case in which a violent movement has collapsed an authoritarian regime and replaced it with a government based on the consent of the
5 people.

How then have we come to the point that three-quarters of the world's nations are democratic? Some have been freed after wars begun by totalitarian rulers have ousted those regimes. Yet there is another force in history that has liberated millions in great waves.

10 Forty years after Lincoln was martyred, the Russian writer Leo Tolstoy, campaigning for an end to conscription, predicted that "public opinion" would change "the whole structure of life" in the world, in the process of which violence would become "superfluous." That echoed the American founder James Madison's insight that "all government rests on opinion," that it cannot function without the people's acceptance.

15 While working as a lawyer in South Africa, Mohandas K. Gandhi said he was "overwhelmed" by Tolstoy's arguments. Inventing a new way for his fellow Indians to fight against hated forms of discrimination, Gandhi enlisted them in burning their racial registration cards and engaging in mass illegal border crossings—all of which derailed the enforcement of a racial law, until it was withdrawn.

20   Gandhi had refined raw negative public opinion into precisely applied political power. He went on to wage 20 years of campaigns against British rule of India, using marches, boycotts and civil disobedience to demolish British confidence in the permanence of their control.

The gratification of those joining a nonviolent struggle is not immediate, and the
25   liberation they attain is hardly ever on the nightly news. Instead, it becomes a fact of history.

The British thought they defeated Gandhi after the Salt March in 1931, but they eventually lost India. The Polish communists thought they had beaten Lech Walesa when they dragged him off to prison in 1981, but he told them: "You idiots, at this
30   moment you lost; you will come back to us on your knees." Seven years later, they did.

Many nonviolent fighters seem to have nine lives. How is their endurance and the success of their movements achieved?

First, the leaders of a civilian-based movement have to articulate clear goals that reflect the people's grievances and animate a sense of the injustice they have borne. Gandhi,
35   Adam Michnik in Poland and Corazon Aquino in the Philippines all said essentially, "This government is running the country for their own benefit. Why should we help them?"

Second, the movement's organizers have to recruit people from all walks of life to diversify its ranks and broaden the scope of non-cooperation with the demands and decrees of the government—and they have to unify the opposition behind the
40   basic objective of ousting the regime, without which any particular political goals are unreachable.

Third, the movement's leaders should develop a strategic estimate of all the material, economic and political sources of the regime's power and devise and employ tactics that dilute that power. The political philosopher Hannah Arendt said, "It is the people's
45   support that lends power to the institutions of a country." When that support contracts, and the people act to shred those institutions' ties to the regime, it cannot cling to power.

Fourth, the movement should multiply acts of small-scale resistance horizontally throughout the country, straining the outermost ranks of the regime's repressive
50   apparatus—and the initial tactics should entail low physical risk, to lessen the fear of participating.

Fifth, all stages of the resistance should remain nonviolent, to insure that the movement gains the upper hand in the contest for legitimacy with the regime, which will inevitably discredit itself with acts of brutality—and to prompt the police and
55   military to realize that the movement is not aiming at them, it's aiming at the top.

Sixth, a campaign to sow doubt about the regime's future should be aimed at policemen and soldiers, to befriend them or soften potential rancor. The inner core of an oppressive regime is usually narcissistic and venal, and its armed defenders know that best of all. They may turn to an increasingly popular movement in a crisis, when
60   defections are conceivable.

Seventh, the movement should seek support from abroad, in the form of direct aid from nongovernmental organizations and foundations, as well as foreign governments so long as that bestows no propaganda benefit on the regime. And international sanctions should be sought, if they are targeted at rulers, not the people.

65   Eighth, a movement must be ready for a last burst of repression, know when to pause to give itself the opportunity to regroup, or be prepared to exploit an opportunity to negotiate, to obtain more defensible political space if it needs more time before pressing forward again. In short, it has to know how to downshift as well as move into overdrive, as circumstances require.

70   Ninth, once the movement has gathered as much momentum inside and outside the country as it can reasonably expect, it should escalate resistance to force the regime on the defensive. If the dictator is ridiculed in cafes and classrooms, if taxes and fees go unpaid, if public administration is in disarray, if police and soldiers are demoralized, and if key industries are grinding down, then a dictator's system for
75 keeping control is jeopardized. His only real power derives from making his own people and the world believe that he cannot be ousted except through violence. Once that belief is destroyed, the end is predictable.

    Since terror is a form of political violence, and most political violence is practiced either by oppressive regimes, or by insurrectionary groups fighting such regimes, any
80 strategy to eliminate terrorism should give substantial new assistance to civilian-based nonviolent movements that are struggling to liberate the people of these nations.

A Force More Powerful: A Century of Nonviolent Conflict (DVD)

Steven York (writer, producer)

1999

Produced by York Zimmerman, Inc.

This film shows six half-hour segments about successful nonviolent social changes:

- Civil Rights Movement in the United States, 1958–1968
- Indian Independence Movement, 1933–1948
- Movement to End Apartheid in South Africa, 1985–1994
- Resistance to the German Occupation in Denmark, 1940
- Polish Labor Movement, 1980
- Struggle Against Pinochet in Chile, 1983

QUESTIONS FOR WRITING ABOUT RISK AND CHANGE

For each writing assignment, use evidence from several of the articles in this Theme to support your position. You may also use evidence from your own experience or additional sources you find.

1. Define what it means to be a hero.

2. What kind of person tries to change society? What is his or her character and motivation?

3. How are cultural attitudes about heroes the same or different? Select two cultures and compare their beliefs about heroes. In addition to evidence from the articles, use your own experience, if appropriate, to support your ideas.

4. What is the difference between a hero and a role model, celebrity or icon?

5. How can people make changes in society? Describe several effective ways to change society in lasting, constructive ways.

6. Why are social entrepreneurs or people with wealth or fame sometimes able to create social change? What qualities besides money do these people need in order to be effective leaders of change?

7. How does nonviolent action work? What are the conditions necessary for this kind of social change to be successful?

8. Looking at history, when has nonviolent resistance been an effective strategy and what has it accomplished? Consider the events documented in the film *A Force More Powerful* and explain the conditions when this approach has worked to create societal change.

MORE QUESTIONS FOR WRITING ABOUT RISK AND CHANGE

To write about these questions, in addition to taking supporting evidence from the articles in this Theme, you will need to use evidence from other Themes in *Sourcework* or find additional sources on your own.

1. Choose a current public figure who is admired by some and disliked by others. Discuss whether this person is a hero.

2. How have gender roles influenced the concept of heroes? You can compare gender roles in one culture across a period of history or look at gender roles and heroism in different cultures.

3. Consider a current or historical event involving social conflict or change. Analyze the people at the forefront of this change. In what ways could these people be considered heroes?

4. How can microcredit and social business enterprises help create social change that is fair and lasting?

5. Find a project currently underway where an individual or a small group is attempting to change the world for the better. Look for such projects at the

websites of nonprofit organizations, such as Global Envision or Habitat for Humanity, among many others. How are the changes being made?

6. How could some of the strategies of nonviolent action be used to combat terrorism?

7. How can some of the strategies of nonviolent action be used to guarantee that globalization is a constructive change for nations and for individuals?

GLOBALIZATION:
Changes That Draw Us Together

GETTING STARTED 1

Globalization is a word frequently heard, but not easily defined. To begin thinking about how this idea is changing our world, bring a short article about globalization to class. Be prepared to give a brief oral summary of the article.

1. In class, working in a small group, take turns talking about your article briefly. Focus on answering these questions:
   • What is the article about?
   • How does this illustrate globalization?

2. After about 15 minutes of listening to your classmates' summaries, choose one article from your group to present to the class.

3. When it is your group's turn to present the article, have a member of your group put notes on the board that outline what happened in the article. Also note why the group thinks it is an example of globalization.

4. When all the groups have presented their articles, work together as a class to brainstorm a definition of globalization.

GETTING STARTED 2

For homework, do an Internet search on the author(s) of each article in this Theme. In class, share what you found.

Introduction to the Theme

Humans have always been curious about each other and looked for ways to exchange things and ideas. With our rapid systems of communication today, this trading happens constantly—sometimes even instantaneously—and influences almost everyone in the world on a daily basis, changing how we think and behave. Globalization, the term often applied to these economic and cultural transformations that are making all the world's citizens more closely connected, means different things to different people. The first two articles in this Theme present several views of the meaning of globalization.

For some, the interconnected world is an exciting opportunity to find fresh ideas, create new products, and blend traditions. Exchanging and combining the arts of many cultures can lead to greater appreciation of diversity and inspiration for new art. Others, however, think that globalization brings damaging changes in lifestyle and creates a dull monoculture. The next three articles look at the influence of globalization on culture.

Increased consumption of goods and growing demands for services, which are both a cause and a result of global interconnectedness, affect everyone. In some ways, it divides more than it unites; it widens the gap between the rich and the poor, between the "haves" and the "have-nots." On the other hand, this interconnectedness could put more money in the hands of more people and lead to better education and higher standards of living for many. Besides the direct economic effect, rising consumerism impacts the environment and, thus, the future quality of life on earth. The last three articles address the challenges of creating a world that is sustainable both socially and environmentally.

Framing Articles: What is Globalization?

Spiritual Perspectives on Globalization

Ira Rifkin

2003

Skylight Paths Publishers

What is globalization, and why do so many people—including many people of faith who see ultimate good, and even God's hand, in the process—share concerns about how it is unfolding, and, like the demonstrators, blame it for so much?

Abstract as it may be, globalization can be said to encompass certain elements. In the economic sphere, globalization refers to the recent decades' unprecedented flow of capital and commerce across national borders, leading to the hegemony gained by international financial markets and multinational corporations, abetted by transnational agencies and organizations such as the WEF, the World Bank, the World Trade Organization (WTO), and the International Monetary Fund (IMF).

On a cultural level, globalization refers to the spread of what has been pejoratively termed "McWorld"—shorthand for the Western-oriented (many say American) global mono-culture that is burying countless regional and even national cultural expressions in an avalanche of MTV, Disney, Michael Jordan endorsements, and, of course, McDonald's-style fast food.

On an individual level, globalization is about the promotion of consumer values that feed on the perception that happiness is rooted in material progress, that choice equals the highest freedom, and that being well connected is more important than being deeply connected. All of this has been pushed at a dizzying pace by the extraordinary recent advances in information and travel technology that seem to mock time and space. The end result is the transformation of human society to a degree and in ways not yet truly understood but deeply disturbing nonetheless to many who worry about the growing divide between rich and poor nations, the commodification of life's basic resources, and consumerism's steady ascendancy.

In truth, though, the only things new about globalization are the phrase and the speed at which it is now occurring. Humans, in the parlance of the day, seem hardwired to seek the next valley and make it their own. We've been spreading around the globe and taking over since our ancient ancestors ventured out of Africa, perhaps as long as a hundred thousand years ago. Hunters and gatherers did it in their day. The early agriculturalists slashed and burned their way across the landscape, in some cases leaving it irrevocably changed. Greeks, Romans, Arabs, Chinese, Columbus, the conquistadors, and the Hudson Bay Company all pushed the globalization envelope, even if they did not always understand the globe's full breadth.

But globalization as we know it may be traced to a 1944 meeting in Bretton Woods, New Hampshire, at which representatives from forty-five nations sketched out a plan for post-World War II economic recovery. In doing so, they created the IMF and the International Bank for Reconstruction and Development, better known as the World Bank—institutions that critics charge are responsible in good measure for the

economic, environmental, and cultural fiascos they cite as proof of globalization's
systematic wrongs. International trade rules were liberalized and the flow of
40 capital turned national borders into sieves. Soon, new media and new modes of
transportation revolutionized the way we defined foreign and distant. A global village
was upon us that more and more resembled an American buffet table-even if chilies,
chutney, and kimchee were added to the mix.

World Publics Welcome Global Trade—But Not Immigration

Pew Global Attitudes Project
October 4, 2007
http://pewglobal.org/

The publics of the world broadly embrace key tenets of economic globalization
but fear the disruptions and downsides of participating in the global economy. In
rich countries as well as poor ones, most people endorse free trade, multinational
corporations and free markets. However, the latest Pew Global Attitudes survey of
5 more than 45,000 people finds they are concerned about inequality, threats to their
culture, threats to the environment and threats posed by immigration. Together, these
results reveal an evolving world view on globalization that is nuanced, ambivalent,
and sometimes inherently contradictory.

There are signs that enthusiasm for economic globalization is waning in the
10 West—Americans and Western Europeans are less supportive of international trade
and multinational companies than they were five years ago. In contrast, there is near
universal approval of global trade among the publics of rising Asian economic powers
China and India.

The survey also finds that globalization is only one of several wide-ranging social
15 and economic forces that are rapidly reshaping the world. Strong majorities in
developing countries endorse core democratic values, but people are less likely to say
their countries are ensuring free speech, delivering honest elections or providing fair
trials to all. Conflicting views on the relationship between religion and morality sharply
divide the world. But on gender issues, the survey finds that a global consensus has
20 emerged on the importance of education for both girls and boys.

Costs and Benefits of Globalization

Overwhelmingly, the surveyed publics see the benefits of increasing global
commerce and free market economies. In all 47 nations included in the survey,
large majorities believe that international trade is benefiting their countries. For
25 the most part, the multinational corporations that dominate global commerce
receive favorable ratings. Nonetheless, since 2002 enthusiasm for trade has declined
significantly in the United States, Italy, France and Britain, and views of multinationals
are less positive in Western countries where economic growth has been relatively
modest in recent years.

30 In most countries, majorities believe that people are better off under capitalism,
even if it means that some may be rich and others poor. Support for free markets has
increased notably over the past five years in Latin American and Eastern European
nations, where increased satisfaction with income and perceptions of personal
progress are linked to higher per capita incomes. But there are widely shared
35 concerns about the free flow of people, ideas and resources that globalization

entails. In nearly every country surveyed, people worry about losing their traditional culture and national identities, and they feel their way of life needs protection against foreign influences. Importantly, the poll finds widespread concerns about immigration. Moreover, there is a strong link between immigration fears and concerns
40 about threats to a country's culture and traditions. Those who worry the most about immigration also tend to see the greatest need for protecting traditional ways of life against foreign influences.

Immigration Fears

In both affluent countries in the West and in the developing world, people are
45 concerned about immigration. Large majorities in nearly every country surveyed express the view that there should be greater restriction of immigration and tighter control of their country's borders. Although Western publics remain concerned about immigration, they generally are less likely to back tighter controls today than they were five years ago, despite heated controversies over this issue in both Europe
50 and the United States over the last few years. In Italy, however, support for greater restrictions has increased—87% now support more controls on immigration, up seven points from 2002.

Concerns about immigration have increased in other countries as well, perhaps most notably in Jordan, where an influx of Iraqi refugees has raised the salience of
55 this issue—70% of Jordanians back tighter immigration controls, up from 48% five years ago.

Religion and Social Issues

Global publics are sharply divided over the relationship between religion and morality. In much of Africa, Asia, and the Middle East, there is a strong consensus that belief in
60 God is necessary for morality and good values. Throughout much of Europe, however, majorities think morality is achievable without faith. Meanwhile, opinions are more mixed in the Americas, including in the United States, where 57% say that one must believe in God to have good values and be moral, while 41% disagree.

The survey finds a strong relationship between a country's religiosity and its
65 economic status. In poorer nations, religion remains central to the lives of individuals, while secular perspectives are more common in richer nations. This relationship generally is consistent across regions and countries, although there are some exceptions, including most notably the United States, which is a much more religious country than its level of prosperity would indicate. Other nations deviate from the
70 pattern as well, including the oil-rich, predominantly Muslim—and very religious— kingdom of Kuwait.

Globalization and Culture

Globalization and Local Culture

no date

The Levin Institute, State University of New York

http://www.globalization101.org/issue_main/culture/

The globalization of the production and distribution of goods and services is a welcome development for many people in that it offers them access to products that they would not otherwise have. However, some are concerned that the changes brought about by globalization threaten the viability of locally made products and
5   the people who produce them. For example, the new availability of foreign foods in a market—often at cheaper prices—can displace local farmers who have traditionally earned a living by working their small plots of family-owned land and selling their goods locally.

Globalization, of course, does more than simply increase the availability of foreign-
10   made consumer products and disrupt traditional producers. It is also increasing international trade in cultural products and services, such as movies, music, and publications. The expansion of trade in cultural products is increasing the exposure of all societies to foreign cultures. And the exposure to foreign cultural goods frequently brings about changes in local cultures, values, and traditions. Although there is no
15   consensus on the consequences of globalization on national cultures, many people believe that a people's exposure to foreign culture can undermine their own cultural identity.

One of the principal concerns about the new globalization of culture that is supposedly taking place is that it not only leads to a homogenization of world culture,
20   but also that it largely represents the "Americanization" of world cultures. The spread of American corporations abroad has various consequences on local cultures, some very visible, and others less obvious. For example, the influence of American companies on other countries' cultural identity can be seen with regard to food, which matters on two levels. First, food itself is in many countries an integral aspect of the culture.
25   Second, food restaurants can influence the mores and habits in societies where they operate. The French are proud of having a unique cuisine that reflects their culture, such as crepes and pastries. Because of their pride in their cuisine, some French people are concerned that U.S. restaurant chains crowd out their own products with fast food. Some French people would argue that fast food does not belong in French society and
30   is of lower quality than their own.

Moreover, restaurant chains not only affect eating habits, but they also influence the traditions and mores in countries where they are located. Starbucks causes cultural concerns in Italy because of the association that Italians make between coffee and leisurely sidewalk cafes. Coffee in Italy is more than a drink; it is part of the way of life
35   and Italian mores. While in the United States it is common for people to buy takeaway coffee for drinking in the street or office, in Italy people usually prefer to relax and chat with peers while drinking coffee. Coffee shops offer a personal, friendly atmosphere that many Italians believe a large chain could not provide. Similarly, many people would prefer to frequent coffee shops that are each unique, while Starbucks offers a
40   standard formula.

Another example can be seen with the introduction of the McDonald's restaurant in China. In the past, it was not considered proper for Chinese children to buy food with their own money, as they were expected to eat what was put in front of them. Because of McDonald's marketing to children, however, kids developed an interest
45 in choosing their own food when going to McDonald's. After some time, it became more of a common practice for children to buy their food with their own money. McDonald's also popularized birthday parties in China. In the past, festivities marking a child's birth date were not celebrated in China. McDonald's established a new tradition by successfully promoting American-style birthday parties as part of its marketing
50 strategy. This example may appear trivial, but it shows that the spread of American companies in foreign countries can have unexpected consequences.

Fittingly enough, the sociologist George Ritzer coined the term *McDonaldization*. In his book *The McDonaldization of Society*, Ritzer states that "the principles of the fast-food restaurant are coming to dominate more and more sectors of American
55 society as well as of the rest of the world." Statistics show that within the last fifty years, McDonalds has expanded to over 31,000 restaurants worldwide.

McDonaldization, Ritzer argues, is a result of globalization and, ultimately, leads to global uniformity, influencing local habits and traditions. Take, for example, the previously mentioned example of Starbucks coffee disrupting the traditional coffee
60 culture in Italy. This sometimes leads to negative reactions, such as in the case of the Starbucks coffeehouse in the Forbidden City in central Beijing. This particular Starbucks branch, which opened in 2000, was shut down in 2007 due to heavy protests. Critics called it a stain on China's historical legacy.

Concerns that globalization leads to a dominance of US customs and values are
65 also present with regard to films and the entertainment industry more broadly. This is the case with French films in France, for example. As will be discussed later in the brief, governments from countries like France have attempted to intervene in the functioning of the market to try to protect their local cultural industries, by taking measures such as restricting the number of foreign films that can be shown. But if a
70 government imposes domestic films, TV shows, or books onto its people, it limits their choice to consume what they prefer. In other words, the government is effectively saying that it does not trust its people to make the choices that are right for them.

Throughout history, cultures have changed and evolved. Globalization may accelerate cultural change. However, because change is driven by the choice of
75 consumers, the elements of a particular culture will inevitably reflect consumer choice.

The Deadly Noodle

Michael Hastings, Stefan Thiel & Dana Thomas
January 20, 2003
Newsweek, Vol. 141, Issue 3

Greasy burgers and processed food may be the most insidious forms of American cultural imperialism. They're making the world fat.

Of all the ways France has resisted the cultural imperialism of the United States, it has arguably achieved its greatest success in the realm of food. Not only is French cuisine the envy of the world, but culinary tradition has allowed the French to consume their
5   sauce velouté and crème brûlée without succumbing to the ills of over consumption that plague the land of burgers, fries and angioplasty. In recent years, however, statistics

have begun to reveal that France is vulnerable to America's junk-food influence after all. Although southern, rural France remains steadfastly healthy, its more urban neighbors
10 to the north suffer more from eating-related problems, not least a rise in childhood obesity. "We can't point our finger at any one thing," says Mariette Gerber, a nutritional scientist at the National Institute for Medical Research and Health in Montpellier. "It's a modern way of life, very urban. And it has come from the United States."

France's growing fat problem underscores how inexorable the Americanization of
15 food habits has become. The problem is even more acute in the developing world, where the taste for American fast-food products like McDonald's hamburgers and Coca-Cola has long been fashionable. Urbanization is leading to more sedentary lifestyles in many places. And more and more, even traditional foods are being prepared from processed flour and other ingredients that yield more calories and less
20 healthy roughage. Nobody ever thought resisting the export of American diets would be easy. But the trend has turned out to be more insidious and more widespread than previously thought. "It's very easy to blame globalization, or the big brands like Coca-Cola or McDonald's," says Derek Yach, executive director of the World Health Organization's disease prevention, nutrition, diet and physical-fitness program. "But
25 the problem goes much, much deeper."

Diet and exercise habits may be complex, but the basic recipe for health problems is simple: a rise in caloric intake and a decline in calorie-burning activities. The number of overweight people in the United States doubled in the past 20 years to 60 percent, and Europe and Asia are catching up. In some developing countries, obesity
30 is increasing faster than in America—the rate is three times higher in Mexico and Egypt. Each year more new cases of diabetes arise in China and India than in all other countries combined.

Where are all the extra calories coming from? One surprising source is the raw grains and other ingredients used for cooking traditional—formerly healthy—dishes. When
35 crops are grown in big farms and processed en masse, much of their nutrient value is taken out, and their "caloric density" rises. Even the noodle, a staple of many traditional diets, is no longer as healthy as it once was. In China, for instance, home-cooked noodles used to be made from whole-grains, ground by hand. Now, households use factory-made "refined" flour, from which the grain husks have been discarded along
40 with nutrients like fiber and minerals. What remains are simple carbohydrates that the body more easily turns into fat.

Cooking oils have taken a similar turn for the worse. Back in the 1960s, Japanese and American researchers discovered an inexpensive way to extract oil from vegetables. Westerners and developing countries alike adopted vegetable oils as a cheaper
45 alternative to butter, healthy if used in moderation. The problem is, the oil is so cheap that in places like India it's used to excess. It's not uncommon for Indian cooks to use vegetable oil for breakfast, lunch and supper, and to throw in an extra 10 or 20 grams to enhance a dish's flavor.

Sugar is another culprit. Diets in some developing countries contain on average
50 about 300 more calories a day than they did 20 years ago, according to Barry Popkin, professor of nutrition at the University of North Carolina. Some of the extra sugar comes from soda, but a bigger factor is the growing adoption of Western manufacturing practices, which allow local companies to sweeten bread and other staples. Brazil now consumes more sugar per capita than even the United States.

55   No part of the world, no matter how remote, is immune from empty calories. Over
the course of 30 years, the native population of Samoa has fallen victim to rampant
weight gain—today more than half its residents are clinically obese. James Bindon, a
biological anthropologist at Alabama University, traced one of the causes to a fondness
for tins of corned beef imported from England. Similar trends have been observed
60   in Fiji. "Where in the past they produced their own fruits and vegetables, now they're
swamped with canned soda and mutton fat imported from New Zealand," says Yach
of WHO. "Call it the Coca-Colafication of the Pacific Islands."

People in both developed and developing countries are also doing less and less
physical activity. It's the couch-potato syndrome. Rather than riding their bicycles
65   and working the fields, people sit on assembly lines, ride in cars and spend their free
time watching television—95 percent of Chinese households now have a TV set.
"We export our jobs, and our wage-labor patterns," says Bindon. "It's a culture-bound
syndrome."

The syndrome is raising health-care costs—$100 billion for obese children in the
70   United States, estimates the Centers for Disease Control. What about the 35 million
overweight kids around the world, not to mention 300 million adults? "The cost
of health care—to feed the hungry and pay for the medical bills of obesity—is
staggering," says Weight Watchers International chief science officer Karen Miller-
Kovach. Unfortunately, obesity and all the illnesses it entails hit the poor hardest of
75   all. High-caloric junk food is cheap enough to afford even on a low income. And the
well-heeled and well-educated tend to be better about hitting the gym. In developing
countries, those leisure activities aren't even an option yet. The popularity of Western-
style food has thus led to an alarming trend: obese parents and undernourished
children living under the same roof. "It's a very attractive lifestyle," says Popkin. But it's
80   killing people all the same.

Paths of Globalization: From the Berbers to Bach

Yo-Yo Ma

Spring 2008

New Perspectives Quarterly

*Yo-Yo Ma is one of the world's most renowned cellists. This article is based on a talk he gave
at the World Economic Forum, in Davos, Switzerland, in January.*

DAVOS—Over the past 30 years as a professional cellist, I have spent the equivalent of
two full decades on the road, both performing and learning about musical traditions
5   and cultures. My travels have convinced me that in our globalized world, cultural
traditions form an essential framework for identity, social stability and compassionate
interaction.

A world changing so quickly as ours is bound to create cultural insecurity, to make
people question their place. Globalization so often seems to threaten the identity
10   of the individual, by subjecting us to someone else's rules. That naturally makes us
nervous, since these rules ask us to change our time-honored habits. So the critical
question for today's global leaders is: How can habits and cultures evolve to join a
bigger planet, without sacrificing distinct identities and individual pride?

My musical journeys have reminded me that the interactions brought about by
15   globalization don't just destroy culture; they can create new culture and invigorate
and spread traditions that have existed for ages. It's not unlike the ecological term

"edge effect," which is used to describe what happens when two different ecosystems meet, for example, the forest and savannah. At that interface, where there is the least density and the greatest diversity of life forms, each living thing can draw from the core
20 of the two ecosystems. Sometimes the most interesting things happen at the edge. The intersections there can reveal unexpected connections.

Culture is a fabric composed of gifts from every corner of the world. One way of discovering the world is by digging deeply into its traditions. In music, for instance, at the core of any cellist's repertoire are the Cello Suites by Bach. At the heart of each
25 suite is a dance movement called the sarabande. The dance originated with music of the North African Berbers, where it was a slow, sensual dance. It next appeared in Spain, where it was banned because it was considered lewd and lascivious. Spaniards brought it to the Americas, but it also traveled on to France, where it became a courtly dance. In the 1720s, Bach incorporated the sarabande as a movement in his Cello
30 Suites. Today, I play Bach, a Paris-born American musician of Chinese parentage. So who really owns the sarabande? Each culture has adopted the music, investing it with specific meaning, but each culture must share ownership: it belongs to us all.

In 1998, I founded the Silk Road Project to study the flow of ideas among the many cultures between the Mediterranean and the Pacific over several thousand years. When
35 the Silk Road Ensemble performs, we try to bring much of the world together on one stage. Its members are a peer group of virtuosos, masters of living traditions, whether European, Arabic, Azeri, Armenian, Persian, Russian, Central Asian, Indian, Mongolian, Chinese, Korean or Japanese. They all generously share their knowledge and are curious and eager to learn about other forms of expression.

40 Over the last several years, we have found that every tradition is the result of successful invention. One of the best ways to ensure the survival of traditions is by organic evolution, using all the tools available to us in the present day. Through recording and film; through residencies in museums, universities, design schools and cities; through performances from classroom to stadium, ensemble musicians,
45 including myself, are learning valuable skills. Returning home, we share these skills with others, ensuring that our traditions will have a seat at the cultural table.

We have found that performing a tradition abroad energizes the practitioners in the home country. Most of all, we have developed a passion for each others' music and developed a bond of mutual respect, friendship and trust that is palpable every time
50 we're on stage. This joyous interaction is such a desirable common greater goal that we have always been able to resolve any differences through amicable dialogue. As we open up to each other, we form a bridge into unfamiliar traditions, banishing the fear that often accompanies change and dislocation. In other words, when we broaden our lens on the world, we better understand ourselves, our own lives and culture. We share
55 more in common with the far reaches of our small planet than we realize.

Finding these shared cultures is important, but not just for art's sake. So many of our cities—not just London, New York or Tokyo, but now even the mid-sized cities— are experiencing waves of immigration. How will we assimilate groups of people with their own unique habits? Must immigration inevitably lead to resistance and conflict,
60 as it has in the past? What about the Turkish population in Germany, Albanians in Italy, North Africans in Spain and France? A thriving cultural engine can help us figure out how groups can peacefully meld, without sacrificing individuality and identity. This is not about political correctness. It's about acknowledging what is precious to someone, and the gifts that every culture has given to our world.

65 ## What Kind of Education for What Kind of World?

What kind of education will prepare a student to live on such a planet? What tools do people need to become architects of their own lives? In a highly competitive hierarchical world driven by tests and measurable results, I would like to propose four priorities for education that are hard to measure and easy to ignore, yet they are vitally

70 important and within reach for all of us.

My conclusions are drawn from my work as a musician, and my first priority is based on a common goal that musicians and teachers share: to make the communication of their content memorable. By memorable, I mean the listeners or students become transported by their experience of the music or subject. The content, then, remains

75 active and accessible in their minds and can grow and connect to future experiences. Our stories will be different, but I'm sure that each of us can recall a teacher whose inspiration transformed our lives.

Content that is memorable becomes a key ingredient in the second priority, passion-driven education. Education driven by passion awakens us to a world bigger

80 than ourselves and makes us curious. Learning becomes self-sustaining as it transforms from a requirement to a desire. Students who are passionate are a pleasure to teach, and teachers who are passionate share their knowledge generously. In fact, teaching becomes learning and vice versa. Passion-driven education liberates students and gives them the self-confidence to discover who they are as individuals and how they

85 fit in the world.

The next priority is the development of a disciplined imagination. Imagination draws on all of our intelligences, senses, experiences and intuition to construct possible scenarios. Through imagination, we are able to transcend our present local reality and envision distant futures. It allows us to think not only about the tools people need

90 today, but about the tools our children will need to contribute to the world they will share. Imagination is the great engine that powers the arts and sciences, and it is an available resource for all to use.

Disciplined imagination leads me to the final priority: empathy. To be able to put oneself in another's shoes without prejudgment is an essential skill. Empathy

95 comes when you understand something deeply and can thus make unexpected connections. These parallels bring you closer to things that would otherwise seem far away. In our world of specialization, compartmentalization and myriad responsibilities, empathy is the ultimate quality that acknowledges our identity as members of the human family.

100 In our complex world, it is crucial that educators have the tools to help students understand not only their own lives but also the broadest possible horizons. An education that incorporates the four priorities of making the subject memorable, inspiring passion-driven learning, developing a disciplined imagination and fostering empathy will result in citizens who are active participants in shaping a future of which

105 we can all be proud.

Globalization and Sustainability

If Poor Get Richer, Does World See Progress?

Brad Knickerbocker

January 22, 2004

The Christian Science Monitor

www.csmonitor.com

In Shanghai this month, bicyclists found themselves banned from certain portions of main thoroughfares. By next year, this ubiquitous two-wheel mode of transportation will have been kicked off such roads altogether. Why? To make way for all the new cars—11,000 more every week—pouring onto Chinese streets and highways.

5   A sure sign of growing affluence in the developing world? Without a doubt. A consumer trend portending a better world? That depends on one's point of view.

"Rising consumption has helped meet basic needs and create jobs," says Christopher Flavin, president of the Worldwatch Institute, a Washington, D.C. think tank. "But as we enter a new century, this unprecedented consumer appetite is undermining the

10   natural systems we all depend on and making it even harder for the world's poor to meet their basic needs."

That's the message underlying Worldwatch's annual "State of the World" report, an influential book-length collection of data-packed chapters that has been used by supporters as ammunition and by critics as a pincushion since 1984.

15   This year's report focuses on the growing global "consumer class"—defined as individuals whose "purchasing power parity" in local currency is more than $7,000 a year (roughly the poverty level in Western Europe). As economies expand—accelerated by globalization that has opened up markets, greater efficiency in manufacturing, and advancing technologies—that consumer class has grown rapidly. It's the main reason

20   there are more than 1 billion cellphones in the world today.

The consumer class now includes more than 1.7 billion people. High percentages in North America, Western Europe, and Japan (85 to 90 percent) are no surprise.

But nearly half of all consumers now are in developing nations. China and India alone account for 362 million of those shoppers, more than in all of Western Europe.

25   That can be a good thing to the extent that it improves health rates, education levels, and social conditions (like the status of women).

"The almost 3 billion people worldwide who barely survive on less than $2 a day will need to ramp up their consumption in order to satisfy basic needs for food, clean water, and sanitation," says Brian Halweil, codirector of Worldwatch's "State of the World

30   2004" project. "And in China, the rush to meet surging consumer demand is stimulating the economy, creating jobs, and attracting foreign investment."

But there are troubling indicators here as well, say Worldwatch researchers:

- Damage to forests, wetlands, ocean fisheries, and other natural areas as resources are used and pollution created.

35   - Higher levels of obesity, personal debt, and chronic time shortages as people work longer hours to satisfy the demand for consumer goods.

- Indications that increased consumption doesn't necessarily mean a better quality of life. In the United States, for example, average personal income more than doubled between 1957 and 2002.

40
- There now are more cars than licensed drivers, and the typical house is 38 percent bigger than it was in 1975, even though fewer people live in it. But when asked to rate how they feel about their lives, the same portion of Americans as a generation ago—only about one-third—describe themselves as "very happy."

- Growing disparities between rich and poor. More than 1 billion people
45   still do not have reasonable access to safe drinking water. More than twice that number live without basic sanitation. (It's estimated that hunger and malnutrition could be eliminated globally for less than is spent on pet food in Europe and the US; universal literacy could be achieved for one-third of what is spent annually on perfumes.)

50   On the other hand, critics argue, the swelling numbers of consumers reflect the improvement in material conditions that has paralleled the progress of nations since the dawn of civilization. And historically, when Malthus and other analysts pointed to factors that would limit future growth, human ingenuity has found ways around those obstacles, these critics point out.

55   "Rather than contributing to global destruction and third-world poverty, consumerism actually promotes technologies that serve to better environmental and human well-being," says Ezra Finkle of the Competitive Enterprise Institute in Washington, D.C.

The question is: Will the growing tide of new consumers in the developing world—
60 joining an increasingly aware body of consumers who've known relative affluence all along—contribute to the solution or simply add to the problem?

The Environmental Benefits of Globalization

John A. Charles
July 14, 2004
Globalenvision.org

Environmental activists who criticize free trade often make two arguments. First, they criticize the American lifestyle as environmentally "unsustainable" and fear that adoption of similar values by other cultures through globalization would result in catastrophic shortages of finite natural resources. As summarized by environmental
5   writer Alan Thein Durning, "If people in third world countries lived the same lifestyle as the average American, we'd need seven more earths" to provide all the natural resources.

While these are legitimate concerns, there is little evidence to support either argument.

10 Is the American Lifestyle Unsustainable?

Many "sustainability" advocates start from the premise that an open, dynamic economy is inherently unsustainable because producers and consumers are primarily concerned with their own self-interest. Without a centralized control mechanism, it is argued, the economy expands infinitely while the earth's resources are finite.

15   Thus, promoting capitalism on a global scale will only accelerate the process towards eventual collapse.

Fortunately, empirical trends of the past 50-75 years suggest a very different conclusion. Economic indicators show that the U.S. economy is becoming steadily more efficient and less polluting over time, and there is no reason this trend should 20   not continue indefinitely.

Measuring Sustainability

The most direct measure of sustainability is the amount of energy consumed per unit of economic output. If an economic system takes increasing amounts of energy over time to produce the same unit of output, then it's unlikely to sustain itself. On the other 25   hand, an economy that actually does more with less energy each year is one that is built for the long haul.

The U.S. economy has shown a remarkable drop in energy intensity during the past 50 years. Between 1949 and 2000, energy consumption per dollar of Gross Domestic Product (GDP) dropped steadily from 20.63 thousand Btu to 10.57. In other words, at 30   the beginning of the new millennium, we were able to produce the same economic output that we had in 1949 using only half as much energy.

This is an important indicator of sustainability, but there are many others as well:

- *Air quality.* Between 1970 and 1997, U.S. population increased 31 percent, vehicle miles traveled increased 127 percent, and gross domestic product
35   increased 114 percent—yet total air pollution actually decreased by about 31 percent.

- *Water quality.* In 1972, approximately 36 percent of American streams were usable for fishing and/or swimming. This had increased to 64 percent by 1982 and 85 percent by 1994.

40   - *Timber supply.* The net growth of timber has exceeded the levels of timber harvest every decade since 1952. According to the U.S. Forest Service, we currently grow about 22 million net new cubic feet of wood per year, while harvesting only about 16.5 million, a net increase of 36 percent annually.

- *Agricultural production.* In the past 30 years, the production of food grains in the United States increased by 82 percent, while the amount of land used
45   for growing remained relatively constant. Planted areas for all crops today in the U.S. is actually lower than it was in 1930; this has freed up land for other noncommodity uses such as wildlife habitat and outdoor recreation.

- *Availability of mineral resources.* Resources that were once considered
50   scarce are now known to be abundant. Between 1950 and 2000, the proven reserves of bauxite went up 1,786 percent. Reserves of chromium increased 5,143 percent, and quantities of copper, iron ore, nickel, tin and zinc all went up by more than 125 percent. The 1970s forecasts of doom for oil proved to be spectacularly wrong; the retail price of gasoline in the late 1990's (adjusted
55   for inflation) was cheaper than at any time in history.

The rise in living standards has had tremendous public health benefits as well. The infant mortality rate in the United States dropped from 29.2 per thousand in 1950 to 7.1 in 1997. Since 1980, the death rate for cancer has dropped more than

60 11 percent for individuals between the ages of 25 and 64. As a result of these and other similar trends, the life expectancy for all Americans rose from 70.8 years in 1970 to 75.8 by 1995.

Wealthier is Healthier

Although it's counter-intuitive to many environmental advocates, rising affluence is an important prerequisite to environmental improvement. Empirical research first
65 published in 1992 by the World Bank showed that the statistical relationship between per capita income and certain kinds of pollution is roughly shaped as an inverted U. In other words, economic growth is bad for air and water pollution at the initial stages of industrialization, but later on reduces pollution as countries become rich enough to pay for control technologies.

70 Wealth creation also changes consumer demand for environmental quality. The richer people become, the more they tend to value environmental objectives such as safe drinking water, proper sewage disposal, and clean air. Once these basic needs are met, they begin raising the bar by demanding such "amenities" as scenic vistas and habitat for non-game wildlife. As their income rises, they increasingly have the financial
75 resources to act on these values by imposing appropriate regulations on polluters and purchasing technologies that provide environmental benefits.

A recent report by the World Trade Organization reinforces these points. The report concludes: "One reason why environmental protection is lagging in many countries is low incomes. Countries that live on the margin may simply not be able to afford to
80 set aside resources for pollution abatement … If poverty is at the core of the problem, economic growth will be part of the solution, to the extent that it allows countries to shift gears from more immediate concerns to long run sustainability issues. Indeed, at least some empirical evidence suggests that pollution increases at the early stages of development but decreases after a certain income level has been reached…."

85 Many so-called "sustainability" advocates argue for greater central control of the economy through government intervention, but every place this has been tried has proven to be a failure. Some of the most polluted cities on the face of the earth are in countries formerly or currently under socialist rule. Leaders of the former Soviet Union and East Germany were as confident in their ability to run the economy as local
90 sustainable development advocates are in Oregon, but they found out that eliminating market competition also eliminated incentives to develop innovative technologies that use resources more efficiently.

Conclusion

It is human nature to seek out others and exchange ideas, products and services.
95 Attempting to limit that impulse, whether in the name of environmental sustainability, fighting communism, or some other moral crusade, is likely to be a costly and futile undertaking. Perhaps nowhere has this been more vividly demonstrated than in Cuba, where the U.S. has enforced a trade embargo for more than 40 years. Despite the embargo, American consumer products are widely available in the Cuban underground
100 economy, and American dollars tend to be the currency of choice. Meanwhile, the primary purpose of the embargo—to oust Fidel Castro—has obviously failed.

The evidence shows that our preference for free trade is not in conflict with our desire for environmental quality. On the contrary, income derived from free trade is a prerequisite for most types of environmental gain. Wealthier people place greater

105 value on environmental amenities, and they have the resources to pay for them. True
environmental advocates should embrace global wealth creation as a fundamental
strategy for achieving environmental sustainability.

*Is Ethics the Missing Link?**

Yolanda Kakabadse

2002

UN Chronicle no. 3

Many governments have decided that liberalizing trade and opening up markets is
the path to prosperity. And, indeed, globalization has brought undoubted benefits
to many countries in all parts of the world. But its benefits have been very unevenly
distributed and as many as one billion of the world's people eke out a living on less
5 than $1 per day. It is not surprising that social tensions are rising as people are so poor
that they need to share a television with their neighbours and watch programmes
celebrating conspicuous consumption by the privileged few.

Globalization has also an unnoticed environmental flaw. Throughout history,
people have been forced to recognize environmental limits because abusing their
10 local systems of resources would immediately influence their lives for the worse. On
the other hand, treating resources with respect and harvesting in a sustainable way
immediately reinforce environmentally appropriate behaviour. But with globalized trade,
the consumers—or at least those fortunate enough to be able to consume—have no
indication of how their consumption is affecting the environment. It is an easy matter
15 for over-exploitation in one part of the world to be financially justifiable by providing
inexpensive goods to growing markets in other parts. But when a mangrove is destroyed
to make a shrimp pond in Thailand, India or Ecuador, the consumers of shrimp salad
in New York or crevettes grillees in Paris or prawn tempura in Tokyo have no idea that
productive mangrove ecosystems have been destroyed, disrupting the way of life of
20 coastal peoples. Even worse, once the ponds have ended their productive life after a few
years, the people no longer have the other resources of the coastal zone upon which
to depend. The consumers simply shift to prawns grown in new shrimp ponds in Viet
Nam, Mozambique or Nicaragua, and the local people suffer. Perhaps the problem is
fundamentally an ethical one, Peru's Francisco Sagasti points out that we are all part of
25 a disintegrated, fractured global order— all connected and at the same time divided
among peoples, ethnic groups and religions—sharing no common understanding of
what we mean by quality of life, equity or development.

We are forcing people to treat their environment as a marketplace, not as the place
where they live. Lawyers are becoming the new priests of modern society as they
30 negotiate over "intellectual property rights" that once were held sacred but freely shared.

Perhaps the concept of sustainability can help us to live in a more reasonable
balance with the environment. We need to find ways of giving higher priority to being
rather than having; consuming responsibly; preventing environmental damage rather
than remediating problems we have created; harnessing science and technology
35 for creation rather than destruction; globalizing values, such as inter-generational
solidarity, especially towards the most vulnerable groups— women and children;
and promoting the concept of diversity as a value as important as freedom. These are
the kinds of changes in our ethical perspective that will be required to ensure truly
sustainable forms of development.

*This article is from a British publication and contains some British spellings.

40   We need to redefine globalization, so that it addresses not only market needs but also seeks to provide appropriate support for social equity, cultural diversity and a healthy environment. Of course, all of these ideals need to be defined locally, helping to meet the needs and aspirations of the people whose welfare is dependent on the politics and policies of those who govern. The interests of the planet in all its diversity
45   must be globalized along with a code of ethics and principles, such as those contained in the Earth Charter. This most certainly does not mean that sustainable development needs to be the same everywhere. On the contrary, sustainable development needs to be a local phenomenon that celebrates the diversity of cultural values, promotes the participation of the people whose lives are being affected, and promotes the
50   forms of government where elected officials listen to the voices of the many, and where solidarity, cooperation, equity and respect replace selfishness, antagonism, injustice and dominance. In short, sustainable development provides an alternative vision where natural systems are intimately linked to the systems created by people to allow life to continue to flourish in many forms. The values of sustainability are the
55   values of life, and this is what we must celebrate at the World Summit on Sustainable Development.

QUESTIONS FOR WRITING ABOUT GLOBALIZATION

For each writing assignment, use evidence from several of the articles in this Theme to support your position. You may also use evidence from your own experience or additional sources you find.

1. What is globalization?

2. What are the positive and negative aspects of globalization?

3. Which is a more widespread consequence of globalization, cultural diversity or a global monoculture?

4. How does globalization influence health and lifestyle?

5. What is consumerism and how is it connected to globalization?

6. How does globalization affect the environment?

7. What is sustainable development and how does it protect local cultures and environments?

MORE QUESTIONS FOR WRITING ABOUT GLOBALIZATION

To write about these questions, in addition to taking supporting evidence from the articles in this Theme, you will need to use evidence from other Themes in *Sourcework* or find additional sources on your own.

1. How does globalization affect human rights?

2. Compare the ways globalization has affected women's rights and opportunities in both developing and developed countries.

3. How can the world community band together to enforce standards for environmental protection?

4. What responsibilities do transnational corporations have toward the people, culture, and environment in the countries where they work?

5. Electronic media make the same information available worldwide almost instantaneously. How does this increased globalization of information affect social change?

6. How does the Internet influence globalization?

 TECHNOLOGY:
Changing Relationships Between Humans and Machines

GETTING STARTED 1

To begin thinking about the topic of how technology affects us, do the following activity with a small group.

1. Brainstorm a short list of five to ten inventions from any time in history. For this exercise, choose inventions such as electric lighting, rather than discoveries such as electricity. Here are a few ideas to get you started:

   written language   clay pottery

   the wheel   the plow

the airplane   the refrigerator

the firepit   the printing press

the loom   television

2. Choose one or two inventions from your list to present to the class. For each, try to imagine how people living at the time of the invention would have responded to the new way of doing things. Make a list of their possible objections to it and also their reasons for adopting it.

3. When you tell your class about the inventions your group has chosen, have one member of your group be the secretary and take notes on the board.

GETTING STARTED 2

For homework, do an Internet search on the author(s) of each article in this Theme. In class, share what you found.

 # Introduction to the Theme

Innovation has been part of human history since our beginnings, and each new way of doing things has had both its supporters and its detractors. Today, as throughout history, some of us welcome innovations in technology for the benefits they will bring, while others are reluctant to accept new ideas because of the damage they may do. The first two articles in this Theme briefly set out some of the gains and losses that come with the adoption of new technologies.

It can be argued that working with new tools—for example, the car—have actually changed us physically, mentally, and emotionally. Some think this is true of the devices we use to acquire information today, such as cell phones and computers. Using new technology may actually change the way we think or lead us to new addictions. At the same time, these devices may be just what we need to keep pace with a flood of information. The next three articles discuss the interaction between the new information technology and the human mind.

In fact, some people even question what it means to be human in this age of rapidly advancing technology. As robots take on more human tasks, such as care-giving and making military decisions, and humans take on more replacement parts, such as artificial organs and neural implants in our brains, one may wonder if robots are becoming more like humans or humans are becoming more like robots. The last three articles examine the relationships between humans and robots.

Framing Articles: Pros and Cons of Adopting New Technologies

Technology, Progress, and Freedom

Edward W. Younkins

January 2000

The Freeman, Volume 50, Issue 1

http://www.thefreemanonline.org/featured/technology-progress-and-freedom/

Technology represents man's attempt to make life easier. Technological advances improve people's standard of living, increase leisure time, help eliminate poverty, and lead to a greater variety of products. Progress allows people more time to spend on higher-level concerns such as character development, love, religion, and the perfection
5   of one's soul.

If people resisted technological change, they would be expressing their satisfaction with existing levels of disease, hunger, and privation. In addition, without experimentation and change, human existence would be boring; human fulfillment is dependent on novelty, surprise, and creativity.

10   An innovative idea from one man not only contributes to the progress of others, but also creates conditions permitting people to advance even further. Ideas interact in unexpected ways, and innovations are frequently used in unforeseen applications. Technological progress involves a series of stages consisting of experimentation, competition, errors, and feedback.

The Problem of Technology

Peter Augustine Lawler

Summer 2005

Perspectives on Political Science, Volume 34, Number 3

Technology is a problem because we cannot do without it and our use of it clearly makes us both better and worse. Human beings are—among other things— technological or tool-making animals. We use our brains and our freedom to transform nature, and in doing so we transform ourselves. We also have a perverse capacity
5   to make ourselves unhappy and a singular pride in our misery. We are both proud of and wish to free ourselves from the burdens of our technological success. So we find it almost impossible to judge how much and what kind of technology would be best for us. In principle, we should be free to accept or reject various technological developments. Technology, after all, is supposed to be means for the pursuit of
10   whatever ends we choose. But, in truth, it might be our destiny to be moved along by impersonal and unlimited technological progress. We do not have much evidence of significant numbers of human beings resisting technological changes for long periods of time. (The peaceful and admirable Amish, for example, are a very small exception to a general rule.)

Technology and the Mind

Addicted to Phones?

April Frawley Birdwell

January 18, 2007

University of Florida News: Health, Research, Technology

http://news.ufl.edu/2007/01/18/cell-addiction/

"Turn off your cell phones and pagers."

For most people, heeding these warnings in hospitals or at the movies is as simple as pressing a button. But for a growing number of people across the globe, the idea of being out of touch, even just for a 90-minute movie, is enough to induce anxiety, says
5   a University of Florida psychologist who studies addictions to the Internet and other technologies.

Although cellular phones and personal digital assistants such as the BlackBerry were created to make modern life more convenient, they're actually beginning to interfere in the lives of users who don't know when to turn them off, says Lisa Merlo, an assistant
10   professor of psychiatry in the UF College of Medicine.

"It's not so much talking on the phone that's typically the problem although that can have consequences too," Merlo said. "(It's) this need to be connected, to know what's going on and be available to other people. That's one of the hallmarks of cell phone addiction."

15   Unlike addictions to alcohol, drugs or even gambling, it can be hard to pinpoint problematic cell phone use. Almost everyone has a cell phone and uses it regularly. But if someone can't get through dinner without sending text messages or furiously typing on a personal digital assistant during a meeting, it may be time to take a step back, Merlo said.

How people respond to being separated from their cell phones or PDAs is another
20   clue. Frequent users often become anxious when they are forced to turn off the phone or if they forget it at home, so much so that they can't enjoy whatever they're doing, Merlo added. Often, cell phone "addicts" compulsively check their phones for voicemails and text messages, she said.

"When (cell phone overuse) really becomes problematic for a lot of people is if they
25   have underlying anxiety or depression," she said. "This can really exacerbate it or (cause) their symptoms to manifest themselves."

For example, someone who already worries about what others think of them could become easily agitated if their phone calls or messages aren't returned right away.

"This is something that is going to affect them on a day-to-day basis," Merlo said.

30   The problem seems to be growing. A Japanese study revealed that children with cell phones often don't make friends with their less tech-savvy peers, a Hungarian study found that three-fourths of children had mobile phones and an Italian study showed that one quarter of adolescents owned multiple phones and many claimed to be somewhat addicted to them. A British study also recently found that 36 percent of college students
35   surveyed said they could not get by without cell phones. But this may be more a sign that students view cell phones as a modern necessity like a car, said David Sheffield, a psychologist who conducted the study at Staffordshire University in England.

"The most shocking figure was that 7 percent said the use of mobile phones had caused them to lose a relationship or a job," Sheffield said.

40   Although experts have pinpointed these problems in frequent cell phone users, studies have yet to show if a bad cell phone habit constitutes an actual addiction. Yet as with traditional addictions, excessive cell phone use is associated with certain hallmark patterns of behavior, including using something to feel good, building up a tolerance and needing more of it over time to get the same feeling, and going through
45   withdrawal if deprived of it, Merlo said.

Cell phone users could start out with one phone and switch to newer models with more advanced features or PDAs that act like mini-computers over time to get the same feeling they had with their first phone, she said. Although withdrawal is typically considered a physical response that occurs when the body goes without a chemical, the anxiety cell
50   phone users feel without their phone could simply be another form of withdrawal.

"Those things lend toward the idea that maybe this is an addiction, but maybe it's manifesting in a little bit different way than you would think of a chemical substance," Merlo said.

Addiction also causes changes in the brain, but scientists have yet to measure what
55   happens in the brains of cell phone users, she said. Even eating and other behaviors have been shown to produce the same effects in the brain as drugs and alcohol in some people, UF studies have shown.

For frequent phoners who do think they have a problem or for parents of children obsessed with their cells, Merlo advises downgrading to a basic phone with fewer
60   features and setting limits about where and when to use the phone.

"Cell phones are a great technology," Merlo said. "They're useful in a lot of situations. (But) one of the most important things is making sure you have some cell phone free time in your day. It's OK to turn it off. Focus on family, homework, knowing that cell phone message will still be there."

Does the Internet Make You Dumber?

Nicholas Carr
June 5, 2010
Wall Street Journal

The Roman philosopher Seneca may have put it best 2,000 years ago: "To be everywhere is to be nowhere." Today, the Internet grants us easy access to unprecedented amounts of information. But a growing body of scientific evidence suggests that the Net, with its constant distractions and interruptions, is also turning us into scattered and superficial
5   thinkers.

The picture emerging from the research is deeply troubling, at least to anyone who values the depth, rather than just the velocity, of human thought. People who read text studded with links, the studies show, comprehend less than those who read traditional linear text. People who watch busy multimedia presentations remember
10   less than those who take in information in a more sedate and focused manner. People who are continually distracted by emails, alerts and other messages understand less than those who are able to concentrate. And people who juggle many tasks are less creative and less productive than those who do one thing at a time.

The common thread in these disabilities is the division of attention. The richness
of our thoughts, our memories and even our personalities hinges on our ability to
focus the mind and sustain concentration. Only when we pay deep attention to a
new piece of information are we able to associate it "meaningfully and systematically
with knowledge already well established in memory," writes the Nobel Prize-winning
neuroscientist Eric Kandel. Such associations are essential to mastering complex
concepts.

When we're constantly distracted and interrupted, as we tend to be online, our
brains are unable to forge the strong and expansive neural connections that give
depth and distinctiveness to our thinking. We become mere signal-processing units,
quickly shepherding disjointed bits of information into and then out of short-term
memory.

In an article published in Science last year, Patricia Greenfield, a leading
developmental psychologist, reviewed dozens of studies on how different media
technologies influence our cognitive abilities. Some of the studies indicated that
certain computer tasks, like playing video games, can enhance "visual literacy
skills," increasing the speed at which people can shift their focus among icons
and other images on screens. Other studies, however, found that such rapid shifts
in focus, even if performed adeptly, result in less rigorous and "more automatic"
thinking.

In one experiment conducted at Cornell University, for example, half a class of
students was allowed to use Internet-connected laptops during a lecture, while the
other had to keep their computers shut. Those who browsed the Web performed
much worse on a subsequent test of how well they retained the lecture's content.
While it's hardly surprising that Web surfing would distract students, it should be a
note of caution to schools that are wiring their classrooms in hopes of improving
learning.

Ms. Greenfield concluded that "every medium develops some cognitive skills at the
expense of others." Our growing use of screen-based media, she said, has strengthened
visual-spatial intelligence, which can improve the ability to do jobs that involve
keeping track of lots of simultaneous signals, like air traffic control. But that has been
accompanied by "new weaknesses in higher-order cognitive processes," including
"abstract vocabulary, mindfulness, reflection, inductive problem solving, critical
thinking, and imagination." We're becoming, in a word, shallower.

In another experiment, recently conducted at Stanford University's Communication
Between Humans and Interactive Media Lab, a team of researchers gave various
cognitive tests to 49 people who do a lot of media multitasking and 52 people who
multitask much less frequently. The heavy multitaskers performed poorly on all the
tests. They were more easily distracted, had less control over their attention, and were
much less able to distinguish important information from trivia.

The researchers were surprised by the results. They had expected that the intensive
multitaskers would have gained some unique mental advantages from all their on-
screen juggling. But that wasn't the case. In fact, the heavy multitaskers weren't even
good at multitasking. They were considerably less adept at switching between tasks
than the more infrequent multitaskers. "Everything distracts them," observed Clifford
Nass, the professor who heads the Stanford lab.

60 **Does the Internet Make You Smarter?**

It would be one thing if the ill effects went away as soon as we turned off our computers and cellphones. But they don't. The cellular structure of the human brain, scientists have discovered, adapts readily to the tools we use, including those for finding, storing and sharing information. By changing our habits of mind, each new
65 technology strengthens certain neural pathways and weakens others. The cellular alterations continue to shape the way we think even when we're not using the technology.

The pioneering neuroscientist Michael Merzenich believes our brains are being "massively remodeled" by our ever-intensifying use of the Web and related
70 media. In the 1970s and 1980s, Mr. Merzenich, now a professor emeritus at the University of California in San Francisco, conducted a famous series of experiments on primate brains that revealed how extensively and quickly neural circuits change in response to experience. When, for example, Mr. Merzenich rearranged the nerves in a monkey's hand, the nerve cells in the animal's sensory cortex
75 quickly reorganized themselves to create a new "mental map" of the hand. In a conversation late last year, he said that he was profoundly worried about the cognitive consequences of the constant distractions and interruptions the Internet bombards us with. The long-term effect on the quality of our intellectual lives, he said, could be "deadly."

80 What we seem to be sacrificing in all our surfing and searching is our capacity to engage in the quieter, attentive modes of thought that underpin contemplation, reflection and introspection. The Web never encourages us to slow down. It keeps us in a state of perpetual mental locomotion.

It is revealing, and distressing, to compare the cognitive effects of the Internet with
85 those of an earlier information technology, the printed book. Whereas the Internet scatters our attention, the book focuses it. Unlike the screen, the page promotes contemplativeness.

Reading a long sequence of pages helps us develop a rare kind of mental discipline. The innate bias of the human brain, after all, is to be distracted. Our
90 predisposition is to be aware of as much of what's going on around us as possible. Our fast-paced, reflexive shifts in focus were once crucial to our survival. They reduced the odds that a predator would take us by surprise or that we'd overlook a nearby source of food.

To read a book is to practice an unnatural process of thought. It requires us to
95 place ourselves at what T. S. Eliot, in his poem "Four Quartets," called "the still point of the turning world." We have to forge or strengthen the neural links needed to counter our instinctive distractedness, thereby gaining greater control over our attention and our mind.

It is this control, this mental discipline, that we are at risk of losing as we spend ever
100 more time scanning and skimming online. If the slow progression of words across printed pages damped our craving to be inundated by mental stimulation, the Internet indulges it. It returns us to our native state of distractedness, while presenting us with far more distractions than our ancestors ever had to contend with.

Mind Over Mass Media

Steven Pinker

June 10, 2010

The New York Times

http://www.nytimes.com/2010/06/11/opinion/11Pinker.html

New forms of media have always caused moral panics: the printing press, newspapers, paperbacks and television were all once denounced as threats to their consumers' brainpower and moral fiber.

So too with electronic technologies. PowerPoint, we're told, is reducing discourse
5 to bullet points. Search engines lower our intelligence, encouraging us to skim on the surface of knowledge rather than dive to its depths. Twitter is shrinking our attention spans.

But such panics often fail basic reality checks. When comic books were accused of turning juveniles into delinquents in the 1950s, crime was falling to record lows, just
10 as the denunciations of video games in the 1990s coincided with the great American crime decline. The decades of television, transistor radios and rock videos were also decades in which I.Q. scores rose continuously.

For a reality check today, take the state of science, which demands high levels of brainwork and is measured by clear benchmarks of discovery. These days scientists are
15 never far from their e-mail, rarely touch paper and cannot lecture without PowerPoint. If electronic media were hazardous to intelligence, the quality of science would be plummeting. Yet discoveries are multiplying like fruit flies, and progress is dizzying. Other activities in the life of the mind, like philosophy, history and cultural criticism, are likewise flourishing, as anyone who has lost a morning of work to the Web site Arts &
20 Letters Daily can attest.

Critics of new media sometimes use science itself to press their case, citing research that shows how "experience can change the brain." But cognitive neuroscientists roll their eyes at such talk. Yes, every time we learn a fact or skill the wiring of the brain changes; it's not as if the information is stored in the pancreas. But the existence of
25 neural plasticity does not mean the brain is a blob of clay pounded into shape by experience.

Experience does not revamp the basic information-processing capacities of the brain. Speed-reading programs have long claimed to do just that, but the verdict was rendered by Woody Allen after he read "War and Peace" in one sitting: "It was about
30 Russia." Genuine multitasking, too, has been exposed as a myth, not just by laboratory studies but by the familiar sight of an S.U.V. undulating between lanes as the driver cuts deals on his cellphone.

Moreover, as the psychologists Christopher Chabris and Daniel Simons show in their new book "The Invisible Gorilla: And Other Ways Our Intuitions Deceive Us," the effects
35 of experience are highly specific to the experiences themselves. If you train people to do one thing (recognize shapes, solve math puzzles, find hidden words), they get better at doing that thing, but almost nothing else. Music doesn't make you better at math, conjugating Latin doesn't make you more logical, brain-training games don't make you smarter. Accomplished people don't bulk up their brains with intellectual
40 calisthenics; they immerse themselves in their fields. Novelists read lots of novels, scientists read lots of science.

The effects of consuming electronic media are also likely to be far more limited than the panic implies. Media critics write as if the brain takes on the qualities of whatever it consumes, the informational equivalent of "you are what you eat." As with primitive

45 peoples who believe that eating fierce animals will make them fierce, they assume that watching quick cuts in rock videos turns your mental life into quick cuts or that reading bullet points and Twitter postings turns your thoughts into bullet points and Twitter postings.

Yes, the constant arrival of information packets can be distracting or addictive,

50 especially to people with attention deficit disorder. But distraction is not a new phenomenon. The solution is not to bemoan technology but to develop strategies of self-control, as we do with every other temptation in life. Turn off e-mail or Twitter when you work, put away your Blackberry at dinner time, ask your spouse to call you to bed at a designated hour.

55 And to encourage intellectual depth, don't rail at PowerPoint or Google. It's not as if habits of deep reflection, thorough research and rigorous reasoning ever came naturally to people. They must be acquired in special institutions, which we call universities, and maintained with constant upkeep, which we call analysis, criticism and debate. They are not granted by propping a heavy encyclopedia on your lap, nor are

60 they taken away by efficient access to information on the Internet.

The new media have caught on for a reason. Knowledge is increasing exponentially; human brainpower and waking hours are not. Fortunately, the Internet and information technologies are helping us manage, search and retrieve our collective intellectual output at different scales, from Twitter and previews to e-books and online encyclopedias. Far

65 from making us stupid, these technologies are the only things that will keep us smart.

Boundaries Between Humans and Machines

Humanoid Robotics: Ethical Considerations
David Bruemmer
May 30, 2006
The Idaho National Laboratory
http://www.inl.gov/adaptiverobotics/humanoidrobotics/ethicalconsiderations.shtml

The world's population of real humans continues to steadily grow. One might ask why we would want to make a machine that looks, thinks and emotes like a human when we have plenty of humans already, many of whom do not have jobs or good places to live. It is important to re-emphasize that humanoids cannot and will not ever

5 replace humans. Computers and humans are good at fundamentally different things. Calculators did not replace mathematicians. They did change drastically the way mathematics was taught. For example, the ability to mentally multiply large numbers, although impressive, is no longer a highly valued human capability. Calculators have not stolen from us part of what it means to be human, but rather, free our minds for

10 more worthy efforts. As humanoids change the contours of our workforce, economy

and society, they will not encroach on our sovereignty, but rather enable us to explore and further realize the very aspects of our nature we hold most dear.

So why should we have intelligent, emotion exhibiting humanoids? Emotion is often considered a debilitating, irrational characteristic. Why not keep humanoids, like calculators, merely as useful gadgetry? If we do want humanoids to be truly reliable and useful, they must be able to adapt and develop. Since it is impossible to hard-code high-utility, general-purpose behavior, humanoids must play some role as arbiters of their own development. One of the most profound questions for the future of Humanoid Robotics is, "How we can motivate such development?" Speaking in purely utilitarian terms, emotion is the implementation of a motivational system that propels us to work, improve, reproduce and survive. In reality, many of our human "weaknesses" actually serve powerful biological purposes. Thus, if we want useful, human-like robots, we will have to give them some motivational system. We may choose to call this system "emotion" or we may reserve that term for ourselves and assert that humanoids are merely simulating emotion using algorithms whose output controls facial degrees of freedom, tone of voice, body posture, and other physical manifestations of emotion.

Most likely, two distinct species of humanoids will arise: those that respond to and illicit our emotions and those we wish simply to do work, day in and day out, without stirring our feelings. Some ethicists believe this may be a difficult distinction to maintain. On the other hand, many consider ethical concerns regarding robot emotion or intelligence to be moot. According to this line of reasoning, no robot really feels or knows anything that we have not (albeit indirectly) told them to feel or know. From this perspective, it seems unnecessary to give a second thought to our treatment of humanoids. They are not 'real'. They are merely machines.

At their onset, all technologies seem artificial, and upset the perceived natural way of things. With the rise of the Internet, we coined the notion of a "virtual world" as a means to distinguish a new, unfamiliar arena from our usual daily life. This once clean distinction between a "real world" and "virtual world" already seems ephemeral. To someone who spends 10 hours a day logged into Internet chat rooms, the so-called "virtual world" is as real to them as anything else in their lives. Likewise, the interactions humans have with humanoids will be real because we make them so. Many years from now, our children will be puzzled by the question, "Does the robot have 'real' intelligence?" Intelligence is as intelligence does. As we hone them, enable them to self-develop, integrate them into our lives and become comfortable with them, humanoids will seem (and be) less and less contrived. Ultimately, the most relevant issue is not whether a robot's emotion or intelligence can be considered 'real,' but rather the fact that, real or not, it will have an effect on us.

The real danger is not that humanoids will make us mad with power, or that humanoids will themselves become super intelligent and take over the world. The consequences of their introduction will be subtler. Inexorably, we will interact more with machines and less with each other. Already, the average American worker spends astonishingly large percentages of his/her life interfacing with machines. Many return home only to log in anew. Human relationships are a lot of trouble, forged from dirty diapers, lost tempers and late nights. Machines, on the other hand, can be turned on and off. Already, many of us prefer to forge and maintain relationships via e-mail, chat rooms and instant messenger rather than in person. Despite promises that the Internet will take us anywhere, we find ourselves—hour after hour—glued to our

chairs. We are supposedly living in a world with no borders. Yet, at the very time we
60 should be coming closer together, it seems we are growing further apart. Humanoids
may accelerate this trend.

If it is hard to imagine how humans could develop an emotional connection to a
robot, consider what the effects would be of systematically imparting knowledge,
personality and intentions to a robot over a sustained period of time. It may well be
65 that much of the software for intelligent humanoid robot control is developed under
an Open Source paradigm, which means that thousands or even millions of developers
will be able to modify the software of their own or other people's robots. Source code
aside, humanoids will be given the ability to develop and learn in response to the
input they receive. Could a cruel master make a cruel humanoid? Will people begin
70 to see their robots as a reflection of themselves? As works of art? As valuable tools?
As children? If humanoids learn "bad behavior," whom should we hold responsible? The
manufacturer? The owner? The robot? Or the surrounding environment as a collective
whole? The ethical question of nature vs. nurture is relevant for humanoids as well as
humans. It will be hard enough to monitor the software and mechanical 'nature' of
75 humanoids (i.e., the state in which humanoids emerge from the factory crate). 'Nurture'
presents an even greater challenge.

Isaac Asimov believed that robots should be invested with underlying rules that
govern all behavior. Although generations of readers have admired and enjoyed
Asimov's ability to depict the theoretical interplay of these rules, it may be that such
80 encompassing, high-level rules are simply impracticable from a software engineering
perspective. Robot intelligence is the emergent effect of layered, low-level mappings
from sensing to action. Already, software developers are often unable to predict the
emergent effect of these behaviors when subjected to a non-Markovian (i.e., real-
world) environment.

85 Whatever else it may be, technological progress flows with a swift current. The Internet
continues to grow with little oversight, offering an incredible wealth of information and
services while at the same time presenting a new and devastating opportunity for fraud,
theft, disruption of commerce and dissemination of misinformation. One lesson to be
learned from the Love Bug virus and Y2K is that the better a technology is, the more
90 dependent we become upon it. Humanoids pose a grave threat for the very reason that
they will be of great service. As our technologies become more complex, more pervasive
and more dangerous, we will be ever more likely to employ the aid of humanoids.
They will not come in to work with hangovers, get tired or demand profit sharing, and
although they will never be perfect, humanoids may someday prove more reliable than
95 their creators.

Most likely, humanoids will never rise up and wrest control from our hands. Instead,
we may give it to them, one home, one factory, one nuclear facility at a time until
'pulling the plug' becomes, at first infeasible and then eventually unthinkable. Even
now, imagine the economic havoc if we were to disable the Internet. We are steadily
100 replacing the natural world with the products of our own minds and hands. As we
continue to disrupt and manipulate the existing state of our world (often for the
better), the changes we make require successive intervention. Technologies engender
and demand new technologies. Once unleashed, it is difficult to revoke a technology
without incurring profound economic, social and psychological consequences. Rather,
105 the problems that arise from new technologies are often met with more complex and
daring technologies.

Yet, no matter how quickly technological progress seems to unfold, foresight and imagination will always play key roles in driving societal change. We cannot shirk responsibility by calling the future inevitable. It is difficult to direct a snowball as it

110 careens down the slope; thus, it is now—when there are only a handful of functional humanoids around the world—that we must decide the direction in which to push. Humanoids are the products of our own minds and hands. Neither we, nor our creations, stand outside the natural world, but rather are an integral part of its unfolding. We have designed humanoids to model and extend aspects of ourselves

115 and, if we fear them, it is because we fear ourselves.

*Smart Robots**

Michael Bond

23 May—5 June, 2009

Engineering and Technology

www.inl.gov/adaptiverobotics/humanoidrobotics/ethicalconsiderations/

It may be an old fantasy, but the basic premise that we will one day engineer machines that are at least as smart as us and whose behaviour is indistinguishable from ours is, according to many roboticists, closer to reality than we might like to think.

Our understanding of the human brain, and our ability to 'reverse engineer' it

5 to analyse how it works and replicate its processes—is increasing dramatically, such that within a couple of decades we should know all about the mechanics of human intelligence and, crucially, learning, and be able to apply this to machines.

Ray Kurzweil, an inventor and writer and one of the leading thinkers on artificial intelligence (AI), believes a profound shift in our capacity to engineer intelligence is not

10 far off. "Extending our intelligence by reverse engineering it, modelling it, simulating it . . . and modifying and extending it is the next step in [human] evolution," he states in his 2005 book 'The Singularity is Near.'

He predicted a vastly accelerated pace of technological change that, in a few decades, would lead to machines that would "encompass all human knowledge and

15 proficiency, ultimately including the pattern-recognition powers, problem-solving skills and emotional and moral intelligence of the human brain itself"—a merger between technology and human biology that would enable us to transcend our biological limits.

Four years on, Kurzweil is just as optimistic. Computing speeds and memory are continuing to improve exponentially, he says, and at the same time "we are making

20 very rapid gains in reverse-engineering the brain, which will be a key source of the software for human intelligence."

The prospect of super-intelligent machine human hybrids will seem fantastical to some. Yet a few decades ago, the notion of AI of any kind seemed unlikely; we are now surrounded by it—in the cars we drive, the computers we use, the video games and

25 toys our children play with.

Devices that respond to their environment and learn from it—the basis of intelligence—are key to everything from speech and text recognition software and spam filters to medical diagnostics and financial trading systems.

We take it all for granted and it seems quite benign. But things look different and a

30 little more unsettling when you apply the thinking behind this AI revolution to the field of robotics. A robot may look like a collection of steel and wires, but watch how people

*This article is from a British publication and contains some British spellings.

cannot help but respond with empathy when one speaks to them or casts sad-looking eyes in their direction and you'll realise the line between human and non-human can seem distinctly opaque.

35   **Robot Clone**

The most graphic example of this is Geminoid HI-1, the android robot created by Hiroshi Ishiguro at ATR Intelligent Robotics and Communication Laboratories near Kyoto, Japan. Geminoid HI-1 is Ishiguro's 'twin'—a near-perfect replica of himself that can mimic his movements and expressions using 46 small, air-powered pistons and air
40   bladders. The air bladders expand and contract to emulate his breathing, fidgeting and other movements, such as turning or nodding of the head, all of which Ishiguro can control from a remote computer.

When he speaks, a system of infrared sensors transmits his lip movements to the robot, while a speaker broadcasts his voice; a built-in camera allows him to 'see' through its eyes.

45   Ishiguro uses his twin to lecture to students while he sits at the controls in his office at the other side of town. People often treat it as real, he says, even when they know it isn't. This is not just a gimmick: he wants to discover the essential human-like social cues that an android robot must possess for people to communicate with it naturally. The idea is to pave the way for the development of robots with more human-like
50   qualities, to enable them to "integrate into human society as partners and have natural social relations with humans." Along the way, he hopes to discover more about what it is to be human.

Geminoid HI-1 is considered a ground-breaking development by many roboticists because it appears to have overcome a problem known as the 'uncanny valley,'
55   whereby we become increasingly comfortable with robots the more they resemble humans but start to get uncomfortable when they look close to humans because the absence of particular movements or behaviour makes them resemble a moving corpse. Ishiguro's twin is sufficiently realistic in its mannerisms that people are not repulsed by it. Yet those who predict a nearfuture in which people daily interact with
60   robots point out that a robot does not have to look much like a human for people instinctively to behave empathetically towards it.

Roboticists have had plenty of chances to observe this. Over the past 15 years, a whole family of 'social robots' has emerged in laboratories in Japan, the US and Europe. One of the earliest, Cog, was developed by a team led by Rodney Brooks at
65   the Humanoid Robotics Group at the Massachusetts Institute of Technology (MIT). Cog, now retired, was programmed to follow movement and to respond to its sensory inputs—for example, it could 'learn' to manipulate objects such as a Slinky toy by adjusting the raising and lowering of its motor arms in response to the weight of the object.

70   Cynthia Breazeal of MIT's Media Lab, who helped design Cog, went on to develop a headrobot called Kismet, which could express basic emotions through judicious manipulation of its eyebrows, eyes, lips and ears.

Kismet had built-in video cameras, microphone and speech recognition software that enabled it to interact with a person at a level similar to that of a six-month-old
75   child. Breazeal's latest project is Leonardo, a nondescript furry creature capable of articulated facial expression and with the apparent interactive sophistication of a five-year-old.

Remarkable Behaviour

80 You might ask whether there's anything remarkable about the way people behave towards robots. Their expressiveness is superficial, even though people respond as if it were something deeper. "Sociable robots inspire feelings of connection not because of their intelligence or consciousness, but because of their ability to push Darwinian buttons in people—making eye contact, for example—that cause people to respond as though they were in relationship with them," says Sherry Turkle, director of the MIT's
85 Initiative on Technology and Self.

People often respond to any mechanical toy with empathy and emotion. Consider the commercial success of robot pets such as the Tamagotchi, My Real Baby, Sony's AIBO dog and the Furby, whose owners—adult as well as children—develop genuine attachment to them, and grieve if they break.

90 Even on the battlefield, a place not known for sentiment, soldiers have been known to humanise the autonomous devices they use for reconnaissance or mine clearance. US troops in Afghanistan and Iraq often treat them as fellow soldiers, naming them, giving them rank or awarding them medals after successful missions.

Given our propensity for bonding with just about anything that moves, is the
95 special allure of Leonardo, Kismet and their ilk all down to sophisticated aesthetics and creative programming? Is there anything going on in there that would have Capek, Asimov, Dick and other AI fantasists rubbing their hands in anticipation? Are modern robots still anything more than machines? Their creators certainly think so.

*My Friend the Robot**

Kathleen Richardson

February 16, 2007

The Times (London)

www.timeshighereducation.co.uk

Worried about being all alone in your old age? A robot companion could be the solution. While roboticists focus on developing humanoid robot helpers for the elderly, other researchers are as interested in building robots for use as human companions and challenging attitudes towards machines as they are in providing practical support for
5 elderly people. But what might be the consequences of giving machines more status?

The baby boom in advanced capitalist economies is long gone; the population is set to age and keep on ageing. In the next 45 years in the US, 20 per cent of the population will be aged 65 or over. By 2050, the proportion of elderly dependent people in Europe is expected to increase to more than 51 per cent. Japan is likely to
10 see one of the largest rises in the elderly dependents ratio, estimated to reach 71 per cent by the year 2050. In light of these forecasts, roboticists see elderly support and care by robots as an important area of their work.

Honda's Asimo (Advanced Step in Innovative Mobility) could be one such robot. It is the size of a small adult, has a humanoid form and is often photographed assisting
15 people—such as collecting a newspaper or delivering the tea. Asimo is held up as an example of robots to come. In the US, researchers at Carnegie Mellon University have developed Pearl, a robot specifically designed to help the elderly. Pearl is about 1m tall and has a mobile base, a video-screen in the place of a torso, a grey face and a hefty price tag—more than $100,000 (£50,800). Its human-like face is designed to encourage
20 the elderly to interact.

*This article is from a British publication and contains some British spellings.

Robots such as Pearl and Asimo could have many uses for ageing populations, reminding them to take medication and assisting with chores. One US-based roboticist explained the advantages of designing robots in humanoid ways.

As human-like robots reflect aspects of the human physical, emotional or communicative repertoire, researchers hope this will make users feel comfortable, safer and able to interact with the technology without any specialised training. A robot with multiple skills, including mobility or communication, might have advantages over technology produced with one specific, inflexible role.

Yet some in the field want robots to be viewed as more than just sophisticated working appliances. Others resent their use as "servants" or "slaves." They talk of developing robot companions that encourage relational bonds between humans and machines. One area where the use of robot companions is under way is among the elderly community, where isolation and depression are major problems.

Japanese researchers lead the way in robotic healthcare for the elderly. As well as funding research in this area, the Japanese Government bestowed an honour on the makers of the robot Paro in December 2006. Paro, which had been in the making since 1993, was developed by the National Institute of Advanced Industrial Science and was one of many robots at the Government-sponsored Robot Awards 2006.

However, Paro cannot help with chores or assist the elderly with mobility issues. This is because Paro is a furry seal-like robot. Its makers refer to it as a "mental commitment robot," or companion robot. Paro was trialled at care homes in Japan, and the results are said to demonstrate how human and machine bonds are possible. The researchers looked to human-animal relations to study human bonds with other kinds of species.

Could companion robots be a technological solution to the problem of elderly alienation? And can technologists convince us that humans could really form relationships with machines?

"We have to be careful how we use the term 'relationship'," says Kerstin Dautenhahn, professor of artificial intelligence at Hertfordshire University. "I have a 'relationship' with my car, but it is not the same as a relationship with a human. Robots are not sentient creatures." But do robotic innovations blur these boundaries? Scientists interviewed in a recently published report sponsored by the UK Government think so.

When surveyed about the future of technology, some scientists thought robots might one day demand rights. In Europe, "robot ethics" is a growing area of research. In fact, studies are under way that examine the treatment of robots by humans. An exhibit at the Boston Science Museum in the US showcases research that addresses this question. Ada Brunstein, a science researcher at the Massachusetts Institute of Technology, says: "It has been reported that children do possess a sense of moral responsibility to Aibo (a robotic dog made by Sony), but this could easily be because kids recognised that Aibo was an expensive and fragile toy, while a stuffed animal is clearly more durable."

Is the very process of humanising machines enough to call into question the boundary between a human and machine?

Dautenhahn thinks not. "Interface" is the term she chooses to explain why she uses humanoid features in her research. "In my work, I employ some humanoid aspects in the design of the robots, but this is mainly as an interface. People like to know where to speak and look when talking to a machine." Yet much research is focused on imparting human behavioural qualities to machines.

The Cognitive Robot Companion, or Cogniron, project aims to design machines with manners. Cogniron researchers believe that a robot with manners could help humans relate to it more comfortably. In addition to "robotiquette," other researchers
70 have embarked on making robots that can trigger human empathy. At the University of the West of England, roboticist Peter Jaeckel is studying how to get a person to feel empathy with a machine. Jaeckel's human-like robotic platform Eva (designed by David Hanson at the University of Texas) does this by mimicking facial expressions. Jaeckel wants Eva to perform the expected facial responses to humans who interact with it.

75 But can companion robots benefit the elderly? In studies of elderly-robot relations, a person's biographical details often reveal a complex picture, with the elderly-robot relationship positively affected, often directly, by illness or feelings of estrangement from the person's family. Sherry Turkle, professor of science, technology and society at MIT, was until last year a distinguished supporter of robot care for the elderly. In
80 her work, she has examined the therapeutic role of robots as relational objects. The robots' use as an outlet for anger or loneliness were some of the positive results found in studies such as Turkle's, but these results cannot be separated from the challenging situations that many elderly people face.

This should not diminish the use of robots as therapeutic tools, but still, a therapeutic
85 tool is quite different from a machine alternative to a human companion.

Robot companions may, in the short term, ease the problem of loneliness in much the way that pets do, but can these robots work over longer periods and connect with deeper human yearnings? For some roboticists, there may be little difference in quality between a human and machine, but for others a human-like robot is nothing more
90 than a machine with a face.

The redefining of robots as companions is imaginative and may lead to some innovative research. But confusing the qualities of human and machine muddy the practical development of this technology.

I think the following examples symbolise the inherent problem in equating robots
95 and humans. While conducting fieldwork at MIT, I was shown a photograph of a robot pushing a wheelchair; behind the robot were several adult males pushing the robot. In another case, a similar scenario was played out when I saw the robot Asimo. The physical form and human mimetic performance of Asimo did seem eerily human-like. But when one steps back from the visual effects of the robot the illusion is revealed.

100 In a recent UK television commercial, Asimo can be seen walking unaided, but Asimo is remote-controlled and requires an army of highly skilled researchers to make it work. Metaphorically speaking, both examples illustrate the ineffective, confused and illusionary nature of the research. Put another way, in the absence of a human-centred vision, the technology's benefits to the elderly will be uncertain and limited.

105 If researchers apply ethics to machines, the potential of the technology will be overshadowed by an uncertainty about who and what it is for. In this sense, machines might be judged less on what they can do and how they are useful and more on how they look, behave and how we relate to them—a very useful sticking plaster, in fact, for our own feelings of alienation from, and responsibility to, other human beings.

QUESTIONS FOR WRITING ABOUT THE IMPACT OF TECHNOLOGY

For each writing assignment, use evidence from several of the articles in this Theme to support your position. You may also use evidence from your own experience or additional sources you find.

1. What are the benefits and the drawbacks of using the Internet as a source of information?

2. How can new technologies such as the Internet and social media be used most effectively? That is, how can we minimize their negative effects and enhance their positive effects?

3. When the written language began to be widely used in Greece in the fourth century B.C., Socrates, a philosopher of the time, opposed it, saying that writing was a lot less flexible than oral language and also that it would have a negative affect on our mind, destroying our ability to memorize. What are some similar objections to the development of the Internet?

4. Consider a definition of addiction and discuss whether it is possible to become addicted to social media.

5. Will using robots as caregivers help or damage relationships within the family?

6. How are robots similar to and different from animal pets?

7. What is consciousness? Is a robot conscious?

8. If robots have emotions and act as caregivers and if people have increasingly more artificial body parts such as neural implants and prosthetic limbs, what does it mean to be human?

MORE QUESTIONS FOR WRITING ABOUT THE IMPACT OF TECHNOLOGY

To write about these questions, in addition to taking supporting evidence from the articles in this Theme, you will need to use evidence from other Themes in *Sourcework* or find additional sources on your own.

1. How have social media affected the concept of friendship among people of different age groups?

2. How has the Internet affected education?

3. How does new technology make it easier for humans to create a lifestyle that sustains the environment?

4. Do inventors of new technologies, especially those that benefit large numbers of people, qualify as heroes?

5. Do advances in technology, such as the Internet and other social media create changes in society or do changes in society, such as more globalization of business, create new technologies? Which is cause and which is effect?

6. How will humanity have enough money and resources to give the benefits of innovative technology to all people? Or, will only the rich benefit from new technologies, creating ever more social inequities?

Appendices

Appendix A: Example Student Research Papers

Students wrote the three essays in this appendix using the writing process presented in Part One of *Sourcework*. The students who wrote the first two essays, "Risky Business" and "Changing Expectations of Marriage," read articles and discussed the theme with their classmates before writing their own essays. For both students, this was the first time they had written a paper using sources. Notice that the papers are short, three to five pages, and refer only to a small number of sources.

The third paper "Vegetarianism?" was written by a student who had already written several guided research papers. In this paper, the student chose her own topic and found her own sources. Notice that the paper is longer and refers to more sources.

All three students worked closely with their classmates throughout the process of writing their papers. This collaboration helped them in each step of the writing process.

Example Essay 1

Research Question: **Why do people take risks?**

Risky Business

What would you do if your friend asked you to try white-water rafting with her? As soon as my friend asked me last month, I answered, "It sounds good. I'll try it!" By comparison, when I told another friend that I would go rafting, she said to me, "How scary! Why do you want to do such a risky thing?" There is a difference between her opinion about thrills and mine. "Risk" has both positive and negative aspects. The positive aspect of risk, that it might give us success in something challenging, makes me try rafting, while the negative aspect, that it might take something important from us such as life or money, makes my friend scared. The uncertain result of risks is sometimes an advantage and sometimes a disadvantage for us. Why do people take risks even though there is a possibility that they may lose something? Biological need, social environment, and psychological satisfaction are three reasons why people take risks.

The first reason why people take risks is to meet a biological need inherited from their ancestors. Some people think the tendency to take risks is just personal taste, but it is not. People are attracted to risk taking, in part, because they have certain genes that stimulate their behavior. The article "For Our Ancestors, Taking Risks Was a Good Bet" (1999) discusses research by Israeli scientists that suggests that people who have a strong interest in taking risks may have inherited what has been called the "thrill-seeking" gene. This gene helps the chemical dopamine enter into nerve cells more easily. Dopamine controls feelings of pleasure and emotion. In addition to this thrill-seeking gene, the study found that risk takers have another gene that influences levels of serotonin, a mood chemical that is linked to feelings of satisfaction. In other words, risky situations stimulate the release of these chemicals and people with these thrill-seeking genes feel a greater sense of pleasure and satisfaction.

These thrill-seeking genes have been inherited from ancestors who lived in a dangerous environment and had to be able to successfully face risk in order to survive. For instance, they had to risk their lives when they had to kill fierce animals for food or find a way to survive during a drought. John Tooby, who runs the Center for Evolutionary Psychology at the University of California at Santa Barbara, writes that the people who survived and passed their genes on, were the ones who did well in risky situations (cited in Taro-Greenfield, 1999). Although now people no longer have to make use of this survival characteristic, they are still very much attracted to risk-taking activities because of these genetic influences.

People may have thrill-seeking genes, but daily life is now so controlled and follows such a safe routine that it is hard to find something exciting and challenging enough to stimulate them. Michael Apter, the author of "The Dangerous Edge: The Psychology of Excitement," points out that our society has become an increasingly safe place to be; however, risk taking is necessary for humans (cited in Bowers, 1995). It is clear that this safety results in boredom and people seek risks in order to escape that boredom. In, "Taking the Bungee Plunge," Ginia Bellafonte (1992, p. 61) writes, "Bungee jumping, the non-art of flinging yourself into midair with an ankle strapped to elastic, can be an exhilarating thrill in an otherwise dreary nine-to-five existence." Through facing the challenge of risky activities, people are seeking some positive thrills, which are missing from their monotonous lives.

In addition to trying to escape the boredom that results from a safe society, people take risks to satisfy psychological needs. The contradiction between human nature that stimulates people to look for thrills and our safe society which lacks thrills causes people to seek psychological satisfaction through risk taking. There are two kinds of psychological needs that are met through risk taking: a feeling of excitement and a sense of accomplishment. First, people escape from everyday life and try risky activities to get excitement (Bellafonte, 1992; Bowers, 1995). For instance, gamblers and investors seek not only money but also the excitement that arises from the risk of losing money. There are also people who find this excitement through extreme sports. Kate Douglas, an extreme sports player, feels that her emotions and awareness are stimulated by bungee jumping (cited in Bowers, 1995).

Moreover, the successful conquest of a risk provides people with a sense of self-accomplishment, the second psychological need. Bowers (1995) writes that meeting the challenge of a risky situation is a way to make life feel more meaningful. For example, I wanted to take the entrance exam for a highly rated high school even though the possibility that I would pass was only fifty percent. My family opposed my effort, telling me it was too risky to focus on entering this high school. Fortunately, I took and passed the exam. If I had taken and passed the exam for a less challenging school, I would not have gained as great a feeling of accomplishment. However, because I pushed my limit and took a risk, my feeling of success was greater. Cathy Hanesworth, an extreme sports enthusiast, wrote, "If you can prove to yourself that you can do something that is very scary, you can carry that confidence with you into any situation because you have pushed your physical and mental limits farther than your comfort zone" (cited in Bellafonte, 1992, p. 61). In short, it is self-satisfaction that attracts us to risk taking.

In conclusion, it is difficult to find risk-taking experiences because modern society has become much too safe and mundane. The challenges presented by taking risks provide us incredible payoffs. We acquire a great deal of self-assurance and self-fulfillment. These social and psychological needs also originate from the genetic traits of our ancestors. When these three factors are combined, it compels someone like me to say yes to an offer of white-water rafting. It may be scary and the outcome may be uncertain, but it is also a way to help make my life feel more valuable. ▪

References

Bellafonte, G. (1992, May/June). Taking the bungee plunge. *Utne Reader,* 61.

Bowers, J. (1995, October). Going over the top. *Women's Sports and Fitness, 283,* 29.

Taro-Greenfield, K. (1998, September 8). For our ancestors, taking risks was a good bet. *Time, 154,* 12.

Example Essay 2

Research Question: **How does culture influence people's concept of marriage?**

Changing Expectations of Marriage in Asia

A young woman in Korea might date fifteen different men before choosing one to be her husband. Her grandmother might be shocked by this. Her mother would probably shake her head in disbelief. Forty years ago, marriages were arranged by the family and a young woman had no voice in who her future husband would be. Once married, she simply accepted her role as a caretaker for her husband and children and did not expect that her own personal interests would be recognized. This attitude toward marriage is changing in Asia as women look for ways to pursue their own dreams. There are three main reasons why women's expectation of marriage is higher than it was 40 years ago in Asian countries: a desire for personal fulfillment, a desire for financial self-reliance, and a simple desire to be able to choose one's husband.

The first thing that contributes to women's high expectation of marriage is that their desire to pursue personal goals has become more important in Asia. This means that they don't want to give up their own lives anymore after marriage. Actually, until recently many women in Asian countries haven't been allowed to have careers. They had to give up their personal lives for their family. In "What Does Life Tell Us About Love?" Kavita Daswani (cited in Wark, 2003, p. 42) writes, "There is an element of sacrifice and obligation: we are expected to make many things secondary once the husband comes along, to devote our energies to him, and his house and the building of another family unit." In other words, married women's first priority is traditionally to spend their time taking care of their husband and children, their house, and the progression of their family. They haven't had enough time to look after themselves and achieve their own career goals in traditional Asian countries like India. The point here, however, is that many women in Asian countries also want their own lives, and don't just want to live for their husband and children. They hope to find a career that enables them to develop as well as earns them money. As a result, they either postpone getting married or look for a more open-minded husband. In "I Take Thee, for Weekends Only," Kay Itoi (1999) discusses how Japanese women's opinion about marriage is changing. "Tired of following in the footsteps of indifferent husbands, Japanese wives are demanding lives of their own" (p. 2). It's true that the typical women who, in the past, gave up their own careers and relied on their husbands are disappearing. Women don't want to be in a rigid traditional marriage. They realize that they deserved to be happy by having and enjoying their lives beyond their marriage.

As a result of an improved economy in many Asian countries, women can become financially independent. This is the second reason why women's expectations of marriage are changing. For example, women in Japan now have more opportunities to get jobs and make money (Itoi, 1999). Having a job means not only making money, but also that women can establish independence. Nowadays, women in Asia have more experience earning, spending, and managing money. As a result, they have learned how to be self-reliant. This financial independence means that women can be more assertive. When they do not need to depend on a man for their financial security, they are able to express and expect that their own desires will be respected. Itoi (1999) writes that young women who were raised with financial security and have their own jobs now, understand that they have choices. They are learning that they are not required to end their arguments on someone else's terms to obtain what they need. They would like to express freely what they want to say and act how they want to act. Now that they have this leverage, they expect the husband to listen to them. So because these women have the ability to get more, they are accustomed to receiving more and have higher expectations of their husbands. Women want to look closely at their potential husband.

Asian women's ability to decide who will be their husband is the last reason for their high expectations of marriage. In the past, they couldn't select their husbands; it was out of their hands. Daswani (cited in Wark, 2003, p. 42) talks about arranged marriage, "[My parents] were brought together by their families, engaged within the day and married within a couple of weeks. That was 40 years ago and all is well." Like Daswani's mother, many women in Asia had to marry an unfamiliar man, picked by their parents or the man's parents. Like India, Korea has a long history of arranged marriage too. It was common that parents chose their daughter's husband or men decided who would be their wives. Women in Korea were required to wait for their husband patiently. However, increased financial independence for women has meant that choosing a partner to live with is becoming one of the most important decisions a woman makes in her life. Single women who have a professional job tend to have high expectations of their future husband and their marriage. Robert Levine (1993), a professor of psychology at California State University in Fresno, writes in "Is Love a Luxury?" that marrying someone for love instead of for practical reasons such as financial security or family status is more common in wealthy countries that value individualism. Women are beginning to look for a husband who will respect their independence and share an emotional bond.

In conclusion, there are several reasons why women in Asia have these higher expectations of their marriage. They are transitioning from the traditional way of thinking about marriage (dependence on husband) to the western way of thinking (seeking their own career in addition to taking care of their family). Women are rethinking not only their own role in marriage, but also their husbands. They are looking for equality and hoping for a new way of living. •

References

Itoi, K. (1999, July 19). I take thee, for weekends only. *Newsweek, 134,* 2.

Levine, R. (1993, February). Is love a luxury? *American Demographics, 15,* 27.

Wark, P. (2003, July 9). What does life tell us about love?. [electronic version] *The Times, 8,* 42.

Example Essay 3

Research Question: **Why do people choose to be vegetarians?**

Vegetarianism?

"Do you want to have this?" I offered the beef jerky to my friend. "No way! Don't you know it's from a dead animal?" I had this conversation when I was at a party in Japan with some foreign friends. Obviously, this person is a vegetarian. She does not eat any kind of animal flesh, does not drink milk or eat cheese, and does not wear leather fabrics. It was my first time to talk to a vegetarian. I was surprised and asked curiously. "Yeah, I know it is from a dead animal, but almost everyone eats it here. Why don't you?" She explained seriously that when she imagined it was from a dead animal, she felt very sick. She did not like depriving anything of its life.

It does not seem easy to become a vegetarian. You have to create ways to cook delicious food without the tastes from animals, like consommé, and bonito soup. Furthermore, you have to be careful of the menu when you order in a restaurant. For me, this activity seems like a pain. I love animals, but I also like eating some of them. So far, I have not felt like I should quit eating meat completely. However, as a result of my conversation with my friend, I began to wonder what makes some people become vegetarian. Improved health, ethical issues, and ecological concerns are three reasons why people become vegetarian.

First of all, many people try to be vegetarians to maintain good health. Vegetarianism can prevent people from getting certain diseases. Castleman (1995) mentions that many studies prove that meat, especially beef, pork and lamb, likely increase the percentages of heart disease and cancer. He states that the number of vegetarians who die from heart disease and cancer is definitely lower than that of the meat eaters. For example, from heart disease, 28 percent fewer vegetarians die than omnivorous do, and 39 percent fewer die from cancer. The National Cancer Research Institute has found that meat-eating women get breast cancer almost four times more than women who do not eat meat or eat little ("Why Be a Vegetarian?" 1999). Moreover, there are other medical conditions which meat eaters are more likely to get than vegetarians, such as hypertension, gallstones, constipation, and diabetes (Cerrato, 1991). Consequently, vegetarians may live longer than omnivores. Dworkin (1999) cites a Loma Linda University study that says vegetarians live an average of 7 years longer than those who eat meat. Another positive health point of vegetarianism that Dworkin gives is the fact that vegetarians tend to be slim and their bones can last longer. Recognizing these health benefits, many people are becoming vegetarians.

However, although people know these positive points of vegetarianism and want to be healthy, there are some opposing opinions concerning the health benefits of vegetarianism. Some people are concerned about the lack of nutrients in a diet without meat. As we know, protein is indispensable to live. Meat, eggs, and dairy products cannot be ignored in one's diet, because they are the only source of vitamin B12 (Cerrato, 1991). The deficiency of vitamin B12 causes anemia and serious neurological damage. In addition, we also need to get essential amino acids, and nine of these can be absorbed from animal proteins. If we eat only vegetables, we have to carefully combine certain kinds of foods, such as red beans or lentils and rice, to get these nutrients. Meat can satisfy nutritional requirements easily, and people who don't like to spend time thinking about their meals prefer the easier way of eating meat.

In addition to health benefits, ethical beliefs lead some people to become vegetarian. Religious practice and animal rights are two ethical arguments commonly made. First, religious belief usually has a powerful influence in the believer's life. In an effort to persuade people to become vegetarian, the People for the Ethical Treatment of Animals (PETA) has argued that Catholic priests, Southern Baptists, and even poultry producers who call themselves devout Christians should be vegetarians because Jesus himself was a vegetarian ("Preaching Christian Vegetarianism," 1998). Another example of vegetarianism in Christianity is in Genesis. Adam named the animals, but he was able to eat only the "green plants" as food in Eden (Gen. 1:29). When these examples are used as arguments for vegetarianism, they imply that Christians have an obligation to follow the examples given in the Bible if they want to consider themselves true followers of Christianity.

A second ethical argument that some people consider is animal rights. Imagine how chickens who are going to be slaughtered are crammed into cages. According to Moran (1989), these chickens have had their beaks cut with a hot knife. This painful process includes destroying sensitive tissue in the beaks. Poultry producers use this method to stop the chickens from committing cannibalism. However, farmers cause this cannibalistic behavior by forcing many into tiny cages. The chickens never fly or walk freely until they are killed. For pigs, it is also a nightmare to be born in factories. Today, many pigs bite their tails off (Why Be a Vegetarian?, 1999). They are bored and frustrated, and finally go insane. In cases where the farmer cannot solve the biting problem, the mauled pig might be attacked and killed by the other pigs in the small pen. This pig cannot be sold, and it becomes troublesome for the producer. As a result, pigs' tails are routinely cut off. They are also forced to stay in darkness until feeding time. I believe that nobody can say that this treatment is humane. People who support animal rights to advocate vegetarianism consider animals as living creatures that are the same as humans. They were not born to be killed or treated in inhumane ways.

On the other hand, in spite of knowing these unethical conditions, some people emphasize the supremacy of human rights which weakens the importance of vegetarianism. Christians who eat meat point out the contradiction of stories in the Bible. According to Witherell (1994), killing and eating animals is not only not forbidden in the Bible, but for some important occasions, it is advocated. For example, after the flood, God announced that there was a difference between humans and all the other creatures. The animals gave their flesh as food for Noah and his families (Gen. 9:3–4). This suggests humans' superiority over all others. In response to the argument that raising animals to kill them is unethical, Achor (1996) points out that some people justify eating meat by thinking this way, "at least the animals had happy lives before they were killed" (p. 68). Actually, we use this phrase when we argue in favor of owning pets, too. "They are fed and living safely. What's the matter?" For people who believe in humans' superiority, even religious and ethical reasons lose their strength.

There is one more practical reason to advocate vegetarianism. Meat eating seems quite wasteful ecologically. In research, it has been proved that raising animals to eat is surprisingly wasteful of land and food (Robinsong, 1995). Every minute, 20 acres of land are collapsed for our meat industry. Calculating the amount, it means that the destruction of the land is 28,000 acres per day. According to other statistics, it is said that cattle require an incredible amount of water to mature (Castleman, 1995). Approximately 50 percent of the water consumed in the United States is used for domestic animals. In some areas, the rate is much higher. For example, 75 percent of the water from the Ogallala Aquifer, which is the main source for the High Plains, is used for raising cattle. Thinking of water, we can compare it with meat. One pound of meat takes almost 2,500 gallons of water ("Why Be a Vegetarian?" 1999). One serving of chicken takes 408 gallons of water, and one pat of butter takes 100 gallons (Achor, 1996). Achor gives the astonishing result of a calculation of the cost for a pound of hamburger. She says that the real price is about 35 dollars. The cost includes, among other things, payment for water, which is required to produce enough greens to feed cattle.

However, somehow, people do not want to be vegetarians. Even though these statistics exist, most people do not want to know the truth or feel ambiguous when they learn what is involved in producing a piece of meat. When they buy a single pound of meat, they see just the "meat," but do not imagine the real cost of the meat.

After I finished this research, I felt that I was in a misty forest. What is important for me? What am I supposed to consider when I think of vegetarianism? Health and animal rights are convincing arguments. However, I still sometimes eat meat without hesitation. I dare to say that I do not even feel pity for the animals that are slaughtered to eat. How am I different from vegetarians? To them I might be a cruel murderer. Even though I do not commit the slaughtering directly, I do indirectly by increasing the demand for meat.

Likewise, if I become a vegetarian, I will indirectly improve life for others. For example, when people decide to become vegetarians in order to improve their health, it may also seem like they care about others. In fact, it is just fortunate that their lifestyle will not be harmful to other creatures. This is also true for people who become vegetarians for ecological reasons. They want to reduce wasteful activity, and it consequently helps animals' lives. Vegetarianism is a habit that allows us to reflect on our life. I cannot say that everyone has to be a vegetarian, but I am learning to respect vegetarians for their reliability as unselfish people. Vegetarianism could be one of the solutions that helps this chaotic world become more humane. ●

References

Achor, A. B. (1996). *Animal rights*. Ohio: Yellow Springs.

Bloyd-Peshkin, S. (1991, June). In search of our basic diet: you may have heard that humans are naturally vegetarian. The evidence is convincing, but is it accurate? *Vegetarian Times,* 46–52.

Castleman, M. (1995, March–April). Flesh wounds. *Sierra,* 26–27.

Cerrato, P. L. (1991, March). Becoming a vegetarian: the risks and the benefits. *RN,* 73–77.

Dworkin, N. (1999, April). 22 reasons to go vegetarian right now. *Vegetarian Times,* 90.

Fossel, P. V. (1994, September–October). Letter from Plum Hill. *Country Journal* 8.

Ireland, C. (1992, February). Vegetarian timeline: a light and lively look at vegetarians through the ages. *Vegetarian Times,* 56–57.

Moran, V. (1989, January). Veganism: the ethics, the philosophy, the diet. *Vegetarian Times,* 50–53.

Preaching Christian vegetarianism. (1998, July 17). *National Catholic Reporter,* 8.

Robinsong, S. (1995, Spring–Summer). The butcher's secret. *Skipping Stones,* 29.

The vegetarian approach. (1991, September). *Current Health 2,* 19–21.

Why be a vegetarian? (1999, May 10). *Vegetarian Education Group of Northern Illinois University* [Online serial]. Available at: http://come.to/veg.

Witherell, T. D. (1994, April 23). Notes from the vegetarian underground. *America,* 16–17.

Appendix B: Vocabulary for Different Types of Focus in a Thesis Statement

Focus	Vocabulary	Example
Cause	reasons, influence lead to cause result in	Cultural values influence expectations of marriage in three ways.
Effect	consequences, results, outcomes, benefits, advantages/ disadvantages	Inadequate transportation planning can have several negative consequences.
Comparison	differences/similarities X differs in these ways X is related to Y in these ways X has these points in common with Y	Attitudes towards marriage in the United States and Iran differ in four ways.
Definition	characteristics, components, qualities, traits	Two qualities of a successful city are strong schools and diverse economic opportunities.
Classification	types, categories	Heroes can be divided into two categories: personal and public.
Process	steps, stages, phases	The change in men's role in the family during the past 50 years has occurred in four distinct phases.
Argument	reasons positive/negative helpful, harmful	Two reasons why standardized testing is a good idea are to increase student motivation and to measure school performance.

Credits

Rebecca Moore, Barbara Baker, Arnold Parker, "*Coping With Procrastination*". From HMCO. *Houghton Mifflin Reading Series, Book 2,* 2E. Copyright 2006 Heinle/Arts & Sciences, a part of Cengage Learning Inc. Reproduced by permission. www.cengage.com/permissions.

Source: Rita Koselka, Carrie Shook, "*Born to Rebel? Or Born to Conserve?*" published 10 March 1997, From Forbes Magazine.

Source: Penny Wark, "*What Does Life Tell Us About Love?*" 2003. From The Times (electronic version, p. 8, 42).

Source: Robert Levine, "*Is Love a Luxury*", 1993. From American Demographics.

Source: Mary Pipher, "*Closing the Gap*", published Nov. 1999. From Reader's Digest.

Source: Phil Sudo, "*Larger Than Life*" published on 2 November 1990, From Scholastic, Inc © 1984.

Source: Joe Bowers," *Going Over the Top*", published Oct, 1995. From Women's Sports and Fitness.

Source: Michael Levin, "*The Case for Torture*", published June 7, 1982. From Newsweek.

Source: Erica Goode, "*Your Mind May Ease What's Ailing You*", published on April 18, 1999. From The New York Times.

Source: Karl Greenfield, "*Life on the Edge*", published on Sept. 6, 1999. From Time Magazine.

Source: Susan Hopkins, "*Bam! Crash! Kapow! Girls Are Heroes Now*". From Evergreen: A Guide to Writing with Readings, Edition, 2007, Cengage.

Source: Janet Wu, "*Lives; Homework Bound*", published on Sept. 5, 1999. From The New York Times.

Source: Susan Fawcett, ""*How Sunglasses Spanned the World*". From Evergreen: A Guide to Writing with Readings, Edition, 2007, Cengage.

Source: Moira MacDonald, "*Does Province-Wide Testing Distort Reality?*". From Toronto Sun, 2001.

Source: Reid, Ewing, et al, "*Measuring Sprawl and Its Impact*". From Smart Growth America/USEPA 2002.

Source: Tommy Lee Lott, "*The 1960's Avant-Garde Movement in Jazz*". From Social Identities, spring 2001.

Source: Nadya Labi, "*A Bad Start? Living Together May Be the Road to Divorce*", published on Feb. 15, 1999. From Infotrac Web: Student Edition.

Source: "*A Bloody War*", published on Dec. 30, 2003. A Special Report from The Economist.

Source: J. White, "*Science, Cloning, and Morality*", published in Oct. 2003. From Science and Christian Belief.

Source: Gina Bellafonte, "*Taking the Bungee Plunge*". From Utne Reader, May/June 1992.

Source: Nelson Mandela, "*Humanity is not Red or Blue*", published on Oct. 25, 2004. From Christian Science Monitor.

Source: Martin Luther King Jr., [many cites, none sourced].

Source: Anne Frank, "*The Diary of a Young Girl*". © Copyright 1952 by Otto H. Frank. From DoubleDay, a division of Bantam Dell Publishing Group, Inc. and Anne Frank Fonds, Basel, Switzerland 1992.

Source: Applewhite, Evans, Frothingham, "*And I quote: the definitive collection of quotes, sayings, and jokes…*". From Thomas Dunne Books, 2003.

Source: Eleanor Roosevelt, "*You Learn By Living*". From Harper & Brothers, 1960.

Source: Mahatma Gandhi, [many cites, none sourced].